Computer Science

A concise introduction

Ian Sinclair

NEWNES

Newnes
An imprint of Butterworth-Heinemann Ltd
Linacre House, Jordan Hill, Oxford OX2 8EJ

PART OF REED INTERNATIONAL BOOKS

OXFORD LONDON GUILDFORD BOSTON
MUNICH NEW DELHI SINGAPORE SYDNEY
TOKYO TORONTO WELLINGTON

First published 1990
Reprinted 1991

British Library Cataloguing in Publication Data
Sinclair, Ian R. (Ian Robertson) 1932-
  Computer science: a concise introduction
  1. Computer science
  I. Title
  004

ISBN 0 7506 0252 X

Printed and bound in Great Britain by
Courier International, Tiptree, Essex

Contents

Preface

The term *computer science* covers a very large range of studies and, like so many other technical subjects, is expanding faster than textbooks can be updated. It is not surprising, then, that many textbooks on this subject are very large and out of date, some of them barely mentioning the use of desktop computers. What is surprising is that very little is available to introduce the subject to the wider range of readers, students, enthusiasts and users of computers who want or need to know more about the subject. In particular, there is little available for the student on courses such as the C&G 424, nor is there much provision for anyone who needs to concentrate on desktop machines as distinct from the vast computers of twenty years ago.

The CGLI course number 424 (formerly numbered 417) was produced in association with the National Computing Centre in 1984 and is geared to modern computers and methods. This book has been written with the 424 course very much in mind, with an emphasis on modern microcomputing methods rather than on long-forgotten devices like punched cards that are used only with very old mainframe machines. The text can therefore be used by students on other courses who want to make use of up-to-date information, and also, since the treatment is at an introductory level, by readers who are not aiming at formal qualifications.

Ideally, a course should be practically based, with each student given a clear set of practical objectives along with enough preparation and computer time to achieve these objectives. This book has been arranged so that each part can lead clearly to a piece of practical work. This, however, cannot be treated in too much detail because of the vast differences between the computers that readers are likely to be using, so that a variety of methods has been illustrated. Textbooks on computing have in the past proved to be very misleading because they described methods that were applicable to mainframe machines at a time when most students were already using microcomputers.

Of the C&G 424 syllabus, some 44 per cent of the examination questions concern filing topics, 20 per cent concern computer hardware, and the sections covering fundamentals, software principles and programming cover 12 per cent each. This is not necessarily reflected in chapter sizes in this book, because the less stressed topics are often fundamental to the understanding of the others. Students who are following the C&G 424 course are expected to take one of the programming options of the C&G 425 set, such as COBOL, PASCAL or BASIC programming, so that details of programming languages and methods are not included here.

The C&G 424 student will be expected to carry out the programming requirements of C&G 425, but the reader who is not aiming at qualifications can make use of any experience of programming, such as a working use of BASIC. This book does not require knowledge of any specific programming language, and the sections that deal with programming can be applied to any language since they are concerned with the principles of planning rather than with details of planning methods or programming languages and coding. Each chapter starts with a list of objectives which, for the convenience of the C&G student, have been indexed with the reference numbers of the C&G 424 course. The chapters include also exercises, which are mainly for thought and discussion, and end-of-chapter multiple-choice tests which are of an easy nature. Answers are provided at the end of the book.

I hope that the resulting text will be of assistance to many students and enthusiasts in years to come, and I thank my past students and readers for all the feedback that they have provided for me over the years. I am also grateful to Star Micronics for information on dot-matrix and laser printers, and to Matmos Ltd for information on a variety of computing hardware.

Ian Sinclair

1 Fundamentals

Objectives

- Describe ways in which information can be represented in digital electronic form (3).
- Convert between decimal, binary, octal and hexadecimal data; represent negative numbers in fixed length binary form; perform simple arithmetic in binary (3.1).
- Explain how numeric, text, sound and graphics information may be coded (3.2).

Number codes

Computers are machines which work with electric signals that we can interpret in any way we want, but which we normally think of as numbers. This comes about because the original uses for computers were as calculating machines, and it was convenient to have the signals representing numbers. Later uses of computers are not nearly so tied to the use of numbers, but we still cling to the idea, mainly because it is so well established. To say that you are nothing but a number to a computer, however, means little more than saying that you are just a few keystrokes to a typewriter or brushstrokes to a painter. Modern applications of computers make use of various forms of numbers to represent the electrical signals in the machine, and we in turn represent data such as letters of the alphabet, numbers, diagrams, and images in terms of numbers. Some of these methods are of a form that has become a standard, others are not.

One of the standards is a code called ASCII, which can be set out in the form of a table as in Appendix 2. The name ASCII comes from the initial letters of American Standard Code for Information Interchange, and in this code each letter of the alphabet, each digit from 0 to 9 and each punctuation mark is allocated a number in the region 32 to 127. For example, the word

ASCII itself would be represented by the numbers 65, 83, 67, 73, 73. ASCII code has become a standard though it has the disadvantage of making no allowance for symbols such as the UK pound sign, Japanese yen sign and other letters or symbols that do not exist in American English. Its use, however, allows a set of words to be translated into numbers by a computer, stored, and read by another computer. ASCII codes are used extensively by word processor programs, allowing text produced on one machine to be read by another. This standardization did not exist in the early days of computing, and was not always followed when microcomputers first appeared. Some computers, notably IBM PC and PS/2 models, make use of codes in the range 128–255 for an additional range of international symbols and simple graphics.

ASCII code is one method of coding letters and digits, but it has severe drawbacks for coding numbers. We can represent the number 79 in ASCII code as 55 57, or in Roman numerals as LXXIX, but neither of these forms is very useful if we then want to add 27 or multiply by 6. To allow arithmetic to be carried out we need to have a number system that corresponds better with the signals that the computer uses. Our everyday number system is decimal or, more correctly, denary, meaning that the scale (or number-base) is 10. We have digits for the numbers 0 to 9, and for the next number we place a digit 1 in a column to the left of the units column. A number such as 275 is therefore 2 hundreds, 7 tens and 5 units, and the columns represent powers of 10, since 100 is 10^2, 1000 is 10^3 and so on. The number 10 itself is 10^1, and 1 is 10^0 because the definition of what we mean by a power of a number includes the idea that any number to the power zero is unity.

A denary number system allows arithmetic to be carried out easily on one column at a time, so that adding 255 to 476 can be done by adding 5 to 6, taking the carry amount (the tens column digit) over to add to the result of $5 + 7$ and so on. Compare this with the effort that a Roman required to add CCLV to CDLXXVI – without the use of columns you have to work with the complete numbers rather than the limited range of 0 to 9. The introduction of the Arabic numbers that we use today was a step forward that was considerably more important to civilization than the invention of the computer.

Calculating machines in the past had no difficulty in working with denary numbers because these machines were mechanical and it is easy to make a gearwheel with ten teeth, for example. Electrical signals are not so easy to deal with. You could imagine a system in which an electrical signal might use ten different levels of voltage or of current to represent the ten digits of a denary number system, but the practical difficulties are immense. It is difficult enough to hold one level of electrical voltage steady, and to hold each of ten at the correct values is out of the question. The only scheme that is workable for anything but the simplest applications is one that makes use of only two levels of electrical voltage or current. One of these values is zero, the other is whatever maximum value the electrical system can use, and the most common of these is +5 V. Since the actual values are not particularly important in a scheme like this, we refer to these as level 0 and level 1, or more briefly to 0 and 1.

The use of just two levels of electrical voltage or current, leading to the use of digits 0 and 1 means that a number system using only these digits must be used for electrical counting. A number system which uses only two digits is called a binary system, and the simplest binary system is one that follows the same pattern as we use for denary numbers, using columns for each power of the base number. Since the base number is 2, this means that we have columns for units, twos, fours, eights and so on, since $2^0 = 1$, $2^1 = 2$, $2^2 = 4$, $2^3 = 8$. Arithmetic can then be reduced to the rules:

$$0 + 0 = 0 \quad 0 + 1 = 1 \quad 1 + 1 = 10$$

all of which can be carried out electrically. This type of binary number system is sometimes called 8-4-2-1 binary to distinguish it from other systems, like the Gray code and Excess-3 code which are used for measuring applications in which arithmetic is not important. Only the 8-4-2-1 code is used within computers. The digits 0 and 1 are often referred to as **bits**, a shortened version of binary digits. Figure 1.1 shows how denary numbers 0 to 15 correspond to binary, using four bits of binary.

Other bases

Though 8-4-2-1 binary code is ideally suited for use by electrical devices which can carry out arithmetic, it is not well suited for human use. Though there is no difficulty in adding 0101100110110111 to 0011101101100101, the size of the numbers looks intimidating, and the pattern of 0s and 1s can confuse the eye and lead to mistakes being made. Binary numbers will inevitably contain more digits than their denary counterparts and because only two values are used, one part of a binary number can look too much like another. Though the machine is not confused, we can be, so that users of binary numbers have adopted other number codes which are less confusing to work with, but easily convertible both to and from binary. The two systems that are used are octal (less common now) and hex. Octal is a scale of eight, using digits 0 to 7 only, and hex (more correctly, hexadecimal) is a scale of sixteen in which the digits 0 to 9 are supplemented by letters A to F in order to have sixteen digits.

Binary	*Denary*	*Binary*	*Denary*
0000	0	1000	8
0001	1	1001	9
0010	2	1010	10
0011	3	1011	11
0100	4	1100	12
0101	5	1101	13
0110	6	1110	14
0111	7	1111	15

Figure 1.1 *Denary and binary numbers* 0 *to* 15, *the range of a four-bit binary number*

The main value of these number systems lies in their close relationship with binary. Any octal number, for example, can be represented by a three-digit binary number, so that converting from binary to octal requires only that the binary digits be grouped into sets of three, starting with the units digit, the **least significant digit**. The table of Figure 1.2 shows the correspondence between binary and octal, and Figure 1.3 shows the conversion of binary numbers into octal. Modern microcomputers use binary numbers of 8, 16 or 32 digits and because none of these numbers divides evenly by three, the most significant digit of an octal equivalent will never make use of more than two bits of a binary code as Figure 1.4 shows. Conversion from octal to binary is as simple as binary to octal, and is illustrated in Figure 1.5. Octal numbers can be identified by using the markers ×Q or a subscript 8, such as 72×Q or 72_8.

Binary	*Octal*	*Binary*	*Octal*
0000	000	1000	010
0001	001	1001	011
0010	002	1010	012
0011	003	1011	013
0100	004	1100	014
0101	005	1101	015
0110	006	1110	016
0111	007	1111	017

Figure 1.2 *A number table showing binary and octal number forms. The table as far as denary 7 can be used for converting denary to octal numbers*

1 Group digits into sets of three, starting at the right-hand side.
2 Convert each group into the corresponding octal digit using the table of Figure 1.1.

Example:

Binary: 10111101101
Break into: 10 111 101 101
Then convert to: 2 7 5 5 in octal

Figure 1.3 *How to convert binary numbers into octal*

Single byte:	10111110	breaks into 10 111 110
Word:	1100111011100110	breaks into 1 100 111 011 100 110

The largest two-bit portion is 011, octal 3, so that no single byte or word will give a most-significant digit greater than 3 in octal
Only three-byte, six-byte and similar numbers will convert with the possibility of the most significant octal digit being fully used

Figure 1.4 *The most significant bit of an octal number is not fully used, because computers generally use one-, two- or four-byte binary numbers*

1 Write down the octal number.
2 Using the table of Figure 1.1, convert each digit to binary.

Example:

Octal 514 converts to 101 001 100 giving 101001100 in binary

Figure 1.5 *Converting octal to binary number form*

Exercise 1

(a) Convert to octal: 1001 0101 1100.
(b) Convert to binary: 12×Q, 26×Q.

The use of numbers with 8, 16 or 32 bits in so many modern computers makes it preferable to use a number system that is based on an even number of bits. Using two bits implies a scale of four, but this is too close to binary to be useful. Four bits, however, leads to a scale of sixteen, representing binary numbers from 0000 to 1111 as digits 0 to F, in which the digits A to F represent numbers 10 to 15 in denary, binary 1010 to 1111. The scale is illustrated in Figure 1.6, which also shows conversions to and from hex. The use of hex has replaced octal for many applications, and a hex number is generally marked in some way to distinguish it from octal or denary. Common methods include the addition of H following the number, the use of # preceding the number, or symbols such as \x or \0x preceding the number. The hex number 02AF might therefore be printed as 02AFH, #02AF, \x02AF or \0x02AF, depending on the requirements of a particular program.

Denary	*Binary*	*Hex*	*Denary*	*Binary*	*Hex*
0	0000	00	8	1000	08
1	0001	01	9	1001	09
2	0010	02	10	1010	0A
3	0011	03	11	1011	0B
4	0100	04	12	1100	0C
5	0101	05	13	1101	0D
6	0110	06	14	1110	0E
7	0111	07	15	1111	0F

Figure 1.6 *The hexadecimal scale for the denary range* 0 *to* 15. *This can be used to convert between binary and hex in the same way as has been illustrated for octal numbers*

> ***Exercise 2***
>
> (a) Convert to hex: 1010, 10110, 11010.
> (b) Convert to binary: OEH, 12H, 1BH.

Negative numbers

The 8-4-2-1 binary system operates with the digits 0 and 1 only, with no provision for **sign** of number, that is, there is no + or − code. The idea of a negative number is a comparatively modern one, and the most traditional users of arithmetic, accountants, always designed bookkeeping so that only positive numbers were shown, and these were always added, never subtracted. Since the computer itself deals only with the 0 and 1 electrical signals, the meaning of a negative or positive sign has to be carried by a 0 or a 1, and the method that is adopted is to make the **most significant bit** (the left-hand bit) of a number carry the sign information. If this bit is a 0, then the sign is positive; if it is a 1, then the sign is negative. The advantage of using this system is that the computer can carry out its arithmetic actions on binary numbers in exactly the same way no matter how we think of the most significant bit being used.

As a simple example, suppose that we use four bits to represent numbers. If all numbers are to be positive, we could use the range 0000 to 1111 to mean 0 to 15 denary. If negative numbers are to be represented, then the set 0000 to 0111 is 0 to +7, and the set 1111 to 1001 is −1 to −8, making the complete range −8 to +7, still a set of fifteen. How does this affect conversion? There are two simple methods, depending on whether you are more familiar with denary or binary. Suppose, using this simple example of four-bit numbers, we want to convert the number −5 to binary. A four-bit number is in base 16, so we add 16 to −5, to get +11. This in four-bit binary is 1011, and this is the correct representation for −5 when we are using the first bit as a sign bit – note that there is nothing in the number itself that can distinguish between a coding for +11 and a coding for −5, so that when you interpret binary numbers you must know whether the number is signed or unsigned. The alternative method, called twos complement, is to convert +5 to binary, which gives 0101. The 0s and 1s are then interchanged, giving 1010, and 0001 is added to give 1011 as before. The two sets of rules are summarized in Figure 1.7.

> ***Exercise 3***
>
> Convert to four-digit binary the numbers −7, −2 and −4.

(a) 1 Add base number (8, 16 etc.)
2 Convert result to binary

Example:
Single byte –97
Base of single byte is 256,
so that 256 – 97 = 159
In binary, this is 10011111

(b) 1 Convert
2 Complement (interchange 1s and 0s)
3 Add 1 to least significant digit

Example:
Single byte is –97
In binary, this is 01100001, and
the complement is 10011110
Add 1 to this to get 10011111

Figure 1.7 *Methods for forming a negative number in binary. Method (a) is easier if you are working in denary, but method (b) is used within the computer*

Binary arithmetic

Binary arithmetic is simpler than denary arithmetic, but considerably more tedious because of the large number of digits. Addition is carried out in exactly the same way as denary addition, with the step 1 + 1 = 10 causing a carry to the next column left. If the sum 1 + 1 + 1 occurs because of a carry in, then the result is 11, with another carry out. Some examples are illustrated in Figure 1.8. Subtraction is normally carried out by making the negative version of the quantity to be subtracted, and then **adding** the numbers. In this way, the computer need not have a subtracting capability as such. For example, using four bit numbers for simplicity, if we were subtracting 3 from 7, we would form the binary equivalent of – 3, which is 1101 and then add binary 7, which is 0111, giving:

1101
0111
(1) 0100

neglecting the 1 that overflows on the left-hand side, because only four-bit numbers are being used. This gives 0100, 4 in denary which is the expected answer.

Taking another example, suppose we subtract 6 from 4, still using four-bit numbers. We form the equivalent of – 6, which is 1010, and then add

01001101	11001011	00111011
00111001	10111010	01101011
10000110	10000101 + 1 carried	10100110

Figure 1.8 *Binary addition examples. These show single byte numbers, and if a 1 bit needs to be carried from a byte, the computer must have some provision for storing the carry or indicating that it has occurred*

binary 4 which is 0100, giving:

```
 1010
 0100
 ----
 1110
 ----
```

which is a negative number. This is converted back to denary **either** by subtracting 1 and inverting, so that 1110 − 0001 = 1101, which inverts to 0010, binary 2, *or* by converting 1110 to its denary equivalent, 14, and subtracting from 16 to give 2.

> ***Exercise 4***
>
> Show the equivalent subtractions in binary for 5 − 2, 2 − 6 and 1 − 7.

Multiplication and division are not quite so simple. Multiplications can be carried out by a process of repeated addition, and divisions by repeated subtraction, and these methods work quite well when only whole numbers (integers) are being used. What would on paper be a very slow method can be done very much more rapidly by a computer, so that the simplicity of the method compensates for the number of times the actions of addition or subtraction have to be repeated. Multiplication can also be carried out by a process of shift-and-copy, as illustrated in Figure 1.9, in which the number being multiplied is copied for each 1 in the multiplier, but shifted the same number of places along. Division can similarly follow the denary long-division methods.

Numbers which are not integers are called **floating-point numbers** and are stored as a binary fraction and a binary multiplier. Just as we can write 102000 as $.102 \times 10^6$, we can write the number 1101.101 as $.1101101 \times 2^4$ (or 0.1101101 E 10000 to put it totally in binary). Numbers in this form can be manipulated by the computer using routines (algorithms) which are very much slower than the methods that can be used with integers. In addition, the use of these numbers that are composed of a fraction (the mantissa) and a multiplier (the exponent) nearly always introduces approximations, because very few numbers convert into a perfect binary fraction no matter how many bits are used. You may find, for example, that asking a computer to add $\frac{1}{11}$ to

```
  11001
    101
-------
  11001
 00000
11001
-------
1111101
```

Figure 1.9 *The shift-and-copy method for binary multiplication*

$\frac{10}{11}$ gives a result such as 0.99999999 rather than 1.00000000, and the difference is due to the approximations using floating point numbers.

Coding to binary

An important feature of computing is the ability to express any form of data in binary form, since this is the 'internal' representation, the form that corresponds to the 0 and 1 electrical signals in the machine. We have seen that alphabetical data, names, punctuation marks and digits that will not be used for arithmetic can be converted into ASCII codes. These ASCII codes are seven-bit numbers and another set of codes is available if another bit can be used. Most small computers handle bits in groups of eight, a byte, so that the additional 128 numbers that correspond to the codes from 128 to 255 (denary) are usable. Unfortunately there is no standardization of these numbers, though many manufacturers follow the pattern used by IBM on the PC machines, and several have agreed on the use of 156 for the UK pound symbol. Another set that is becoming a standard is the Lotus set, as used on programs such as Lotus 1-2-3 and Lotus Agenda.

In computer programming languages, numbers are dealt with either as integers or *floats*, meaning floating point numbers. The range of integers depends on how many bytes can be used for an integer, and this depends on the computing language rather than on the computer. Several programming languages allow a large choice of number formats, such as short integers using two bytes and long integers using four bytes. A two-byte integer allows a range of − 32768 to + 32767, and a four-byte integer a range of − 2147483648 to + 2147483647. Addition, subtraction and multiplication of integer numbers are always performed with perfect precision provided that no number or result of an action exceeds the limits of the integer. Division, however, cannot be guaranteed to be perfect because only the whole number part of a division will be obtained. No matter what type of integer you use, $\frac{8}{3}$ in integer arithmetic always gives 2 because no fractions are permitted. Float numbers can be of single or double precision, depending on how many bytes are allocated for the mantissa. Since single precision can lead to errors of the order of 0.015 per cent, many programming languages specify that all arithmetic on floats is carried out with double precision, though the number can be displayed in single precision, which means that the number is rounded off to six decimal places, fewer if you so specify.

The office uses of computers are mainly satisfied by the coding of alphanumerical data in ASCII code and the use of integer and float numbers. Computers are used for a great variety of other purposes, however, particularly since the development of microcomputers, and many other types of data need to be converted into binary form and used in this form. You might, for example, have a computer connected to a set of test equipment (wind tunnel, rolling road, concert-hall acoustics analyser, whatever you like) being used to gather and analyse these test results. How can this type of data be converted? Since the output of practically all test or measuring instruments is electrical, or can be converted to electrical form, this requires a conversion from electrical voltage to binary number. A converter of this type is called an A-to-D (written as A-D) converter, meaning analogue to digital. The electrical voltage from the test or measuring instrument is an analogue quantity, meaning that its value can vary by as small or as large an amount as the instrument can cope with. Digital counters, by contrast, deal with integers only, you can have a value of 4 or 5 but not 4.2 or 5.6. The A-D converter must therefore convert voltages into a set of numbers in which a change of unity will represent the smallest change of a quantity that can be used. For example, if you were converting temperatures from 0°C to 100°C into digits, then using a scale of 0 to 100 would allow you an accuracy of 1°C only, the difference between any two integers. If you convert the temperature range of 0°C to 100°C into a number range of 0 to 1000, then a difference of 1 in a number represents 0.1°C change of temperature, a much better resolution. Using a scale of 0 to 10,000 might allow you to measure a change of 0.01°C – but would this ever be necessary?

The A-D converter must therefore be chosen so that its range and resolution are suited to the application, and by connecting the voltage output of the measuring instrument to the input of the A-D converter, and the output of the A-D converter to the computer (Figure 1.10), the data from the instruments can be used by the computer. This is possible, however, only if the computer is at the time running a program which will identify the signals that are coming in and take whatever action is required. In addition, the computer must possess a suitable connecting point or port for these signals. Some computers have such ports, a few have a port which will also perform the necessary A-D conversion. Many will have to use the serial port connection which is one that is common to most computer types. The connection of computers to measuring devices is seldom straightforward, and only a few machines are equipped for dealing with such connections easily. The most important point, however, is the program. Correct connections are essential in order to transfer signals, but the computer can do nothing with the signals unless a suitable program is running, or is made to run each time a signal is entered.

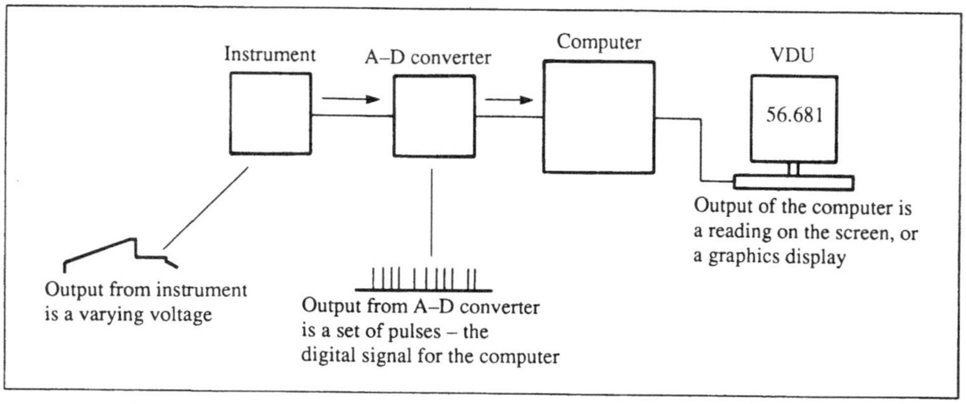

Figure 1.10 *Using the A-D converter to provide a computer input from a varying voltage level. The computer must be programmed to deal with this input in whatever way is required*

Sound signals that can be used by an amplifier and loudspeaker consist of electrical signals that have been produced by a digital to analogue converter, the opposite of the A–D converter. For each digital number input, the D–A converter will generate an electrical wave whose frequency (corresponding to the sensation of pitch) is controlled by the digital number. A simpler method is to use digital numbers simply to control the electrical signals (square waves) that exist in the computer, and many computers contain a small loudspeaker which will convert these signals into sound. A digital to analogue conversion, however, allows much better quality of sound to be generated, with a choice of the type of waveform (sharply-changing or smooth) and the envelope of the waveform (the way that the loudness varies in the course of each note).

Another method of dealing with sound is to use the MIDI (musical instrument digital interface) system. This allows the computer to send signals which can be used by synthesizers and other electronic instruments, specifying note frequency, waveform, envelope and special effects. The MIDI system allows a whole set of electronic instruments to be linked together under the control of the computer, using a code system so that each instrument responds only to signals intended for that instrument.

Graphics can also be coded by the computer, either on screen or on a printer. A picture, colour or monochrome, can be analysed as a set of dots, the number of which will depend on the capabilities of the computer system. A typical set would be 640 across the width of the picture by 320 down. For each dot or pixel (picture element), a number can be used to represent the colour which will either be foreground or background. The complete set of numbers will represent the complete picture, but to work with pictures in this way demands a large amount of memory to store the numbers and a large amount of computing effort to ensure that the numbers are correctly converted into colours on the screen or dots on a printer. Office computers in general are not so well-equipped for graphics handling as the machines which have been specifically designed for graphics, like the Atari ST and Amiga, or the multipurpose Apple Macintosh.

Suggestions for practical work

1. Carry out binary arithmetic using an eight-bit adder.
2. Carry out arithmetic in hexadecimal.
3. Encode simple graphics shapes into coordinate form for a simple graphics display (such as is available in many versions of BASIC).

Multiple-choice test questions

Note: In this and subsequent test questions in later chapters, pick the answer which in your opinion is the most suitable.

1 Computers use binary counting scales because:
(a) it makes the numbers longer
(b) the simplest type of electrical signal is on or off
(c) it makes the numbers more precise
(d) 0 and 1 are the only numbers that can be represented by electrical signals

2 Octal and hexadecimal scales are used because:
(a) they can also be represented by electrical signals
(b) they make arithmetic easier
(c) they are easier for a programmer to use
(d) they are more precise than binary

3 A negative number in binary is represented by using:
(a) a negative sign
(b) a 1 in the least significant place
(c) a 0 in the most significant place
(d) a 1 in the most significant place

4 Arithmetic with integer numbers is perfectly precise with the exception of:
(a) addition
(b) subtraction
(c) multiplication
(d) division

5 Electrical quantities can be converted to digital form using:
(a) a D–A converter
(b) a A–D converter
(c) a hex to binary converter
(d) a binary to hex converter

6 So that a computer can display graphics on a screen each dot is represented by:
(a) numbers for position, brightness and colour
(b) a position number only
(c) numbers for position and size
(d) numbers for size and colour

2 Programs

Objectives

Explain the concepts of programming (4).

- Illustrate concepts of constants, variables, assignment statements, numbers, strings and arrays (4.1).
- Give examples of types of instruction executed by computers (4.2).
- Explain execution of programs using flowcharts or pseudocode (4.3).

A program is a set of instructions to a computer. These instructions are set out in order and will be obeyed in that order, because computers at present are **serial devices** which carry out commands one at a time and in sequence. However, we shall soon have in general use computers which are capable of **parallel processing**, carrying out several actions simultaneously, and requiring a very different form of processing. When present-day computers appear to be doing more than one action at a time, this is done by switching rapidly between one task and another, not by genuinely working on both at the same time. The type of construction for computers which demands that tasks are carried out in sequence is known as **Von Neumann architecture** and, until very recently, this principle has dominated computer design.

Before a program can be written for a computer to use, then, the action of the program must be planned so that it can be carried out by a sequence of steps. For very simple tasks, like making the computer operate a printer direct from the keyboard so that it acts like an electric typewriter, this can be done in one step with very little effort by one person. For large-scale tasks, like automating the stores system of a warehouse or controlling a production line, the planning must be on a much larger scale, with several people each allocated a section of the work and one person responsible for the overall plan. By dividing the work into sections, then breaking down these sections into smaller and more manageable pieces, each piece can be made small enough for a single programmer or a small team to work on (Figure 2.1). The most difficult part of such a programming task is to ensure that all the pieces

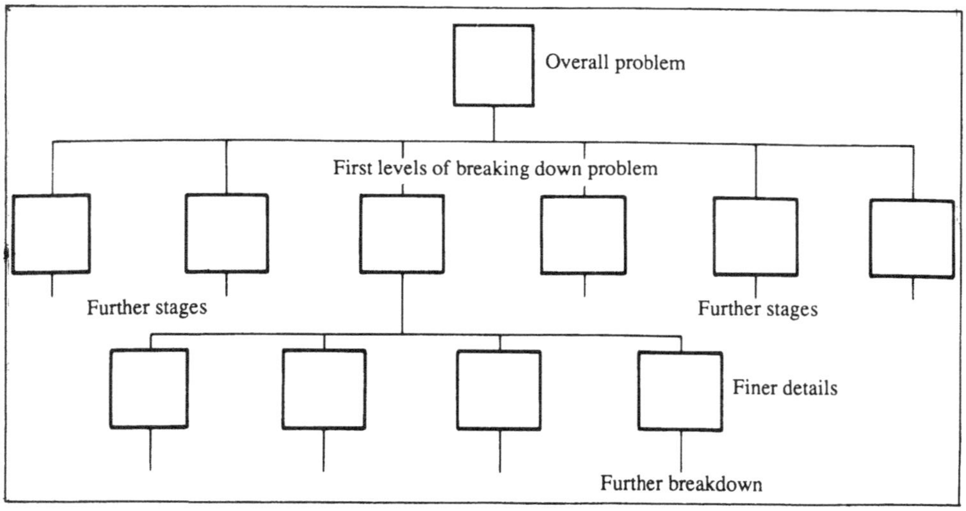

Figure 2.1 *Breaking down a problem into pieces small enough to work on. This must be done in stages (levels) of importance*

of the program fit together afterwards, and this can be made much easier by choosing a suitable **programming language** which is designed to be used in this way.

The actual **coding** of the program, writing down the instructions for the computer, is the least important part of the act of programming. Many newcomers to computing place a lot of emphasis on learning a programming language, and worry about whether their chosen language is the most suitable for their future uses. This is a mistake, because learning to break down problems into small pieces is the most fundamental part of programming, and the chosen language is much less important, though the correct choice of language can make the final conversion of plan into program much easier. It is most likely that you will have to learn more than one programming language, simply because languages tend to be suited to specific purposes. A language that is well suited for writing programs for office routine work may be unsuited for working on engineering calculations; a language that is admirable for learning the principles of programming may be quite useless for writing fast-moving graphics routines for animated displays that demonstrate the working principles of a new invention.

Programming fundamentals

No matter what programming language is used, the task has to be broken down into pieces that are small enough to work on without confusion, and these pieces are called **modules**. Some programming languages demand that the pieces are very small, others are less fussy, but the types of pieces are much the same for all languages, and it is these types that we have to look at now. We have already seen that the computer may have to deal with numbers, with letters and words, measured quantities, sound or graphics; all of which will be represented within the computer by number codes. Most programming languages are not concerned with the details of the codes, but they do work with the quantities that are converted into these codes. The exception is the type of programming we call **assembly language** or **machine code**. This deals directly with the number-codes that the machine uses, and it is the most tedious, most difficult and most troublesome form of programming. For that reason, programming in assembly language is done only where it is absolutely necessary, a topic that will be dealt with in Chapter 8.

One common item in programs is the number constant. In the course of the use of a plan, there are likely to be several numbers used that never change, or are likely to change very seldom in the time that the program is likely to be used. The rate of VAT, for example, is a quantity that stays constant for years at a time, a firm's VAT registration number certainly remains unchanged, and even rates of income tax stay constant for a year. The ratio of the circumference of a circle to its diameter, the quantity that we call pi, is a natural constant that never changes, as compared to the artificial constant of VAT and income tax rates. A firm of paper suppliers may work with 500 sheets of paper to a ream, a trucking firm may be able to fit sixty-four boxes into a container so that these numbers are constants for their respective programs. Natural constants include conversions, the number of millimetres in a foot, the number of litres in a gallon or square metres in an acre.

Any programming language must therefore provide for dealing with constant numbers like these examples. The method that is followed is to convert each constant into code form, and then to allocate a place in the memory of the computer for each coded constant. The programmer must then have some way of tracing where each constant can be found, and this is done by using a reminder in the form of a **name** for each constant. This name can be one that reminds the programmer of what the constant is used for, and is much more useful than just knowing the memory location. Computer memory is divided into units with each unit numbered, but referring to a constant as LBTOKG or LB_TO_KG rather than as number 275116 is a better way of remembering that it is used to convert pounds to kilograms. The code form of a number uses a fixed pattern, so that no matter how small or large the number, each number takes up the same amount of memory space.

Not all constants are numerical, however, though they will always be stored in the memory as number codes. A constant can consist of a set of letters, making a word or phrase, and this type of constant is known as a **string** constant. The name of a firm might need to be used in a program that printed contracts, invoices and other paperwork, and this, since it is not likely to change from day to day, would be stored as a constant. The names of directors of a firm might be less permanent, but it would be better to store them as constants rather than having to type them each time the names were required or having to enter the names from a file kept on the disk. Everything that is stored as a constant means that keyboard work is reduced when the program is used, and so the possibilities of mistakes are reduced. The converse, of course, is that if a name is misspelled and then stored as a constant it is likely to be some time before the mistake is rectified. On the whole, though, storage of words and phrases as constants in a program, available instantly when the program runs, is an easier and more reliable way of making use of these words and phrases, providing that these quantities are not likely to change in the life-time of the program. A string uses one unit of memory (a byte) for each character in the string, so that the size of a string constant is not fixed, unlike the size of a number constant.

The constants can also represent measured graphics and even sound. The identifying logo for a firm might have taken hours to put into number-code form, and it certainly ought to be stored as a constant rather than have to be re-coded each time the computer is switched on or even loaded in from a separate disk. Not all users approve of computers that honk and beep each time something is entered, but the sound is sometimes necessary as a confirmation to the operator, and if several distinctive sounds are needed (entry approved, entry invalid, wrong key) then these should be stored as constants.

Variables are the most important type of stored item. A variable, as the name suggests, is something that can vary from day to day, possibly hour to hour, minute to minute, or even each time the program deals with the quantity. If a program deals with export billing, for example, then the conversion from local currency to foreign currency has to be done, and this conversion rate should be the rate prevailing on the day. A constant cannot be used here, because the rate is not fixed and will have to be entered by the operator each day, perhaps twice per day. If your program writes letters to clients, the name of the sender is a constant, but the name of the recipient is a variable, entered by the user or drawn from a list that is held on a disk.

Simple variables are mainly number or string in nature, and, like constants, they are stored in the memory and referred to by name. The difference is that when the program starts running each day the storage places for the variable contain nothing. A name for a variable means nothing until the operator, the program, or a value read from the backing store has supplied a number, word or phrase, and the program can be designed so that the operator will be asked to supply this information, either by typing or by inserting a disk. A variable is an **assigned** quantity, meaning that the place where it is stored is fixed, and a name is provided, but a quantity, number or words, has to be placed in the memory and so assigned to the name. The action of assignment of a value to a variable name is therefore a very important part of any programming language.

Variables can be used also for measured quantities, for graphics and for sound; all, of course, coded into number forms. If the computer is being used as part of a control system in a chemical process, the input might be a set of signals that expressed the results of an analysis. These signals would be coded and stored as a variable to be used by the program. When a new set of signals became available, the variable value would be accordingly changed, and the program would now use this new value. This is how the program can be arranged to control the process, by taking the results of analysis and using the stored variables from these results to adjust an earlier part of the process. This is an example of automation of a procedure that would once have been performed manually, and the advantage of computer control is that the sequence of analysis and adjustment can be carried out at much more frequent intervals, giving closer control and so less likelihood of reject product. Graphics variables can be used to store drawings that might be made up from constant pieces (like architectural drawings) or by the use of a light-pen which allows freehand drawing to be made on screen, or a graphics tablet that allows lines on a drawing board to be converted into variables stored in the computer, along with a program that reproduces the results on the screen. Sound might be stored as a variable in order to compose a short jingle for a TV commercial, which would later be played on synthesizers by way of a MIDI interface. Like constants, variables follow the pattern of a fixed length of numbers, and one byte per character for strings.

Exercise 1

Decide the classification of the following items of data for a program you are about to write for your own use. The classes are number constant, string constant, number variable or string variable.

(a) Your birthday.
(b) Your age.
(c) Your name.
(d) Mortgage interest rate.
(e) Conversion of feet to millimetres.
(f) Conversion of pounds sterling to dollars.

Constants and variables as we have considered them so far can be simple, like the number pi or complex like a complete graphics image. All programming languages allow for certain types of organized variables or constants, meaning patterns rather than single items. The most common pattern of variable or constant is the **array**, which simply means a list. Suppose, for example, that you need to store a set of fifty names. You could store each of these as a simple constant or variable, but by doing so you would lose one very important advantage of an array. When you store items individually, you have no control about how they are arranged in the memory of the computer. Though it is likely that they will be stored in consecutive parts of the memory there is no guarantee that this will happen, and each value will have to be referred to by a separate name to which it is assigned.

An array (Figure 2.2) is like a single variable in the sense that it uses just one name for reference, but can store a set of single items. It is rather like the difference between writing a name on each of a set of fifty cards, and having all fifty names on a list on a sheet of paper. When a set of names is stored as an array, the name of the array refers to all of the names, and you can find each individual name by specifying its place in the array, as a number. You might, for example, have an array of fifty names which was assigned to the name NAMLIST, and the tenth name in this list could be found by using NAMLIST[10] if the first name was NAMLIST[1]. It is very common, however, to find that the first name on a list is referred to as number 0 rather

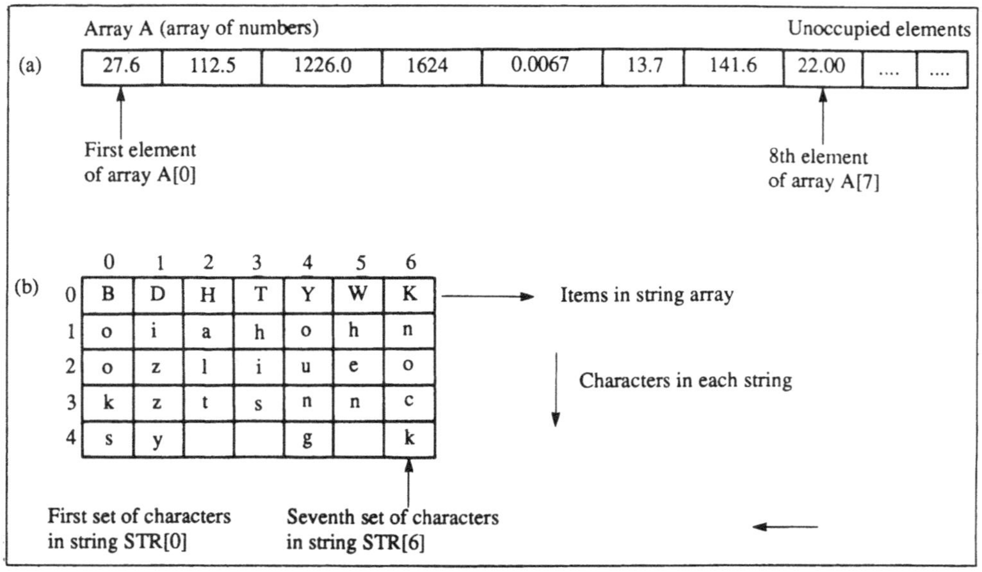

Figure 2.2 *The form of an array (a) of numbers, (b) of strings. The string array that is shown here is a two-dimensional array*

than 1, so that the tenth item would be NAMLIST[9] rather than NAMLIST[10]. Some versions of programming languages allow you to choose whether a list starts at 0 or at 1, others have the starting number built-in so that you have no choice, but you can always choose for yourself whether or not you use the zero.

We have illustrated arrays with strings (letters, words or phrases), but we can also use arrays of numbers, and some languages provide for arrays of other quantities. Many languages, however, make no provision for other arrays so that if you want to have an arrays of sounds, you will have to store your sound codes as if they were string items, and the same applies to graphics, though measurements can often be stored in number form because one measurement is usually one number rather than a whole collection as you might have for a sound or a graphics shape.

A simple list, whether of names or numbers, is called a one-dimensional array because each item can be found by specifying just one number, the position from the top of the list. We might, however, have a list which in written form had two items in each line, a name and a phone number. This is a simple example of a set of information which can be stored as a **two-dimensional array** (Figure 2.3). On a printed list we could locate an item by using instructions like line 24, right or line 35, left. The computer, confined to working with numbers will use 0 for the first item in the line (the left hand) and 1 for the next (the right-hand one), so that for the computer this could be coded as 24, 1 or 35, 0. If the array is called TELLIST, then the items could be referred to by the use of brackets as TELLIST[24][1] or as TELLIST(35, 0), depending on how the programming language requires the location numbers to be arranged.

Column 0 → 6

							Row
5	22	31	7	44	6	71	0
21	3	7	66	2	21	8	↓
8	12	41	71	16	14	9	↓
18	6	22	16	5	9	22	3

Figure 2.3 *A two-dimensional array, or matrix, illustrated as lines and columns. We can refer to any element in the array by using its line and column numbers*

You can imagine a two-dimensional list like this as a sheet with rows and columns and it is just about possible to think of a three-dimensional list in terms of several sheets of paper with rows and columns on each, so that you had a number for the sheet, one for the row and another for the column. Most languages allow arrays of more than three dimensions to be used; the main problem is in finding any sort of way of imagining these arrays. An array with more than one dimension is sometimes referred to as a matrix (plural *matrices*).

Exercise 2

A list of twenty-six names, each starting with a different letter of the alphabet, is maintained in alphabetical order, using the array variable name NAMLST[1] to NAMLST[26]. Outline how the computer could find a given name such as SMITH in this list and print also the names just before and just following this name.

Several modern programming languages provide for a different form of organization of data, called a **record** or **structure**. A structure uses a reference name and consists of more than one item, but unlike an array, it can consist of more than one data type (Figure 2.4). When you store an array, you have to choose a number array or a string array. If you choose a number

Pending	Name – string or array of characters
Pat	Name – string or array of characters
44	Age – short integer or cardinal
1.87	Height – short floating-point number
1070625	Ref. no. – long interger

Figure 2.4 *A record or structure, which can consist of more than one data type. Not all computer programming languages make provision for the use of records*

array, the array must consist of numbers only, and names or symbols cannot be stored. If you wanted to store a telephone number in a number array, for example, you could not store it in the form 01-55504-71615 because the hyphen (-) is not a digit. In addition, because of the way that a number is coded and stored, you might find that the telephone number was read out of the memory as -127118 (if you were lucky) or even as 1.271E5, meaning 127100. Number coding is intended to make it easy for the machine to carry out arithmetic, and if your numbers are not for this purpose (like telephone numbers, address numbers, departmental reference numbers) then they should be stored as strings. Conversely, if you use a string array, each item in the array must be a string, and this can include a number put into string code, one code for each character.

The structure, by contrast, can contain mixtures of strings and numbers, with each coded in its own form. If you have a structure that contained a name, a tax code number and an amount of money all contained in a structure, then the tax code and money amounts could be used by the program to calculate a tax amount without any need to make any conversions from string coding to number coding, because the numbers are held already in number-coded form. You could not form an array in which you had for each name these two numbers in number form – they would have to be coded as strings and converted into number coding to be used as numbers. By using a structure, you can hold a set of items together in whatever form is suitable. Languages that permit the use of structures directly (without any special programming effort) will also permit you to use an array of structures, so that you can pick out one set of data from a list in the usual array manner.

Types of program instructions

A programming language can look very complicated until you see that all of the instructions can be put into a few groups. We usually distinguish between commands and instructions, reserving the word **command** to mean something outside a program, a direct request to the computer to do something like run a program or produce a list of the programs on a disk. This reserves the word instruction to mean part of a program, one of a list of instructions that will carry out the actions of the program. A complete instruction (instruction and data together) makes up a **statement**, and most languages are organized so that there is one statement on each line of the program.

One important class of instruction is assignment, meaning that a value, number or string, is assigned to a name of a constant or variable. Once assignment has been carried out the name can be used in place of the number or string, so that, for example, typing PI will always mean the number 3.1416 and typing CONM will always mean **Pottlehurst Die and Tool Co. Ltd.** Assignment in most languages makes use of the = sign, sometimes along with the colon as := but more often by itself.

Once assignments have been made, actions can be carried out on the assigned quantities. Some of these actions will be carried out by **operators**, the familiar + − * / symbols, and other actions are carried out by **functions**, another class of instruction. Most computing languages divide their functions into several groups such as number functions, string functions and logical functions. Number functions include such actions as taking logarithms, finding the sine of an angle and finding a power of a number, along with others which will vary from language to language. Some languages are constructed so that you can add to the functions for yourself. All allow you to combine functions in such a way as to create a new action so that if you want to take each number in a list and find its cube, then take the square root, then your programming language will have ways of setting out this set of instructions.

String functions include such actions as shortening a string, extracting from the left, right or centre of a string, finding the number of characters in a string and converting a number that is in string form into number code form. Some languages are notoriously ill-equipped for string handling, so that a string has to be treated as an array of characters, others are blessed with an excellent range of functions that allow strings to be handled without any reference to arrays. If much of your programming work is concerned with numbers and graphics, then string handling may be unimportant, and it does not necessarily follow that a language with easy string handling is necessarily the best language to program in even if most of the programming effort concerns strings. Making string handling easy for the programmer can often result in programs that run slowly or are inconvenient for the operator.

Logical functions allow tests and comparisons to be made, and always have a result that consists of a code for TRUE (usually −1) or a code for FALSE (usually 0). You can, for example, create a test for the number assigned to the name TAXCODE to be compared to the number assigned to ALLOWANCE, so that the TRUE or FALSE result of the comparison determines whether or not tax will be deducted (Figure 2.5). You can also compare the word stored as string variable DECISION with the word YES, and use the TRUE or FALSE result to carry out the printing of a name or the omission of the name. The logic functions are a very important feature of a language because they determine how easy it will be to carry out the implementation of a programming plan.

Decision steps are used to make the result of a test perform some action, such as carrying out an action (including repeating an action), altering data, performing an input or output, or ending the program. The way that decision steps are implemented varies from one language to another, but the most common method is to supply in the program the name of a module which should be run if the test is true, and possibly another module to run if

Test:	**IF (A = 5)**	Result:	**TRUE** (A is equal to 5) **FALSE** (A is not equal to 5)

Coding: TRUE = −1, FALSE = 0. For single-byte numbers this means that TRUE is 11111111 in binary and FALSE is 00000000. This makes it easy for the computer to interpret NOT (TRUE) = FALSE and NOT (FALSE) = TRUE

Figure 2.5 *A test which gives a TRUE or FALSE result. All tests must be formulated so as to give this type of result (a* **Boolean** *result)*

the result of the test is false. The way that tests and decisions are implemented determines what the program will do, and is a very important part of the planning of the program.

Another very important set of instructions deals with inputs and outputs. All languages provide for input from the keyboard and output to the screen, and usually output to the printer will be reasonably simple to provide for. A few languages do not have any standard provision for the use of disks for inputs and outputs, however, so that each version of such languages has a non-standard set of instructions for these essential actions. Languages designed in the 1970s and since provide for disk input and output in the normal set of language instructions, but many languages were designed well before the modern microcomputer era, and have only the most primitive provision for storage outside the memory of the computer itself.

Finally, we have the system control actions which consist mainly of direct commands to the machine, but which in many languages can also be used as program instructions. If, for example, your program requires you to insert a floppy disk into the drive it would be ridiculous to have to leave the program in order to find out what was on the disk. If the language contains suitable control actions, then the contents of the disk can be checked. The contents might be displayed on the screen so that you can check for yourself, or the program might search the disk for a set of data and report in the form of a message such as WRONG DISK if this data is not found.

Exercise 3

Decide how you would classify the following command words and commands of a programming language:

(a) REPEAT
(b) OUTPUT
(c) IF A <B
(d) NAME = "SINCLAIR"

Algorithms

An algorithm is a routine for solving a problem. To take a simple example, the VAT on an amount is found by multiplying the amount by 0.15, and this tax will then be added on. An algorithm for VAT, put into words, might read:

add to number the quantity (number × 0.15)

or this could be written as a formula:

$$X + (X * 0.15)$$

and either way this is a form of algorithm, a description of how to solve a problem or carry out a process.

The design of any computer program must start with an algorithm, because unless you know a method for solving a problem, you cannot write a computer program for solving it. Computer programs cannot solve problems that are impossible for humans, all they can do is carry out an algorithm very much faster than a human, so that problems that might take a team of humans many years to solve can be solved by the computer in minutes – provided the method of solving the problem is known.

One particular advantage of using a computer is that it can deal very well with algorithms that require a lot of repetition. For example, there is a well-known way of finding the square root of any number which is noted in Figure 2.6. This depends on guessing a number, substituting that number into a formula, and obtaining another number which is in turn substituted into the formula. When the formula produces the same number on two consecutive tries, the number is the required square root. This is a simple example of an **iterative** method, one that depends on the same set of steps being repeated with just one alteration (the inserted number) each time. The repetition or iteration is continued until some condition is met, like consecutive answers being identical or within some set limit.

Program flow

Since a program on a conventional serial computing language consists of a set of instructions that must be carried out in sequence, the order of the instructions, called the **program flow** is of vital importance. In the early days of computing, program flow was expressed in chart form, using the flowchart symbols of which a few are illustrated in Figure 2.7. A flowchart showed how each small section of a program would be arranged in sequence,

x is number whose square root is to be found
n is a guessed number which is used as an approximation

Formula is: $\dfrac{n + \frac{x}{n}}{2}$ for a closer approximation.

Example:

Find the square root of 52

A reasonable guess would be 7, so that the formula gives: $\dfrac{7 + \frac{52}{7}}{2}$

which is 7.2145 (taking four decimal places)

Repeating this, using 7.2143 as the approximation gives: $\dfrac{7.2143 + \frac{52}{7.2143}}{2}$

which is 7.2111.
Using this quantity in the formula again gives 7.2111 once again, so that this is the required value of square root, correct to four places of decimals. Checking, 7.2111 squared is 51.999963, as close as you are likely to get using four places of decimals

Figure 2.6 *A method of finding a square root which depends on repeating the use of a formula until the result is constant*

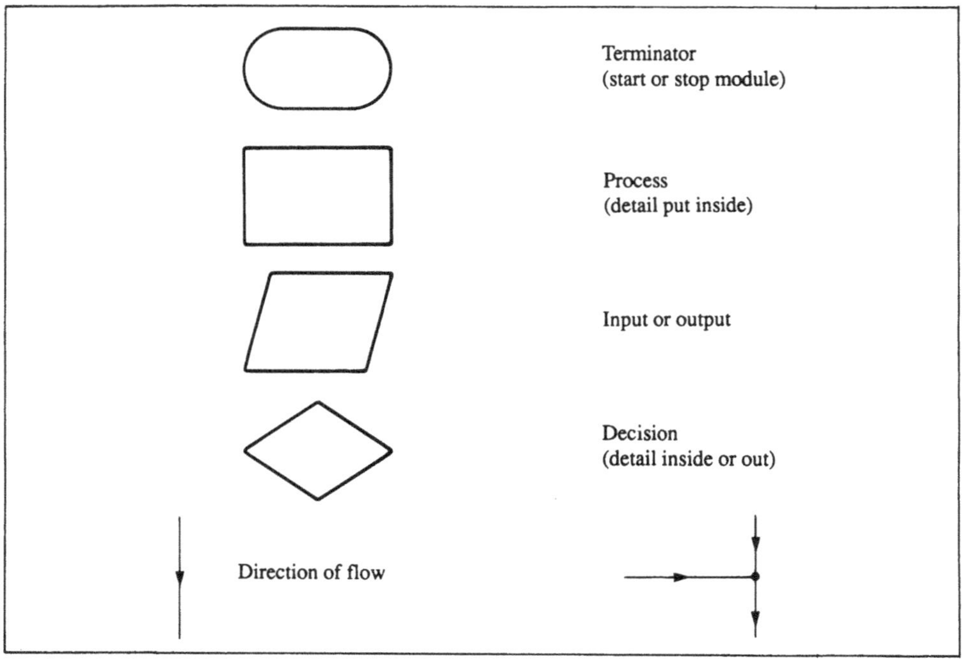

Figure 2.7 *Some of the standard flowchart symbols, seldom used nowadays*

giving an appearance as shown in Figure 2.8, and the programming could not start until this flowchart was drawn up. The spread of microcomputers, often calling for programming to be carried out in days rather than years (before the program became obsolete) called for more direct and quicker methods to be used, and one popular method is **pseudocode,** also known as **structured English** (Figure 2.9). This has the advantage of looking more like a program, yet not specifying a programming language. The actions are shown in sequence in abbreviated form, so that the flow appears clearly along with the steps of the program. There is no fixed form of pseudocode, unlike flowcharts, so that each user can incorporate his/her own variations. Though this makes it less easy for one programmer to take over the work of another, it allows for easier and quicker expression of ideas and its use has contributed greatly to speeding up the process from planning to coding.

Suggestions for practical work

1 Use flowchart or pseudocode to explain a program which converts a lowercase character into an uppercase character.
2 Work out the square root of 50 using the iterative formula of Figure 2.7.

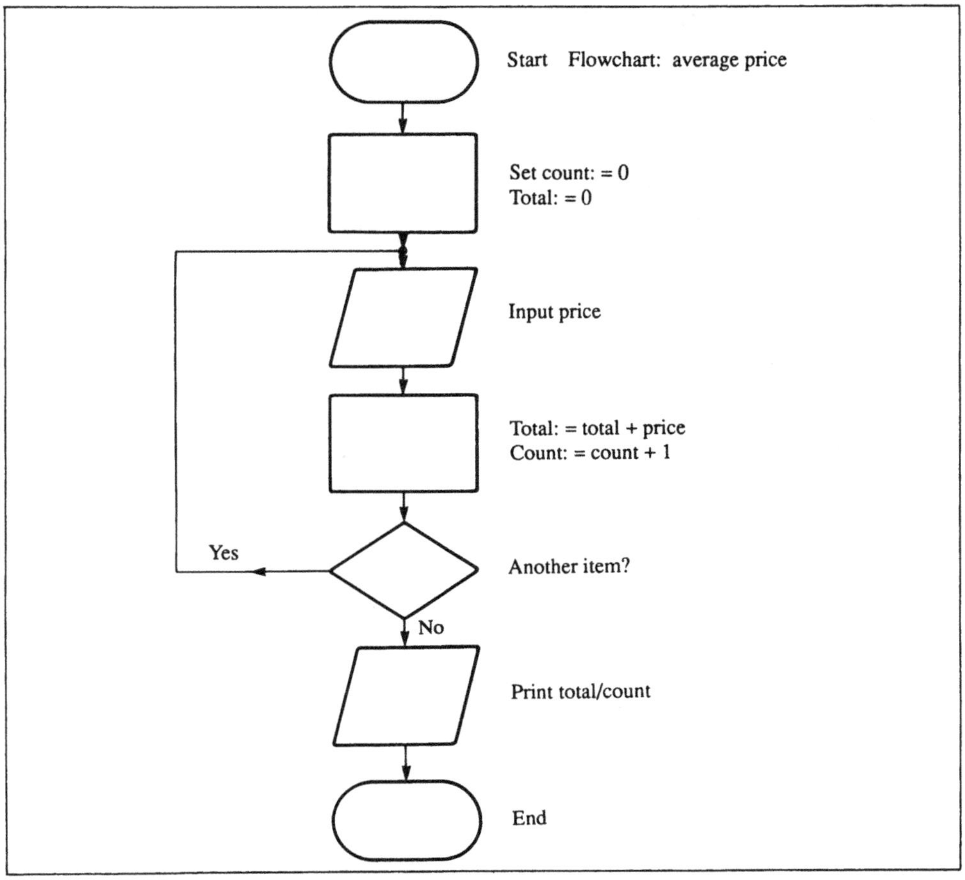

Figure 2.8 *A small piece of flowchart to illustrate the use of the symbols*

```
Module average price

Count: = 0
Total: = 0
Repeat
   Input price
   Add total, price
   Increment count
Until another item = false
Print total/count
```

Figure 2.9 *A piece of program described in pseudocode, or structured English. This is often easier to follow than a flowchart, and corresponds much better to the form of the program that will be written*

Multiple-Choice test questions

1 The ratio of width to height for a TV picture is called the aspect ratio. This would be coded as a:
(a) number variable
(b) number constant
(c) string variable
(d) string constant

2 The value of 22.76 is to be represented in a program by the name NUM1. This will require the use of a:
(a) logic statement
(b) string function
(c) number function
(d) assignment statement

3 A computer is to work with a set of book titles and prices. A suitable data type would be:
(a) string variable
(b) number variable
(c) string and number matrix
(d) number array

4 A statement such as IF X = 5 THEN K = MAX is an example of:
(a) assignment only
(b) test and assignment
(c) test only
(d) string function

5 The disk controller of a computer deals with:
(a) input and output
(b) output only
(c) input only
(d) none of these

6 The order of planning before writing a program is to:
(a) draw a flowchart and then write pseudocode
(b) find an algorithm and then write the program
(c) find an algorithm and then write pseudocode or draw a flowchart
(d) write the pseudocode and then the program

3 Computers and programs

Objectives

- Describe micro-, mini- and mainframe computers and their uses (1).
- Describe the ranges and types of computers and peripherals currently available (1.1); distinguish between batch, on-line and real-time systems (1.2).
- Describe applications to numerical computation, commercial data processing and industrial control processes (1.3).
- Describe the tasks undertaken in DP and the organization of these tasks (2).
- Describe the functions of data preparation, data control, computer operations, applications programming, systems analysis and design, database administration and network control (2.1).
- List the phases of a DP development project (2.2).
- Explain how an applications programmer interacts with other specialists (2.3).

Types of tasks

Some computers are required to handle only batch work. This means that a collection of data is presented to the computer, nowadays usually in disk form but sometimes as magnetic or paper tape, and the computer then processes this work, printing out results. A large store might, for example, keep details of all the transactions of one day on magnetic tape which would be collected after closing time. This tape would be fed into the computer which would calculate the total takings, analyse which items were selling best, calculate what orders would be needed to maintain stock levels, and possibly automatically send out these orders. The essence of batch processing is that the data is gathered up, often away from the computer, and is then processed at a different time. Most of the early applications for digitial computers were for batch work, and this influenced the design of computers because a batch machine does not need a viewing screen (a **visual display unit**); its output is entirely on a printer or by way of command signals (to cause re-stocking orders, for example).

Real-time computing applies when the computer is used in automation control. The data that the computer needs is fed into the machine continuously, and the computer analyses this data and sends out the signals that make any necessary corrections to the process. This requires the computing part of the action to be carried out quickly, because if a correction is applied too late, the effect may be worse than not applying the correction at all. Slow reaction time can even cause instability of the form called 'hunting', in which too much correction is applied, but always too late (Figure 3.1). Real-time computing requires only signal inputs and outputs, and if a video screen or printer were used, it would be only to monitor the action and not as a vital part of the action. In many cases, no keyboard is required either except for diagnostic work.

On-line computing or interactive computing, means that the computer is being used with inputs and outputs that come from a terminal, a combination of keyboard and video screen. The terminal may be part of the computer itself, as in microcomputers, or it may be remote, in another room, another building, even in another country. The familiar microcomputers are interactive, and it is possible to gain access to a remote computer from a terminal which is then said to be on-line to the remote machine. When a travel agent uses a Prestel terminal, for example, to look up the availability of holidays, a large computer is being used on-line, giving responses to the keys that are being pressed on the terminal. On-line computing using a remote computer is a much more recent development, and the uses of computing have developed enormously since low-cost machines of this type became available. Because a machine is on-line, however, does not exclude it from the other types of use, and most machines that are designed for on-line use can be used for batch work and in many cases for real-time work as well.

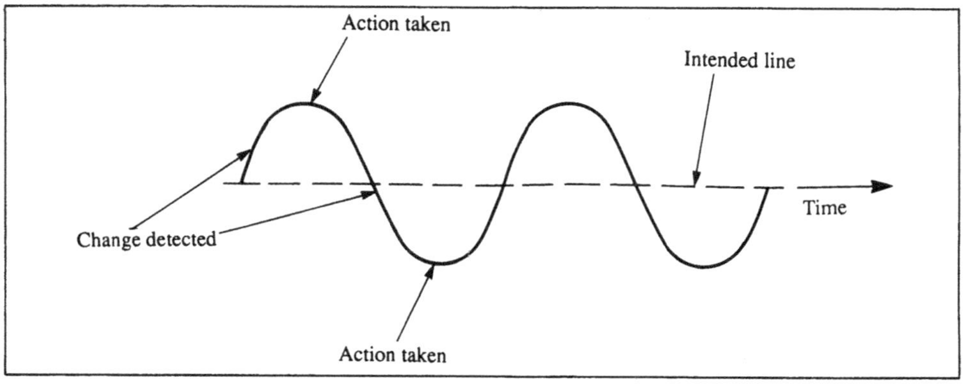

Figure 3.1 *Applying a correction to a changing output too late can result in the form of oscillation called hunting*

These different forms of computing determine the type and variety of computers that are available. The use of batch processing for very large amounts of data demands the use of machines which can cope with these quantities, and this is a task which is still filled by the larger machines, the mainframe and minicomputers. Mainframe machines are physically large, often require air-conditioned surroundings and rely on the use of magnetic memory which retains its data when power is switched off. The input to such computers is from magnetic tape and, today, only a few very old machines rely on the use of paper tape. Computing speeds are high, and the output is to a lineprinter, a wide-carriage machine which prints a complete line of characters in one impression, using a set of printwheels in each character position. The position of the mainframe machine for this type of work has been eroded by the appearance of floor-standing minicomputers which take up only a portion of the room and do not require air-conditioned surroundings. These are in turn being replaced by the most recent generation of desktop microcomputers.

The speed and capacity of the large mainframe, particularly the more advanced designs, are the features that keep up a demand for this type of machine. Batch processing does not require great computing speed, because the speed at which data can be processed is always greater than the speed at which it can be read into the machine or printed out. For real-time use, however, very high computing speed is essential. There is little point in taking ten minutes to plot and predict the course of a missile if the missile can reach you in four minutes, and if the time needed to analyse a factory process is too long, then the corrections that are applied will be too late and will probably over-compensate. Some mainframe machines are designed for the highest possible speeds, to the extent of making the machine of a circular pattern so as to reduce the distance that the signals have to travel between sections (Figure 3.2). Electrical signals take about 1 ns (one thousandth of a millionth of a second) to travel a distance of 20 cm, and in very fast computers, times in the nanosecond range are taken for computing actions. Computers (super-computers) of this type are used for research work that involves fast real-time calculations and for applications like weather forecasting which require a vast number of calculations, but even for everyday use like booking airline tickets a fast response is needed from a computer and this, combined with the amount of data that has to be handled, makes the use of a mainframe computer essential.

For the smaller scale of data and a slower time response, the minicomputer has superseded the mainframe, taking much less space and using a lot of the techniques that were developed for microcomputers. The medium-sized business, operating on one site and handling a few thousand customers can use a mini- rather than a mainframe. Another advantage is that the modern minicomputer will be interactive, allowing the operator the choice of using it for purposes other than batch or real-time computing. Like the mainframe, the modern minicomputer permits use by a number of terminals, all connected to the central unit and all working independently. One user may be typing letters, making use of a word-processing program, another may be working on accounts, using a spreadsheet program, a third may be working on customer records using a database. To all intents and purposes they

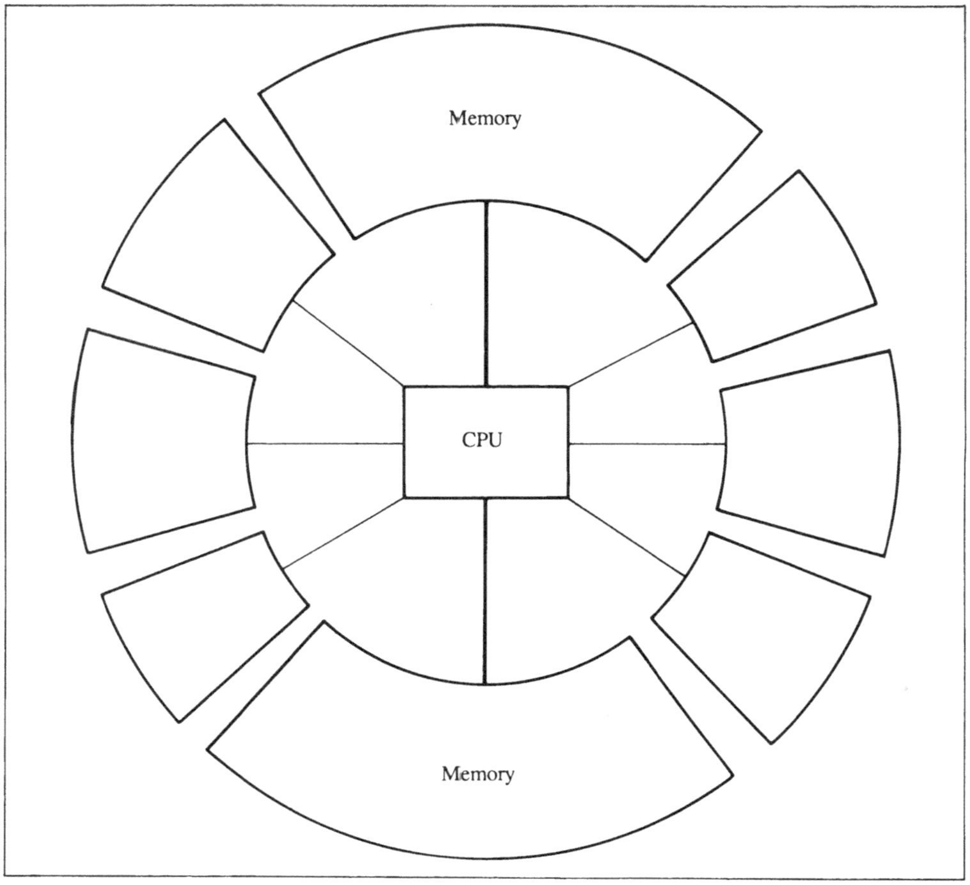

Figure 3.2 *A computer designed in circular form so as to minimize the time that signals take to travel from one section to another. The CPU is located centrally, since most signal paths are between the CPU and other units*

appear to be making simultaneous use of the computer but they are, in fact, **timesharing** the machine. The computer is servicing each activity for a few thousandths of a second in rotation, making full use of the fact that where the input to a program comes from a keyboard, there is a large (in computing terms) time interval between pressing one key and pressing the next. This method of working is ideal when the machine has ample memory and operates fast, because unless the number of users becomes very large, the timesharing is never obvious. With too many operators, there can be obvious pauses between pressing a key and seeing a character appear on the screen.

The microcomputer is a desktop machine which has the speed and memory capacity that a few years ago would have been the province of a minicomputer. The main advantage of the micro is the availability of distributed computing, allowing each office to work with its own data bank and independently of all others. The use of microcomputers removes the problems of what happens when a single main computer fails, because there is little likelihood of ten to one hundred microcomputers all failing at the same time for any reason other than a total failure of power. The micro also ensures greater confidentiality of data, because the user can keep confidential records on a disk which can be carried about, with no central records kept on a machine to which many others have access. Though micros can be operated with timesharing and in networks, in which several computers share data stores and printers, the greatest advantage of the micro is obtained when it is used as a stand-alone machine, and the use of modems to link machines through telephone lines makes it possible for the first time to have work done anywhere, bringing the promise of an end to the business of moving thousands of people twice a day to sit at a desk and press keys which they could press on a similar computer at home.

Exercise 1

Discuss the probable computing needs of:
(a) a small hardware store
(b) an agent for a mail-order catalogue
(c) the mail-order catalogue company
(d) a technical college

Computing work

One application of computers which is still a major requirement is numerical processing. The solution of problems in engineering and science, particularly examples like the stresses on bridges, the path of airliners, the positions of planets and weather forecasting all demand equations to be solved at a rate of up to several millions per second. This calls for very fast processing, and the speed of a computer for such work is measured in a unit called the megaflop – the number of millions of floating-point arithmetic operations per second. Work at megaflop speeds requires the use of specialized mainframes, and for less intensive work, a minicomputer can cope. The most recent generation of microcomputers are also capable of respectable rates of data processing, making them suitable for numerical work.

Apart from the suitability of the machine, the program that is being used has to be capable of high performance. The program must be written in a language that allows for fast arithmetic, and languages are far from equal in this respect. Some languages allow for this type of work to be carried out by subprograms that are written in a faster language (assembly language), others can make use of specialized co-processors. A co-processor is an extension to a computer circuit that consist of a specialized plug-in module which will deal with calculations separately, allowing the main unit to concentrate on input and output. The use of a co-processor can often speed up arithmetical work by ten to thirty times, depending on the application. In the earlier days of programming, a programming language called

FORTRAN (from formula translation) was extensively used for numerical work, and versions of FORTRAN are still available and in use for such purposes, although other languages are by now more fashionable. The language BASIC was devised as a method of learning FORTRAN, and most varieties of BASIC permit the same numerical abilities as FORTRAN.

Commercial data processing has always been one of the main applications for computing. The daily transactions of any large firm generate a huge amount of data on sales, purchases, stock changes, hours worked, overheads and other information of a financial and numerical nature, and the use of the computer to replace clerks by putting this material in order was one of the earliest uses for computers outside research laboratories. In the UK much of the pioneering work in commercial computing was done by Lyons, and the LEO (Lyons Electronic Office) machine that was developed for the purpose, since suitable computers could not be bought at the time, incorporated several innovations that were widely copied by later computers.

The traditional commercial data processing (DP) operation is a batch process, with tapes placed inside secure boxes being left outside shop doors to be picked up by processing specialists after hours. The trend now, however, is to make such computing in real-time, so that each transaction is noted by the computer and processed at once. This allows stocks to be kept at lower levels, since trends can be picked up earlier and ordering done a day before it could be done with batch methods. Tighter management control is also possible when the computing is carried out in real-time. This requires that each till shall be a computer terminal and that the actions of ordering are carried out either by way of the computer or are notified to the computer at the time of ordering. The programming for such real-time applications is very much more difficult than for the traditional batch use, and programming languages such as Cobol which were suited to the leisurely pace of batch computing are not exactly ideal for use with real-time work. It is also difficult to test a program for real-time DP other than in a live situation, because unlike batch processing, it is not easy to create dummy data for testing. Stores also make use of on-line computing to process credit cards by scanning the card through a reader rather than by laboriously writing down the details on to a form.

The third traditional area for the larger computer is industrial control, with the computer once again used in real-time. Inputs are taken at points in a process which allow quality and quantity checks to be expressed in number terms, and the results are used to produce output signals that control the process. This leads to much tighter control than is ever possible manually, and if the processing is fast enough it is possible to operate a 'nil reject' system, with every product within specification. Programming for this type of use is extremely difficult because of the need to maintain speed as well as precision, and testing of the software other than under operating conditions is impossible unless simulation inputs can be provided. A fault in a DP program might lead to a cheque for £000.00 being issued, but a mistake in a control system could result in a process running out of control, possibly causing damage, even injury to users.

The traditional areas of use of large computers have been joined by a by-product of the microcomputer revolution, the personal office system. We are

Date	Name	Amount	VAT	Raw goods	Services	Other
12 Oct	Berringer Ltd	£230.00	£30	£200		
13 Oct	Catalytical Inc	£805.00	£105		£700	
14 Oct	Post	£22.50				£22.50
15 Oct	D. Grimshaw	£57.50	£7.50		£50.00	

Figure 3.3 *The form of a spreadsheet, a form of computer ledger which recalculates totals each time a new entry is made. Each 'cell' can contain a formula that refers to other cells, but only the result of this is shown. For example, a cell D3 might contain the formula C3*0.15, but what appears at that position is the result of multiplying the number in C3 by 0.15*

so accustomed to the use of word-processing and spreadsheets (Figure 3.3) that it is difficult to remember that these are very new applications which, unlike the use of databases, never existed on mainframe machines in the past. The first spreadsheet, Visicalc, appeared in 1978, running on the Apple-2 microcomputer, and several manufacturers of larger machines thought at the time that it was a hoax, that such computing power could not exist on a small machine. The use of spreadsheets, word-processors and databases for microcomputers has been the main growth area of computing in the years since 1978 to the extent that an office without a microcomputer is an odd and unusual sight. Microcomputing is interactive, requiring more of the time of the user than the traditional type of machine, but providing information very soon after receiving data. The days of taking a reel of tape to a computing room along with a request to have results at the end of the week have been replaced by typing a few instructions to a program running on a desktop machine and seeing the results on the screen as soon as they are processed.

Exercise 2

Decide which of the following applications will require fast numerical processing:

(a) Keeping records of books borrowed from a library.
(b) Using a program which created technical drawings by computer.
(c) Working out monthly salaries.
(d) Allocating landing 'slots' for aircraft.

Work classifications

The work that is involved in the day to day use of a large mainframe computer cannot be carried out by one operator and will normally be the responsibility of a team of specialists. By contrast, the user of a desktop micro will as often as not carry out all of these tasks single-handed, demanding that the machine should be easier to use and that the user should know more about the machine and the use of its programs than the more remote mainframe user. The main impact of the microcomputer has been to make computer users aware that computing need not be a mysterious activity that needs to be farmed out to specialists, because microcomputer manufacturers and software specialists have pioneered systems which, though providing as much computing power as the mainframe of a few years back, are nevertheless easier to use and understand. The functions that have to be carried out in order to keep the computer running are therefore not necessarily carried out on the basis of one specialist or team to each function, but the distinctions are still useful in understanding how much is required in the running of a computer system.

Data preparation is the start of any batch processing operation, and some form of data preparation is involved in any type of use of a computer. The main effort lies in the collection of the data and its arrangement into a form that is suitable for the computer to use. Just to take a very elementary example, this might involve collecting the names and departmental numbers of several hundred employees and arranging them with surname first, then initials, then number for typing into the memory of the machine. It is possible to arrange during typing, but this is likely to lead to more mistakes being made and not all users of the machine necessarily know how to correct a wrong entry once it has been entered into the machine. Data preparation is usually considerably more elaborate than this and for large batch-operated machine can include the actions of typing in the data to be recorded on magnetic tape or disk for later batch processing. Data in the form of such tape or disk is said to be **machine readable**, meaning that it can be fed automatically into the computer without any need for human intervention once the tape has been loaded. The aim of data preparation, then, is to change the data into machine readable form.

For a machine that is used in real-time, the data may be provided automatically in readable form, from electronic tills, from digital measuring equipment or from remote keyboards, so that there is no separate data preparation action. The amount of data that is used along with a desktop computer is comparatively small, so that no separate data preparation is needed in this case either and any rearrangement of data is carried out by the user as the data is typed in. Data preparation can be labour-intensive, and should be avoided if possible and minimized if it cannot be avoided. When data is being gathered by the filling in of forms, then the forms should be designed so that the data must be entered in a way that makes it suitable for easy transcription into the machine without further preparation. This is done by designing forms with the answer spaces divided into one square for each printed character and with the answers in separate boxes in the order that will be used for entering the data into the machine. Very often these boxes are numbered to correspond with codings that are used by the data-processing program.

Data that is gathered and arranged in this way is **raw data**, and as such will provide the main source of any errors that will appear later. Unless a program is grossly faulty, the computer will not make mistakes with this data but if a name is misspelled at this stage then it will remain misspelled until someone notices the mistake and corrects it. For desktop machines this is a relatively simple process, but programs for large mainframe machines are designed so that changes to data are far from easy to carry out. This makes it particularly important to ensure that the raw data is valid and correct as far as it is possible to check, and this is the data control function.

Some data control can be carried out by the program itself. Each item of data that is entered can be checked against reasonable criteria so as to catch gross mistakes, particularly typing errors. It is easy, for example, to test a data of birth and reject anything earlier than 1880, or dates like 30th February. Spelling mistakes in names cannot be caught in this way, however, because there is an infinite variety of names and spellings. It should be possible to ensure that a demand for one million pounds is not sent to a small business that never orders more than £20 worth of goods per month (by coding this as a small-scale trader and querying anything over some set amount), and it should be equally possible for the program to avoid sending out demands for £0.00 and demanding payment. The more that can be intercepted by the machine itself, the simpler the task of data control.

For much of the activity of data control, however, there is no substitute for human intervention. The machine can check a list of names against an older list, but new names have to be scrutinized. You cannot easily program a machine to query a name like M. Mouse or D. Duck, but a human operator can be alerted to the possibility of error or fraud by such names. A human operator might also spot that there was no number 36 in Whistleton Drive, or that a written telephone number could not exist; these are checks that could not be incorporated in any simple way into a program for the smaller type of machine – a large mainframe might contain details of each address in a town and be able to find an error by comparison. When errors or anomalies do find their way into data and are entered into the machine, then the other function of data control is to extract such entries and either amend them or cancel them. This requires sufficient knowledge of the program, and for DP programs running on mainframes this may require the use of a password, putting as many obstacles as possible in the way of altering data. The purpose is to avoid the accidental alteration of data which might occur if the data were easy to change, or the deliberate changing of data in order to carry out fraud. The protection measures, however, often have the effect that errors are not corrected for some considerable time.

Computer operation is a separate function nowadays only for users of mainframe and the larger minicomputers. Operation includes switching up and switching down of computer systems which are not operated full time; so that the operator is responsible for saving any data that would otherwise be lost when the machine is switched off, and reinstating that data when the machine is later switched on again. The operator also attends to the operating system of the computer, ensuring that the correct data is present and keeping records of where data is stored when not being processed. The most obvious task is entry of data and programs into the computer and the running of the programs, together with printing out results.

The extensive use of desktop machines implies that the user of each machine is its operator, as well as providing data preparation and control. Even on the larger machines, the role of the operator is changing in the direction of the more technical side of operation, with data entry being done by anyone with access to a terminal. This calls for a higher level of skill on the part of operators which at present is not reflected in the salaries paid to operators, some of whom are carrying out the tasks that once were assigned to maintenance engineers or programmers.

Exercise 3

Which of the following errors could easily be detected by a suitably programmed computer, and which would probably require human intervention.

(a) Today's date.
(b) Name of a client.
(c) Income-tax coding.
(d) Post code of an address.
(e) Day on which Christmas 1995 will fall.

Higher-level functions

The functions that we have been looking at are sometimes described as being low-level, because none of them requires a great deal of knowledge about the computer or the programs. Even the work of the operator has in the past been fairly routine, requiring nothing more that a sequence of tasks which are not difficult to learn. The higher-level functions concern the programming of the computer and the management of how it is used, but these functions are just as much undermined by the spread of microcomputers as are the lower-level ones. Offices that make intensive use of microcomputers require no programmers, because they will use the ready-made packages that are in such abundant supply for these machines. One of the most noticeable results of the growth in the use of desktop machines has been the appearance and rapid growth of software houses which publish and distribute off-the-shelf software for a fraction of the price of custom-designed software. The great variety of such software that exists now means that it would be very difficult to put forward a convincing case for employing programmers in any firm that used microcomputers mainly.

The applications programmer, where such a job title still exists, is concerned with developing individual programs, each of which carries out a specific task. At one time, an applications programmer might develop programs such as stock control or word-processing, but it is much more likely now that off-the-shelf software would be used for such tasks if desktop machines are being used. The applications programmer is most likely to be found where the machine that is used is a mainframe or a large mini, and the task of the applications programmer is to design and implement the individual programs that are needed, such as accounts processing, billing systems, wages statements and so on. In a small-scale system, the work of the applications programmer might be virtually complete when these programs had been written, tested and put into use, but in a large-scale business the work is never complete, because continually changing needs mean that programs have to be altered and updated. Where a lot of different applications programs are in use, this requirement for updating can result in almost as much work as was involved in the original design of the programs.

Systems programming is not concerned with individual programs but with how the complete system is used. A systems programmer will, for example, devise programs that allow several users to time-share the use of the computer, with password protection for each user to protect his/her data. The scope of the systems programmer is the entire use of the computer rather than individual programs, so that the individual programs can run without interfering with each other, using resources like printers and databanks in a predictable way that does not cause problems such as a printer listing one line of accounts followed by a line of stock entry and a line of personnel records. Once again, on desktop machines the function of systems programmer does not exist, because such machines come with their own operating systems ready provided in the form of industry standards like MS-DOS and Unix. On the larger machines even if a standardized operating system is used, the systems programmer is still required to ensure that the computer system is suited to the user rather than the other way round.

The systems analyst is at the top of the hierarchy of computing functions, particularly for very large enterprises. The task of the analyst is to decide on the best way to make use of the computer, and implement this design. The analyst will have to find out from each user of the computer system what will be required, and if the users are inexperienced to suggest what might be possible. At this stage, the amount and type of data that will be used can be assessed, and the pattern of forms for input of data and the way that data will be filed can be determined. The systems analyst then writes specifications for programs which will subsequently be written by the systems and applications programmers. When these programs are produced, the systems analyst takes charge of testing the individual programs and the complete system, followed by ensuring that each user is taught how to take advantage of what is available. The final task is complete documentation of the system so that anyone who later wishes to make changes can do so without wasting time in discovering how the existing system works.

The systems analyst, like the moving finger, writes and moves on, because only a very large scale and expanding computer user would need a systems analyst permanently. At the other end of the scale, microcomputer users perform their own systems analysis, determining which tasks can be carried out by off-the-shelf software, and setting up this software for use. The weakness at this level is that there is often no documentation of what has been done, and this is particularly serious when the programs that are being used require a large amount of installing or contain 'macros', which are mini-programs that control the action of the software. Though a user of desktop machine may have no need of a systems analyst, there is a definite need for someone to take overall control of the programs and how they are used, and to document what is being done.

The containing work after a large computer system has been set into operations is carried out by the database administrator and the network controller. As the name suggests, the database administrator is concerned with the management of the data bank, which for a large-scale user might amount to millions of items. Even with the compact nature of storage of data for computers this requires a large amount of space, and whatever method of storing data is used there will have to be some form of backup, meaning that data must be copied at regular intervals in case of any fault developing in the storage systems. Of all the methods of storing data, only punched paper tape is **archival** in the sense that a paper tape kept in a dry cool place is likely to be unchanged in ten, twenty or fifty years time. Magnetic tape and disks offer much more compact storage, but no one can be quite certain for how long, since no one has used magnetic tape storage for fifty years. Certainly the tapes that were made in the distant past have exhibited corruption (random changes), and for this reason one of the main tasks of a database administrator has been to set up a routine for copying any data that is held on magnetic materials. The method that is used is known as the grandfather–father–son method, and it involves cycling three copies of each set of data so that at any given time you have a fresh copy (the son) along with its immediate predecessor (father) and in turn the copy (grandfather) from which this was taken. This three-part backup system has proved reliable if well maintained and is still in use even now that magnetic storage materials have improved to the extent that data corruption has become quite rare.

The database administrator also has to ensure that the database programs are providing what is needed. The data might, for example, contain data on the accounts of 120,000 customers and yet a user might find that it was impossible to find if older customers were running larger accounts. It is the responsibility of the database administrator to uncover such deficiencies (which arise because the need was not evident at the time when the system was analysed) and to see that the program is modified so as to cope with this requirement. More mundane tasks include ensuring that records are kept up to date, so that no one is billing a customer who died three years ago or sending goods to an address that is now a three-lane motorway.

Network control is a more specialized function, and one which has arisen since the use of microcomputers became common. A network is a connection path among several computers which allows the computers to share data and facilities such as printers and databases. Computers of any size can be networked, but the advantages of networking are greater for the users of desktop machines, because networking, unlike the timesharing of a single computer among several users, does not reduce the speed of each individual machine to any noticeable extent. A network usually includes one machine, the **server** which has considerably more capacity than the others and which can act as a controller. On request from a remote machine, the server will read a program from its disks and send the program along the network cables to the remote machine to be used. Contrast this with the timeshare system in which the program stays in the main machine and the user has access to it only through a terminal. By using networking, several machines can be running different programs or be at different stages in the same program without interference. Control is needed when there is a request for a new program or for access to a printer, and the network control must be designed to all such tasks to be carried out without interference or undue delay.

Steps in a program project

Suppose that a company has decided to implement the use of computing to simplify its service to the public of spare parts for electrical domestic equipment from a central depot. The systems analyst would normally first have to decide whether the problem *could* be solved, but since this is a straightforward type of problem no time needs to be spent on feasibility at this stage, only on the design of a system. This is not always so, and in some projects almost as much time needs to be spent in assessing whether a solution is possible as in creating the solution, particularly when fast real-time computing is required. Most projects that involve commercial data processing are of a type for which there is an existing solution, so that their feasibility is not a problem.

The system requirements then need to be studied. How will a request for spares be made? One possibility is to identify the part number from a catalogue, or on microfilm, and then key in the part number to the computer. A bolder possibility is to keep part illustrations and numbers on computer files, so that the computer screen will show the shape of the part and its number, and pressing an 'ACCEPT' key will carry out the ordering. This seems to be a neater solution which is easier to use and to keep up to date, but is it feasible? The system of keying in the number is traditional but archaic, and it does nothing to avoid the immense amount of time that is wasted in identifying the part in the first place. With the advances that modern microcomputers have brought, the more modern approach sounds better. A discussion with potential users shows that they would much prefer to make the computer do the work of searching, though this requires considerably more computer capacity than the straightforward method.

The next step is to find out what will be involved in this solution. How many parts do we have to be able to identify, how many need drawings, and how would the drawings be held in the computer. Unlike the conventional microfilm system, in which the parts maker usually provides the microfilm and the dealer needs only a reader, this system calls for some method of entering this data into the computer. As it happens, **scanners** exist which can encode drawings, and there are programs that can scale such drawings up or down in size so that they can be fitted into a page. The finding system will consist of locating a page, pointing to the correct part using a **mouse** or keys, and then pressing an ACCEPT key. This will print out a request form in the warehouse. Perhaps at this stage, we could think of extending the scheme later to a fully automated warehouse, so that the correct parts-bin could be placed on a moving belt automatically.

This in turn leads to specifications being drawn up for the various parts of the program; the input of the parts data, the specification of a required part, and the method of passing the request on for action. We have to assume that since this method has been chosen, the analyst knows of a computer system on which such work is possible. The specifications can now be passed to the programmers who will start to break down each specification into programmable parts. Most programmers nowadays do not 'reinvent the wheel', so that they will be able to use sections of programs they have designed or used before in similar circumstances. Many programming textbooks assume that every program has to be designed from the beginning, but this is now very rare. Modern programming languages are **modular**, meaning that they can be used to create pieces of program which are independent of each other but which can be assembled into a program with comparatively little effort.

When each program section is ready, it can be tested on the computer system – in some cases it will be possible to test the programming on a desktop machine with a small amount of data. Thorough testing is extremely difficult, and it is always better that someone with very little knowledge of computing should participate, because programmers undertaking testing have a habit of being able to avoid faults rather than finding them. At this stage, the program should be free of gross errors, the type that cause the computer to seize up, so that the programmers can concentrate on improving the ease of use of the system – the man–machine interface as it is called. As the system moves towards acceptance, the people who will use it can be trained; if the design principles have been well implemented the amount of training should be quite small.

All through this work, the systems analyst will have been keeping notes and will by this stage have started on the documentation for the system. This will be in several parts, one of which will show both outline and detail plans. Another set of documents will deal with the work of the programmers, showing the program coding along with notes on how the sections of program fit with each other. The third part will be the user instructions for routine use of the system and also for coping with problems. A fourth set of documents cannot be compiled yet – they will list the user history of the system. The applications programmer will at all times need to consult extensively with the other specialists. It would be impossible, for example, to devise suitable data entry steps without consulting the data preparation manager, and there has to be particularly close collaboration between the applications programmer and the systems analyst, because the applications programmer is trying to implement what the systems analyst has designed.

Suggestions for practical work

1 Arrange to see computers used commercially for batch processing, numerical analysis and process control.
2 Devise and test data preparation methods for a proposed new tax on all personal possessions worth over £1,000.
3 Use a simulated industrial control system and check the effects of putting delays into control loops.

Multiple-choice test questions

1 A computer user has to prepare six reports and then transmit them to a head office. This requires a combination of:
(a) on-line and real-time computing

(b) real-time and batch computing
(c) batch and on-line computing
(d) batch computing only

2 A firm prepares local area maps. Its computer can be used:
(a) to store map drawings
(b) to process orders
(c) to control printing machines
(d) all of these actions

3 An essential part of data preparation is:
(a) weeding out useless data
(b) putting data into alphabetical or numerical order
(c) checking additions of numbers
(d) counting the number of data items

4 An applications programmer is required particularly where the computing is done by:
(a) microcomputers running off-the-shelf software
(b) a mainframe running custom-written software
(c) a minicomputer and several networked micros running off-the-shelf software
(d) a minicomputer running software serviced by an agency

5 The overall planning of a program for a large-scale requirement is primarily the responsibility of the:
(a) systems programmer
(b) applications programmer
(c) systems analyst
(d) database administrator

6 In the course of a data processing project the applications programmer will work most closely with:
(a) the systems programmer
(b) the data preparation officer
(c) the database administration officer
(d) the systems analyst

4 Inside the machine

Objectives

- Explain the basic concepts of computer architecture (5): Instruction execution cycles (5.1); bit, byte, word (5.2); addressing memory (5.3); interfacing and peripherals (5.5).
- Describe the differences between mainframe, mini- and microcomputers (6).
- Describe the characteristics of main memory and backing storage devices (7.1).

The working core of any computer, of any size, is the unit called the central processing unit (CPU). The CPU for a large mainframe computer will be a large electronic circuit constructed using transistors which have been chosen for outstandingly fast operation. A desktop microcomputer will use a CPU which is a single silicon chip, the type we call a microprocessor. Minicomputers use a mixture of techniques, and one very common method of constructing the CPU is to use a set of chips that are called bit slice microprocessors. Whatever the size and construction, the purpose of the CPU is to organize and control all of the actions of the computer.

We have seen in Chapter 1 that any form of information can be coded into the form of numbers, and that numbers can be converted into binary form as a set of 1s and 0s. Each digit of a binary number is called a **bit**, and the handling of binary numbers in a computer is in units that are formed from groups of bits. These units are always multiples of eight bits. Mainframe computers often use sets of forty-eight, fifty-six or more bits, but the early microcomputers used eight bits, forming a unit called a **byte**. The byte is the smallest group that will accommodate the ASCII codes that are used for letter and number coding. Minicomputers have tended to use 32-bit groups, sometimes known as a double-word or Dword. Developments in desktop microcomputers have led first to the adoption of sixteen bit groups (a **word**) and more recently to the use of 32-bits, so that the boundary between the techniques of the microcomputer and of the minicomputer is continually shifting, and similarly many minicomputers are now as powerful as mainframe machines of only a few years earlier.

The CPU of a microcomputer may work with eight bits, sixteen bits or thirty-two bits, and the number is fixed by the type of chip that has been chosen. Minicomputers generally make use of specialized single-bit microprocessors, the bit-slice type, and use whatever number, 32 or 48, is required to make up the size of group that the machine is designed around. The mainframe type of machine still uses an assembled CPU, as distinct from the silicon chip type, so as to obtain the highest possible operating speed, and such units can be constructed for as many bits of grouping as are required by the design, usually forty-eight or sometimes fifty-six.

The size of unit that the CPU works with is not necessarily the size of unit that the computer program works with. Some of these units might be strings, others are numbers, but none of them can be guaranteed to fit neatly into the bit-grouping that the CPU uses. We have seen, for instance, that ASCII codes fit neatly into single byte units of eight bits each, so that a microcomputer working with single byte units can handle strings one character at a time. The use of word units of sixteen bits does not necessarily improve the handling of strings, because the choice is either to use single characters, using only half of a sixteen-bit unit, or to work with two characters at a time, which is not always desirable.

The use of a machine which handles larger groups of bits, therefore, does not automatically lead to faster and more efficient computing unless the conversion of data into these groupings is carried out efficiently. One aid to the efficient handling of data, for instance, is to use groups, called blocks, of typically 128 bytes (or 256 or 512 bytes), even if the size of each data element is smaller than that of the group. A block size unit can be located and worked with more quickly than smaller units, and the larger the grouping used in the CPU, the better it can deal with these blocks.

The CPU

The CPU itself is an electronic circuit which can carry out a limited number of actions on the chosen unit, whether byte, word or double-word. To avoid having to refer to groupings in this way we shall use the term **word** from now on to mean the grouping that the CPU uses. The important feature of the CPU is that each action is initiated by an instruction in the form of a word, so that the CPU works in a repeating sequence of instruction, then action, then instruction again. The speed of operation is very fast, so that the sequence of instruction words and data words cannot be supplied from the keyboard or even from a spinning disk, but from the memory of the machine, so that the CPU must be able to read words from the memory and also to place words into the memory. This is done by a system called **addressing**.

The memory of the computer is constructed from units, often single-byte units even if the CPU deals with larger words, and each unit is numbered consecutively, starting with 0. The numbering uses the binary scale, so that the unit of memory size for the smaller machines is the kilobyte (K) which is 1024 bytes rather than the 1000 which the use of the letter k would imply.

The reason for the use of this number, of course, is that 1024 is 2^{10}. If we take one K of memory as a simple example, the numbering of the bytes in such a memory unit will be from 0000000000 to 1111111111 (in denary, 0 to 1023), using ten binary digits. Within the computer, these digits are represented by electrical voltages, so that a 0 is represented by zero volts and a 1 by (usually) +5 V. Our example of a 1 K memory could be connected to the CPU by ten connecting lines, and if each of these could carry either a 0 or a 1 signal, then each and any of the 1024 bytes in the memory could have its number placed in binary code on these lines. This is termed addressing, and the lines are called address lines, or collectively as the **address bus**.

Memory banks for a computer are arranged so that when the address number for a byte is placed on the address lines, that byte is opened for access, allowing a byte of data to be placed into the memory (written) or copied from it (read) (Figure 4.1). Only writing changes the content of memory, because reading, like playing a tape, does not erase the memory but simply allows the stored signals to be shared along connecting lines (called the **data bus**) with other units, usually the CPU. The number of lines of the data bus determines the size of memory unit, byte or word, that the computer uses, and the number of lines of the address bus determines the size of memory that can be used.

Early microprocessor CPUs had sixteen address lines and eight data lines. This permitted the use of single byte memory units, and allowed the maximum size of addressed memory to be $2^{16} = 65536$ (64 K) bytes. Later, methods were developed of switching between banks, each of 64 K, of memory so that such machines could operate with 256 K or 512 K, switching from one set of 64 K to another as required and using some of the memory as if it were a disk (RAM-disk). Later types of microprocessor have used greater numbers of lines, typically sixteen data lines (allowing the memory unit to be a word) and twenty-four address lines, and more recently thirty-two data lines and thirty-two address lines. The use of a twenty-four-line address allows memory sizes up to 2^{24}, 16777216 bytes of memory, equal to 16384 K. If we define a megabyte of memory (M) as being 1024 K, then twenty-four address lines permits the use of 16 M of memory. Some types of CPU chips, in order to reduce space, use shared lines, so that twenty lines

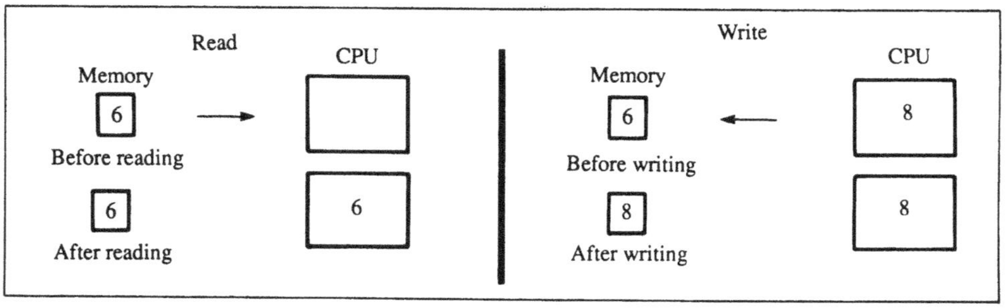

Figure 4.1 *The actions of reading and writing in a computer memory. Reading does not alter the content of memory, but writing replaces the older byte by the new one*

are used for addressing, and then sixteen of these lines are switched over to be used for data. This technique requires more complicated connections between the CPU and the memory and is less common now that manufacturing processes have improved.

Minicomputers and mainframes have much more choice about the use of address and data lines, and CPU sections with thirty-two lines of data and twenty-four or thirty-two lines of address have been used frequently in the design of these machines. The larger machines are also more likely to take up the full number of address lines, because the smaller desktop machines are often limited to the use of less memory than the number of address lines could cope with. Many sixteen-bit microcomputers, for example, have a memory limit of 640 K imposed not by the number of memory lines but by the inability of software to cope with memory beyond this limit. Both mainframe and minicomputers will generally have their memory 'fully populated' meaning that the machine contains as much memory as the number of address lines can cope with.

Exercise 1

A CPU uses sixteen data lines and twenty address lines – how many bytes can be addressed and how many are read for each address number?

Managing memory

Having a memory system in which each byte or word is located by placing a set of binary number signals on lines allows any byte or word in the memory to be contacted at random, so that this form of memory is a **random-access memory**. The abbreviation, RAM, is used for one specific variety of memory, however, which allows both reading and writing once the address number has been used. All of the memory of a modern computer allows random access, and the phrase is a hangover from earlier days when some types of memory (serial memory) required the complete contents of memory to be read in order to gain access to any one byte. The use of random access requires some method of placing the electrical signals on to the address lines, and this is one of the functions of the CPU.

The way that this is done is surprisingly simple. Each CPU contains a number of units called **registers**, which act rather like banks of switches which can be set. If we imagine that each switch in a register allows a 1 or a 0 signal to exist, then connecting these switches to the address lines will place the required electrical voltages on the lines. The CPU maintains one register, called the **program counter** which is used specifically for the purpose of addressing. When the CPU is switched on, this program counter register is set to an address number, which can, for example, be 0. The actions of the CPU are then regulated by a set of clock pulses, electrical signals which are delivered from another circuit at a fast and regular rate, typically 8 to 50 million times per second. Each instruction is carried out in steps, with one step for each clock pulse, and the action of the program counter register is to add 1 to its address number at the last clock pulse of each instruction. In this way, if the register starts at 0, then after one instruction has been completed its address number is 1, after the second instruction it is 2 and so on. The fast rate of the clock pulses means that the program counter will have cycled through all of its possible addresses in a very short time. For example, if twenty address lines are being used, with twenty switch units in the program counter register, then there are 1048576 possible address numbers, and if no instructions were being carried out (so that each clock pulse caused the register to increase its stored number by unity) at the rate of 8 million per second this would mean that all of the addresses would be covered in about 0.13 seconds if nothing else were being done by the CPU.

This provision for the address in the program counter to increment (increase by 1) automatically in the absence of any other instruction is the method by which the CPU starts its operations, since it provides for an automatic search through the memory to be made until an instruction byte is found, and also for the automatic address change from one address to the next when an instruction has been completed. It also provides for the use of any address at random, because moving a binary number from any other register in the CPU to the program counter will have the effect of placing that number on to the address lines (Figure 4.2).

CPU action

The way that the program counter operates can be understood better by a simplified description of a typical action: the addition of two bytes. There are many ways in which this can be done, but we shall concentrate on the simplest, making use of a memory which consists of single byte units and the simplest forms of use of that memory. Like all CPU actions, the addition is done in a sequence of steps, and the necessary preparation is illustrated in Figure 4.3, with part of the memory being occupied as shown. The steps are then as follows:

1 The address in the program counter (PC) is set to the first of the memory addresses, the one containing the read instruction.
2 Because this address is in the PC, the instruction byte for READ is copied along the data lines to the CPU.
3 The READ instruction byte is stored in a register and analysed. The byte used in this example specifies that the data to be read is in the following memory address.
4 The PC increments, and reads the byte in the next memory address. This is placed in a general-purpose register called the accumulator.
5 The PC increments again, and reads another instruction byte, specifying an ADD operation. This instruction byte is placed in a register and analysed.

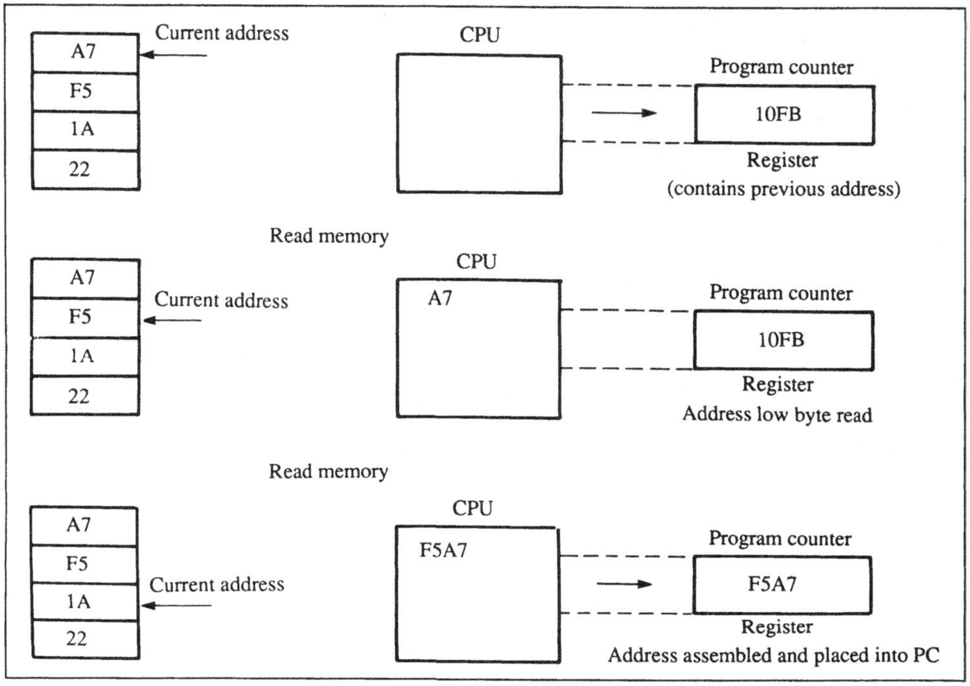

Figure 4.2 *Moving a number to the program counter in order to use it as an address number. The number is read in stages from the memory (illustrated by single-byte reads here) and assembled, then transferred to the program counter register*

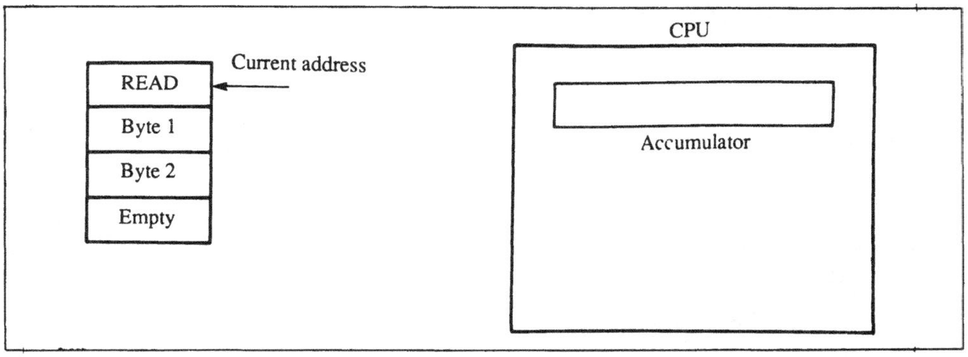

Figure 4.3 *The set-up steps that are needed prior to adding two numbers in the CPU, making use of the automatic incrementing of the address number. If the numbers to be added are not adjacent, then the CPU will have to be supplied with an address for each, which takes more time*

6 This particular ADD instruction specifies that the byte in the next memory address is to be added to the content of the accumulator.
7 The PC increments again and reads the second data byte.
8 The second byte is added to the first, and the result of the addition is held in the accumulator.

9 The PC increments, reading another instruction byte which specifies a WRITE.
10 This particular instruction specifies that the byte in the accumulator is to be written into the next memory address.
11 The PC increments and writes the byte.
12 The PC increments and looks for the instruction byte in the new current address.

From this list you can see the importance of the automatic incrementing of memory. This is carried out each time an instruction or a portion of an instruction has been completed, so that writing a program for the CPU consists of placing bytes in the memory arranged in the correct order. If data has to be obtained or written at some other memory address then the CPU can read in the bytes of that address and then transfer them to the PC so that the address is activated; then at the end of the instruction the addressing will revert to the usual sequence.

Exercise 2

If the CPU carries out each instruction in a sequence of steps, one for each clock pulse, how can a computer run two programs simultaneously with only one CPU?

Interfacing and peripherals

A computer system that consisted only of CPU and memory would be of very little practical use because it would lack any way of putting in data and reading out results. A computer must be able to make use of keyboards, VDUs, printers, disk drives and other such units, called **peripherals**. Unlike the memory of the computer, these units are not connected directly to the address and data lines, and the form of the connection is known as **interfacing**. The interfacing involves:

1 A method of making connections between some or all of the data lines and the peripheral equipment.
2 A method of selecting a time at which the signals can be transferred into or out of the computer, enabling or disabling the connections.
3 A method of storing signals until they can be transferred.

The use of temporary storage and time selection is very important. A printer can cope with perhaps a few hundred characters per second, while a CPU can shift characters around at the rate of at least one million per second. When a computer is driving a printer, then, a character or set of characters can be delivered into a temporary store, and the computer instructed to 'mark time' until the printer has dealt with all of the codes. The method of marking time is either to cycle through a set of instructions that do nothing, or to get on with another computing task. The computer has to send a signal out through the interface to the printer to find when the printer is ready, and the printer has to place an electrical signal in part of the interface store to signal when it can accept more characters to print. This method of signalling ready to send and ready to receive is referred to as **handshaking**.

The use of a keyboard is rather different. Even a fast typist is unlikely to press keys at a rate faster than four or five per second, and a time of one-fifth second is vast by CPU standards, long enough to cycle through all of the memory. The scheme that is usually followed is to allow the CPU to concentrate on other tasks, and interrupt it when a key is pressed. At the interruption, the CPU then runs a small piece of program that will find which key has been pressed and place the code for that key into the CPU to be dealt with as the program requires. The CPU then resumes whatever task it was carrying out before the key was pressed. This system, called **interrupt processing** ensures that the CPU attends to the keyboard only when attention is required. In the course of running many types of programs, the keyboard is not required, and these interruptions are suppressed so that the CPU is free to get on with its main task. By contrast, some programs, notably word processors, require much more frequent attention to the keyboard, and the CPU spends its spare time organizing and rearranging the contents of the memory and the screen display.

Nowadays, interrupt processing is used for virtually all interaction between the CPU and the peripherals. An older type of process is **polling**, in which the CPU checks each peripheral at intervals to see if any attention is necessary. The use of polling wastes CPU time, and polling is nowadays used only for a few tasks, like checking whether a BREAK key has been pressed.

The most basic peripherals for a computer are the keyboard and VDU, along with a backing store and probably a printer. The keyboard is an input device, the means by which you pass instructions and data to the computer. The VDU is purely an output device, if we exclude the touch-sensitive screens that are part of a few computer systems. The VDU screen shows the results of computing, and is often (but not always) arranged so that it shows the character corresponding to the key that has been pressed. The VDU is not a simple device, because to display one single character on the screen requires a set of electrical signals that are delivered in sequence. Though this can be done by the CPU, it is wasteful of CPU time to make it control the VDU so that modern computers normally have a separate chip controlling the VDU. In some cases the provision for the VDU can even extend to a complete microprocessor system, particularly if the screen is expected to be able to display graphics in colour.

The backing store refers to the ways in which large quantities of data can be stored outside the memory of the computer. When the computer is switched off, any memory that is electrical as distinct from magnetic will lose its contents, and in the mini- and microcomputers all of the internal memory is of this type, called **volatile** memory. Programs and data must therefore be held on other forms of memory, usually magnetic, such as a floppy or hard disk system. This form of storage is called a backing store, implying that it backs up the computer's memory, holding data when the memory of the computer is inactive or working on other data. Interfacing to a suitable backing store is a very important computer function, and data can be passed very quickly between the backing store and the main memory, though not as quickly as between sections of the internal memory. The main methods of constructing a backing store are magnetic, using magnetic disks, magnetic drums, or magnetic tapes. When tapes are used, they are usually wide tape, recorded with several channels of data, one bit of a byte on each channel. Where cassette tapes are used, their recording is done digitally, allowing much more data to be packed on to the cassette than was possible on the cassette tapes that were used along with early small computers. The early types of small computers used ordinary audio cassette recorders, which were incapable of data recording other than converting **1**s and **0**s into musical tones. Such recording methods are not used on data cassettes.

The costs of backing storage are important. Backing storage for the larger computers is always expensive, but the cost per megabyte of data is roughly comparable for the various systems using fixed disks or drums, the more costly removable (hard) disks or tapes. At the microcomputer level, the price of hard disk drives has dropped to such an extent that the price per megabyte is very much lower than that of a floppy disk drive, and tape is used only as a method of a backing-up disk (see later).

The factor that makes the use of a backing store so important is that a computer is totally unusable unless a program is running. Without a program, all that the CPU can do is cycle through the memory addresses. There can be no response to the keyboard, nor any output on the screen, because these actions require the computer to be running an input/output program. It is not even possible to make any use of the backing store to load in a program, because simply to make use of the backing store requires a program to be running. No form of activity is possible unless under the control of a program, and if no program is running, there can be no form of computing activity.

The use of a computer would therefore be difficult unless some form of permanent memory could be arranged. This type of memory is called read-only memory (ROM) – dealt with later in this chapter – and the design of a computer provides for addresses in a ROM to be read when the CPU is first switched on. Some early desktop machines used a comparatively large fraction of their addressable memory as ROM, so that the control of the machine and also its programming language (usually BASIC) was established as soon as the machine was switched on. Later desktop machines, in common with mainframes and minis, use only a small piece of ROM memory as a **boot** program. This means that the instructions in this piece of memory are just sufficient to control the use of a disk system or other backing store, and to load a much longer program, the **operating system** into the main memory of the computer from the backing store. Control is then passed to this operating system, which looks after all the inputs and outputs, taking charge of peripherals such as disks, printers, VDU, keyboard and any other items that are connected. By using an operating system in this way, changes in the operating system can be made easily without having to alter any part of the fixed memory of the computer. At the time of writing, desktop machines use mainly the operating system called MS-DOS, with OS-2 becoming established, and larger machines use a variety of systems, with UNIX one of the few that is found almost universally.

In the early days of desktop machines, each manufacturer tended to use a different operating system, though a standardized system called CP/M was available. The use of incompatible operating systems meant that a disk created using one type of machine could not be read on any other, and even when CP/M was used on different machines only the 8 in type of disk could be guaranteed to be usable on any CP/M machine. The manufacturers of computers intended for serious business applications therefore used CP/M and often specified the use of an 8 in disk drive, and the manufacturers of machines intended mainly for entertainment used either cassette tapes or 5.25 in disks with incompatible operating systems and data formats. The success of the IBM PC machine in the 1980s has encouraged standardization on the MS-DOS operating system and a 5.25 in standard disk format (forty track double-sided, double-density) and this has done much to restore confidence, and avoid the large upheavals that used to take place when one computer had to be replaced by another which could not make any use of the data that had been gathered by the previous model.

Incompatible operating systems still exist among mainframe and mini-computers, but in general when one machine is replaced by one from the same manufacturer it is possible to transfer data without too much difficulty. An operating system called UNIX can be used by most mainframe and mini machines, though it is still common for such machines to run only an operating system designed for them by the manufacturer. Even when operations are switched to an entirely different machine, some cross-transfer of data is usually possible because 'translation' programs can be written (or bought) for the purpose. Where desktop and the smaller mini machines are used, the value of the software, programs and data, often considerably exceeds the value of the computer hardware, so that it is important to maintain compatibility. The original specification that the BBC laid down for a computer bearing the BBC name was that it should run the CP/M operating system, but for some reason this specification was relaxed so that many educational users of computers never had experience of the CP/M system which by that time was universal for office use of microcomputers, and have never used the MS-DOS system which is standard on business PC machines.

Memory types

The most common forms of internal memory for desktop and minicomputers are termed ROM, RAM and EPROM, all of these names being acronyms (formed from initial letters). Mainframe machines have relied in the past on magnetic memory systems that used tiny rings of magnetic material threaded with signal wires. Though this system allows memory to be non-volatile, retaining its data when the power is switched off, this type of memory (**core memory**) is expensive, bulky and dissipates a considerable amount of heat when in use. Memory of this type is therefore used only where its advantages of very high speed operation and its ability to retain data with no power applied override other considerations.

RAM memory is the ordinary read/write memory that is used to hold program or data information for as long as power is applied to the computer. Though the name means random access memory, it really ought to be called read write memory, because all memory for a modern computer uses random access. A RAM for a microcomputer will be constructed from a set of chips (Figure 4.4) often using one single chip for each bit in the data group (eight chips for a single byte memory, sixteen for a word), or with the memory already organized into bytes within the chip. The size to which a memory chip can be made has been steadily expanding over the years from 1977 when the first microcomputers appeared. In the early days, a memory capacity of 1 K was regarded as usable, but a figure of 512 K is now commonplace. The early 1 K RAM chips allowed 1024 single bit units to be addressed in each chip, so that wiring up eight of these chips allowed access to a byte-wire 1 K memory. Chip sizes of 256 K and 512 K are now becoming commonplace.

Each RAM chip will provide for a number of connections. Some of these will be address connections, and modern RAM chips make as much use as possible of methods that will reduce the number of connections, such as having four row and four column connections in place of sixteen separate address lines. As well as the address lines and the data lines, a RAM chip needs a read/write connection. The voltage on this pin will determine whether the memory is to be read or written, and the control voltage, like the address, originates at the CPU. Another connection that is used is a chip-enable, so that the voltage on this connection determines whether the chip responds to other signals or not. By turning off the chip-enable voltages, a set of memory chips can be switched out of use so that another set can be used, and this is the basis of the **bank-switching** method that is employed to allow a CPU with only sixteen address lines to work with memory sizes greater than 64 K.

Since the data in RAM chips is lost when the power supply is switched off, a computer needs to be able to take its instructions from ROM when it is first switched on. Read-only memory (ROM), can exist in several varieties, and when the word ROM is used it normally refers to **masked ROM**, meaning that the internal connections are made at the time when the chip is

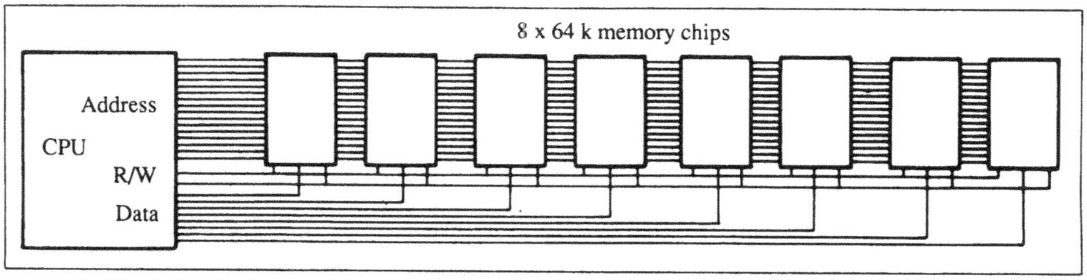

Figure 4.4 *How a memory, in this case of* 64 $K \times 8$*-bits, is constructed from single-bit memory chips. Each memory chip shares the address lines, and contributes one data line*

manufactured. These internal connections are either to earth (zero voltage) or to the supply voltage connection (the one voltage), and are made using conducting silicon.

Because a masked ROM is manufactured using very expensive tooling and the contents of the ROM are unalterable, this method is used only when the contents are well tested and required in large numbers. When the ROM is used only to boot in an operating system, this is by far the cheapest method, because the requirements are simple and unchanging. The desktop computers which used their own operating systems often placed them in ROM, but this had the disadvantage that changes required retooling for the masking process. This led to the use of EPROMS for this purpose.

The EPROM is an electrically-programmable read-only memory. As the name suggests, the connections to levels 0 and 1 within the chip are created electrically rather than mechanically, so that these ROMs can be programmed after manufacture, allowing much more flexibility. This allows an operating system to be tested from disk until all the obvious faults have been corrected, then transferred to EPROM. The later type of EPROM uses conducting paths through silicon which can be established by selecting memory addresses and applying higher than normal voltages. These conducting paths that are formed in the material can be erased by allowing ultra-violet light to shine on the material. This allows these EPROMS to be reused and reprogrammed as required, and some desktop machines used EPROMS to carry programs in place of any other form of backing store. Nowadays, the use of EPROM is more likely to be associated with a system under test, for which a final version has not yet been fixed.

Both ROM and EPROM are addressed in exactly the same way as RAM, so that in any working computer system, some of the address range will be used by ROM and/or EPROM and the rest by RAM. In a 1 Mb system, for example, typically only 640 K will be used by RAM and the remainder by ROM, EPROM and for future expansion.

Exercise 3

Some machines maintain a 'real-time clock' which keeps current time and date stored in the computer. This system makes use of RAM whose memory is maintained by a battery. Why is the battery needed and why could ROM or EPROM not be used for this memory?

Backing stores

When you insert a floppy disk of the 5.25 in or 8 in type into a drive, and activate the drive, a hub engages the central hole of the disk, clamps it, and starts to spin it at a speed of about 300 revolutions per minute. The disk itself is a circular flat piece of plastic which has been coated with magnetic material on each side. It is enclosed in a floppy plastic envelope to reduce the chances of damage to the surface, and the hub portion of the disk is also built up in plastic to avoid damage to the disk surface when it is gripped by the drive. The surface of each disk is smooth and flat, and any physical damage, such as a fingerprint or a scratch, can cause loss of recorded data. The jacket that surrounds the disk has slots cut into it so that the disk drive head can touch the disk at the correct places. There is a slot to allow a disk head to touch the magnetic surface on each side of the disk, and also a hole for locating the disk position. The disk surface can be seen and touched through this slot, and you should not touch the disk surface, sneeze on it, or do anything which could leave any marks on the surface. The later 3.5 in type of disk is encased in a plastic holder, and access to the disk surface is possible only when a spring-loaded shutter is pulled back. This shutter is pulled back when the disk is inserted into the drive, so that this type of disk is much better protected than the older type of floppy. Because of this, these small disks are used with a higher density of recorded data.

Through the slot that is cut in the envelope, the heads of the disk drive can touch the surface of the disk, one head on each side. These heads are tiny electromagnets, and each head is used both for writing data and for reading data. When a head writes data, electrical signals through the coils of wire in the head cause changes of magnetism. These in turn magnetize the disk surface. When the head is used for reading, the changing magnetism of the disk as it turns causes electrical signals to be generated in the coils of wire. The larger-capacity hard disk units use multiple disks with two heads per disk.

Unlike the head of a cassette recorder, which does not move once it is in contact with the tape, the heads of the disk drive move quite a lot. If the head is held steady, the spinning disk will allow a circular strip (sometimes referred to as a 'cylinder', a word derived from the use of magnetic drum memory) of the magnetic material to be affected by the head. By moving the head in and out, to and from the centre of the disk, the drive can make contact with different circular strips of the disk. These strips are called 'tracks' and unlike the groove of a conventional record, these are circular, not spiral, and they are not grooves cut into the disk. The track is invisible, just as the recording on a tape is invisible. What creates the tracks is the movement of the recording/replay head of the disk drive. A rather similar situation is the choice of twin-track or four-track on cassette tapes. The same tape can be recorded with two or four tracks depending on the heads that are used by the cassette recorder. There is nothing on the tape which guides the heads, or which indicates to you how many tracks exist.

The number of tracks that are used therefore depend on the disk drives. The standard that has been established by the IBM PC is of 5.25 in disks with forty tracks on each side. These forty-track disks use forty-eight tracks per inch, so that the usable width of the disk surface is only $\frac{40}{48}$ inch, about 0.83 in. The data is recorded on each side of the disks, and is recorded at twice the density (amount of data per linear inch) of older types. These disks are therefore known as double-density, double-sided, abbreviated to DDDS. Once you have accepted the idea of invisible tracks, it is not quite so difficult to accept also that each track can also be invisibly divided up. The reason for this is organization – the data is divided into 'blocks', or sectors,

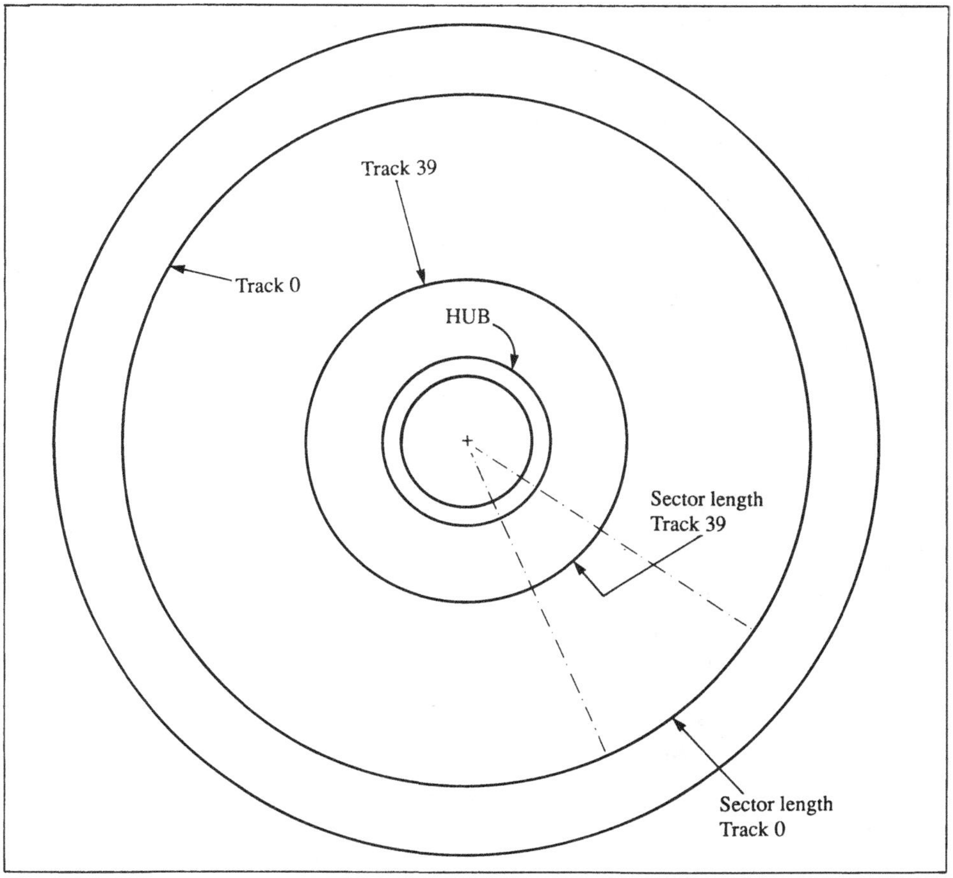

Figure 4.5 *The organization of a disk surface into sectors, using a forty-track disk example*

each of 512 bytes (Figure 4.5). Each track of the disk is divided into a number of 'sectors', and each of these sectors can store 512 bytes of data.

The next thing that we have to consider is how the sectors are marked out. Once again, this is not a visible marking, but a magnetic one, a system called 'soft-sectoring' to distinguish it from an earlier hard-sectoring system. Each disk has a small hole punched into it at a distance of about 25 mm from the centre. There is a hole cut also through the disk jacket, so that when the disk is rotated, it is possible to see right through the hole when it comes round. When the disk is held in the disk drive, and spun, this position can be detected, using a beam of light. This is the 'marker', and the head can use this as a starting point, putting a signal on to the disk at this position, and at eight others, equally spaced, so as to form sectors. On hard-sectored disks, there is one hole for each sector. This sector marking has to be carried out on each track of the disk, which is part of the operation that is called 'formatting'. Modern 3.5 in disks do not use a sector hole because the shaft of the disk drive is shaped so that it can engage the disk in one position only.

When you load a program from a disk, or save data on a disk, you do not have to worry about the tracks and sectors. You do not, for example, have to specify at which sector and on which track the recording must start, and what to do if there is already something recorded on some of the sectors. All of this is the main action of the disk operating system (DOS), a sort of good-housekeeping system for disks. The action of the DOS is to ensure that a disk is of the correct format, to keep a record of what sectors are used for what files, and to allocate sectors as needed when data is recorded. The simplest types of DOS, as were supplied in the early days of microcomputers, did little more than this, but were still a very considerable aid to effective use of computers. Systems such as CP/M (which first emerged in 1972) added very much more to disk operating systems. The aim of CP/M was to provide an operating system which could be used by a variety of different computers and which would allow software to run on any machine that used the same DOS. The other point about CP/M was that it provided for much more than just disk operation. It provided a complete system for the control of all inputs and outputs, so that the computer manufacturer could concentrate on designing a machine, knowing that the use of CP/M would allow any of the vast range of software written for the machine to be used. It also incorporated a number of commands and 'utility' programs that were intended to make programming and computer use considerably easier than it had been in the past.

The arrival of sixteen-bit computers meant that the older type of CP/M, based on the Z-80 microprocessor, had to be supplemented by a newer version. Two competing systems emerged: MS-DOS from Microsoft; and CP/M 86 from Digital Research. The difference in the licensing prices proved to be the deciding factor, and most sixteen-bit machines adopted MS-DOS, with the result that most business software for the IBM and similar machines was written so as to run with MS-DOS.

Hard disks

The floppy type of disk has several limitations. The main limitation is that the disk spends most of its life out of the drive, subject to the dust and smoke in the room where the disk is housed. This, along with the quality of the disk surface, means that the recording and replaying heads of the computer cannot make very close contact with the head. At the same time, the disk cannot be spun at a very high speed because of the friction of the sleeve which partially protects it. The distance between the head and the disk restricts the speed at which data can be written and recovered, and the comparatively slow speed of the disk has the same effect. If we want to place more data on to disks, we need smaller heads, closer spacing between the head and the disk surface, and much higher rotational speeds.

The hard disk, sometimes called a Winchester disk, is a way of obtaining a much larger amount of information packed into the normal size of a disk. The older name of Winchester was used because this was the IBM name for a project that called for the development of a hard disk in a sealed unit in the early 1970s. Like other types of hard disks, Winchesters keep the disk itself and the magnetic read/write heads sealed inside a container that ensures a dust-free environment for the disk. Unlike some other types of hard disk units, however, the Winchester is permanently sealed – the disk is not removable, and the sealing will be disturbed only if repairs are needed – and that will require an air-conditioned workshop. This sealing into a clean dust-free space allows the gap between the head and the disk to be made much smaller than could be contemplated for a floppy disk, smaller than a grain of dust or a particle of smoke. Technical leaflets refer to the head as 'flying' and this is not advertisers talk – the head actually floats on a thin film of air between the head and the disk. This very small gap between the head and the disk allows a much higher packing of information on to the disk so that the most obvious effect of using a hard disk is the much greater number of bytes that can be stored.

Unlike the comparatively slow-spinning floppy disk, which cannot be rotated fast because the disk rubs against its envelope, the hard disk spins at a very high speed, around 3600 revolutions per minute. This means that the rate at which data can be written to the disk or read from it is much greater, some twelve times as fast as a floppy disk. This speed of recording or recovery of data has been helped by the progress in reducing the size of these hard disks. The first units used 14 in disks, and by the late-1970s, 8 in units were in full production. The modern 5.25 in hard disk started to appear by the early 1980s, and the 3.5 in size in the mid-1980s. The advantages of the smaller size have been lower costs, and faster access to data, because the head needs to move over a much shorter path on a 5.25 in disk than on the 8 in disk. Even smaller hard disks are now available, and form the basis of the hard disk on a card that allows a twin floppy-drive machine to be upgraded to hard disk use with the minimum of installation and without removing an existing drive. The hard card units that are now available use multiple disks with two heads each, and about 615 tracks on each surface. The sectors are also recorded to a much greater density of data, with 2 K per sector rather than 512 bytes (0.5 K) as on the ordinary floppy so that fewer tracks are needed for a long program, and some programs will fit within a single sector. The sector size also means, of course, that a ten-byte piece of data might occupy a single sector with nothing else recorded there.

Hard disks for microcomputers range in size from 20 Mb (1 Mb = 1024 K) to more than 600 Mb, and both mini- and mainframe computers use much larger capacities, often in the form of removable cartridges. The larger capacities make use of both larger disk diameters and multiple disks, and where a unit is removable, the disks, heads and motors are all part of the removable unit.

CD ROM

A more modern form of backing store is CD ROM which makes use of the techniques that have been evolved for recording high-quality sound as digital signals, using a laser to create patterns of dots on surface of a plastic disk that is then coated with aluminium. The CD recording method makes use of a beam of light from a miniature semiconductor laser. Such a beam is of low power, a matter of milliwatts, but the focus of the beam can be to a very small point so that low-melting point materials like plastics can be vaporized by a focused beam. Turning the recording beam on to a place on a plastic disk for a fraction of a microsecond will therefore vaporize the material to leave a tiny crater or pit, about 0.6 μm in diameter – for comparison, a human hair is around 50 μm in diameter. The depth of the pits is also very small, of the order of 0.1 μm. If no beam strikes the disk, then no pit is formed, so that we have here a system that can digitally code pulses into the form of pit or no-pit.

Reading a set of pits on a disk also makes use of a semiconductor laser, but of much lower power since it need not vaporize material. The reading beam will be reflected from the disk where no pit exists, but scattered where there is a pit. By using an optical system that allows the light to travel in both directions to and from the disk surface (Figure 4.6), it is possible to focus a reflected beam on to a detector, and pick up a signal when the beam is reflected from the disk, with no signal when the beam falls on to a pit. The output from this diode is the digital signal that will be amplified and then processed. Only light from a laser source can fulfil the requirements of being perfectly monochrome (one single frequency) and coherent (no breaks in the wave-train) so as to permit focusing to such a fine spot. The CD system uses a beam that is focused at quite a large angle, and with a transparent coating over the disk surface which also focuses the beam as well as protecting the recorded pits. Though the diameter of the beam at the pit is around 0.5 μm, the diameter at the surface of the disk, the transparent coating, is about 1 mm. This means that dust particles and hairs on the surface of the disk have very little effect on the beam, which passes on each side of them – unless the dust particles are a millimetre or more across. This is just one way in which the CD system establishes its very considerable immunity to dust and scratching on the disc surface, the other being the remarkable error detection and correction system.

The pits are arranged in a spiral track, like the groove of a conventional record. This track, however, starts at the inside of the disk and spirals its way to the outside, with a distance between adjacent tracks of only 1.0 μm. Since there is no mechanical contact of any kind, the tracking must be carried out by a servomotor system. The principle is that the innermost track can be located automatically, and this carries the position of the various tracks in the usual digitally coded form. Moving the scanner system radially across the tracks will result in signals from the photodiode unit, and with these signals directed to a counter unit, the number of tracks from the inner starting track can be counted. This therefore allows the scanner unit to be placed on any one of the possible 41,250 tracks.

Positioning on to a track is a comparatively slow operation because part of each track will be read on the way before the count number is increased. In addition, the motor that spins the disk is also servo controlled so that the speed of reading the pits is constant. Since the inner track has a diameter of 50 mm and the maximum allowable outer track can have a diameter of 116 mm, the number of pits per track will also vary in this same proportion, about 2.32. The disk rotation at the outer edge is therefore slower by this same factor when compared to the rotational speed at the inner track. The

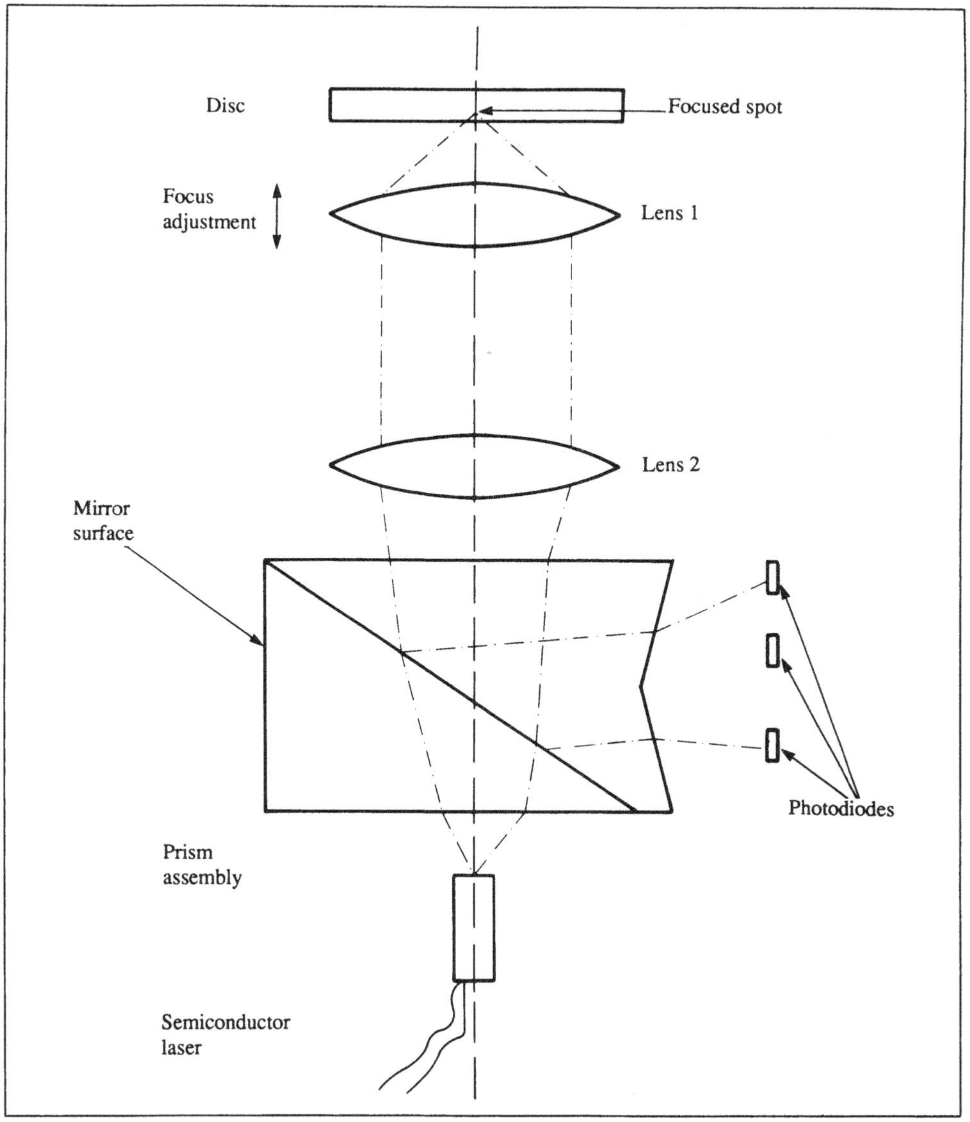

Figure 4.6 *The reading of the pit-marks on the surface of a CD ROM*

rotational speeds range from about 200 r.p.m. on the inner track to about 500 r.p.m. on the outer track – the actual values depend on the servo control settings and do not have to be absolute. The only criterion of reading speed on a CD is that the pits are being read at a correct rate, and that rate is determined by a master clock frequency. This corresponds to a reading speed of about 1.2 to 1.4 m of track per second.

The most complicated features are the modulation method, the error-detection and correction, and the way that the signals are assembled into sets for recording and replay. The exact details of each of these processes are released only to licensees who buy into the system. This, added to the difficulty of creating a master disk, restricts the use of CD ROM for very large amounts of information whose value is high enough to justify the cost of production. A typical example is the disk which contains all the addresses and postcodes of businesses in the UK; or of an encyclopaedia in CD form. This is all ROM data, because at the time of writing, despite considerable effort, no suitable read-write system has yet been evolved. The CD ROM drive is not costly, and the price of a disk is usually greater than the price of the drive, because of the large amount of information on a disk, of the order of 600 Mb.

Suggestions for practical work

1 Point out the main components in a block diagram of a modern computer.
2 Work through an addition sequence using a machine-code trainer.
3 Working from manufacturers specifications, compare the following chip types: 8080, 6800, 80386, 68020.
4 Make use of floppy and hard disks for storing and retrieving a standard amount of data, such as ten pages of text. Compare speeds of storing and access.
5 Find what is required to back up the contents of a 20 M hard disk on to tape.

Multiple-choice test questions

1 A CPU uses 32-bit data. This means that its normal addressing sequence:
(a) will be one byte after another
(b) will be in pairs of bytes
(c) will be in groups of three bytes
(d) will be in groups of four bytes

2 The clock speed for a computer is 10 MHz, 10 million pulses per second. If each instruction requires an average of eight clock pulses, the number of instructions completed per second will be:
(a) 18 million
(b) 1.25 million
(c) 0.8 million
(d) 2 million

3 The first actions of the CPU when a machine is switched on will be to:
(a) read the keyboard
(b) read the disk
(c) read a ROM
(d) read the RAM

4 A computer uses separate microprocessors to control the VDU and the keyboard. This has the advantage of:
  (a) requiring less memory
  (b) allowing the CPU to work faster
  (c) requiring no ROM memory
  (d) using less power

5 A machine permits 2 Mb of addresses to be used. Of these 2 Mb:
  (a) some will be ROM, most RAM, some unused
  (b) all will be RAM
  (c) all will be ROM
  (d) all will be unused

6 An advantage of using a hard disk compared to the use of a floppy (removable) disk is that the hard disk:
  (a) keeps its data more securely
  (b) retains data when the machine is switched off
  (c) allows data to be used immediately at any time
  (d) does not allow data to be erased

5 Outputs and inputs

Objectives

- Describe the main characteristics of common types of input, output and input/output devices used in commercial computer applications (7.2).
- Explain the encoding of information for data transmission and describe components of a data transmission system, including networks (7.3).
- Describe common methods of preparing data for input to commercial computer systems (7.4).

Printers

The reasons for using a printer are obvious if the computer is used for even the smallest business purposes. It would be unreasonable to expect accountants or an income-tax inspector to look at accounts that can be shown only on the screen. It would be a total waste of time to keep stock records with a computer, and then have to write down each change on a piece of paper, copying everything from the display on the screen. For all of these purposes, and particularly for word-processing and for programming, the printer is an essential part of the computer system. Output on paper is referred to as **hard copy**, and this hard copy is essential if the computer is to be of any use in business applications. For word-processing uses, it is not enough just to have a printer, because a printer with high-quality output must be used, whose characters are as clear as those of a first-class electric typewriter. A lower quality of output can be tolerated for listings of programs.

The choice in printers lies among three basic types: character printers; line printers; and page printers. Of these, character printers are most often used with desktop machines, though page printers (laser printers) are now becoming much more common thanks to a dramatic fall in prices. Line printers are used mainly with the larger types of mainframe machines. Whatever type is used, the connection between the computer and the printer will either be a parallel connection or a serial connection. The parallel type of connection is much more commonly used for microcomputers, because it allows for much simpler and faster printer operation. Parallel connection means that each character is sent to the printer by using electrical signals along eight lines, making use of the ASCII codes that exist for each character. The ASCII set, in fact, uses only seven lines, but most printers can make use of eight-bit signals to provide a range of graphics characters or special print effects in addition to the standard ASCII range.

The form of connection that has been standardized is one that was originally used on printers manufactured by Centronics Inc., and which is universally known as the Centronics port. This makes use of a multi-wire cable which takes the eight-bit signals and several handshaking signals so that the printer is always correctly synchronized with the computer. This ensures that, for example, if printing is started with the printer switched off, the computer will hang up, waiting until the printer is switched on, and when this is done, printing will start with no loss of characters. The main drawback of using a parallel printer connection is that the cable must be comparatively short, up to about 2 m. If a longer cable is to be used, an amplifying interface has to be fitted to ensure that the signals do not interfere with each other.

The serial interface sends the signals out to the printer one bit at a time. This means that at least seven signals have to be sent for each character, and in practice this number must be ten or eleven, to allow for 'start and stop' signals which are used to mark where the signals for each character start and finish. This system uses less cabling, because only two strands need to be used for signals, and the cables can be longer, because there is no risk of one signal interfering with another. The standard system is called 'RS-232', and has been used extensively in the past to link mainframe and minicomputer with printers that might be some distance away. Unfortunately, a lot of systems that are described as being RS-232 are not strictly to the old standard, so that it is seldom possible to plug in a serial printer and expect it to work without some adjustments to the connections.

There are also software requirements quite apart from the hardware aspect of ensuring correct cable connections. To take one obvious point, since the signals for each character are sent out in sequence, the printer must be set to receive these signals at the same rate as the computer sends them. The standard rates are shown in Figure 5.1, and the most common rates for printers nowadays are 2400 to 9600 bits per second. In addition to using the same rates, the printer and computer must use the same number of start and stop bits for each character, and must agree on whether to use parity or not. Parity is a simple error-detecting system that makes use of a count of the 1 bits in a signal. In an even parity transmission, the number of 1s in a character (using seven-bit ASCII code) is checked, and if this number is odd, the eighth signal in the byte will be another 1, making the total into an even number. At the printer, each byte is checked for an even number of 1s, and if an odd number is found an error is signalled. The odd parity system works in the same way, but uses the eighth bit to make the total number odd

75	110	150	300
600	1200	2400	4800
9600	19200		

Note that the values shown here are not all of the possible rates but main rates used in the past as well as those used by equipment today.

Figure 5.1 *The standard baud rates (taken as being equal to bits per second) for use in computer serial inputs and outputs*

rather than even. Parity is not used unless the printer is at a considerable distance from the computer, but if parity is used, then both computer and printer must both be using the same parity type, odd or even. The combination of rate, use of parity, and start and stop signals is known as the **serial protocols**.

Another problem that can arise in the use of a printer is that of line feed and carriage return. Some computers send out only one code number, the carriage return code (ASCII 13) at the end of a line. Other machines send both the line feed (ASCII 10) and carriage return codes. Printers are arranged, therefore, so that either possibility can be catered for by a switch. If when the printer is connected everything is printed on one line, then a switch on the printer that alters the line-feed setting has to be changed over. If, on the other hand, each printed line is double-spaced, then the switch will have to be set to the opposite position.

Character printers that are used with small computers will use one of the mechanisms that are listed in Figure 5.2. Of these, the impact dot-matrix type is the most common. A dot-matrix printer creates each character out of a set of dots, and when the print is examined closely the dot structure can be seen. Most of the dot-matrix printers are impact types, meaning that the paper is marked by the impact of a needle on an inked ribbon which hits the paper. There are also thermal dot-matrix printers which use non-moving

Impact mechanisms:
- Dot matrix
- Daisywheel
- Line printer

Non-impact line mechanisms:
- Thermal
- Electrostatic
- Ink-jet

Page printers:
- Laser printer
- Crystal shutter printer
- LED printer

Figure 5.2 *Mechanisms for computer character printers*

hot needles to make marks on heat-sensitive paper. The advantage of this method is silence, but competition from equally silent and more convenient ink-jet printers has reduced the number of thermal printers that are sold for connection to computers. The ink-jet printers use the signals from the computer to guide tiny globules of ink into the correct pattern for each character. The printers are silent and can print at high speeds with laser quality, but the tiny jets can clog easily, a problem that now seems to have been overcome by a few leading manufacturers such as Hewlett-Packard, Canon and Epson.

The ultimate in print quality for impact printing is provided by the daisywheel printer. This uses a typewriter approach, with the letters and other characters placed on stalks round a wheel. The principle is that the wheel spins to get the letter that is required at the top, and then a small hammer hits the back of the letter, pressing it against the ribbon and on to the paper. Because this is exactly the same way as a typewriter produces text, the quality of print is good, but the rate of printing is unacceptably slow. In any case, 24-pin dot-matrix printers can now produce equal print quality with the advantage of allowing print design (the **font**) to be changed easily.

The full-page type of printer is the laser printer. A laser printer is a development of the familiar electrostatic photocopier of the Xerox (TM) variety. In an electrostatic copier, the original paper is pressed against a material which is electrically an insulator until it is struck by light. This material is electrically charged, making it able to attract small particles, and then the master copy is illuminated. This makes the material conduct where the light has reached it, so that the electric charge leaks away except in the dark areas, which will be the inked areas of the original. A dry powder ink (toner) will now stick to these areas when blown over the plate, and this pattern of dry ink can be transferred to a clean sheet of paper. Finally, the paper with its dry ink is passed under a heater which melts the powdered ink into the paper, leaving a permanent copy.

In a laser printer, the removal of the electric charge from an insulating plate or belt is carried out by moving a laser beam across the plate or belt, and this laser beam is under the control of a separate computer which is built-in to the printer. Unlike ordinary computer printers, the laser printer deals not with characters, or lines, but complete pages. The principle is that the appearance of each dot on a complete sheet is held in the memory of the printer, and the printing is therefore very fast, around eight seconds for a complete A4 page. This implies that a laser printer needs a large memory, because the definition can be very good, of the order of 300 dots per inch. For a piece of paper measuring 8 in × 10 in, this implies that the memory must hold information on the state of 7,200,000 dots. Since the memory must also hold the state of the page in ordinary form (as a set of ASCII or other codes), this means that a lot of memory is needed. The minimum memory for a laser printer is 512 K, and many offer 1 M or more.

Laser printers can be divided into two types: those which offer page description languages and those which do not. The simpler and cheaper laser printers are in use rather similar to dot-matrix printers, and can produce results that do not look all that much better unless suitable software is used. Many laser printers can be set to emulate the print of popular daisywheel or dot-matrix printers (like the Diablo 630 and the Epson FX), and some offer their own print fonts, either built-in or in the form of plug-in cartridges. Print speed is a feature of laser printers, and most machines will print eight pages of A4 size per minute if the computer can send text to them at this speed. In practice, when laser printers are used for publishing work, the amount of computing effort that is needed within the printer to organize the printing of text and graphics can slow the rate down very considerably.

A slightly different approach to page printing is taken by the 'crystal shutter' type of printers, which are often classed with the laser printers. The principle is still based on the electrostatic copier, but with the charge laid in a photoconducting drum or belt as it is in a photocopier, and exposed to light through a liquid-crystal transmission shutter which is controlled by bits stored in the memory. The shutter is a variant on the liquid-crystal screen type of display as used in calculators and in portable computers, and it can be produced and controlled at much lower cost than the laser type of 'engine'. This allows a printer of the same resolution as a laser type to be produced at much lower cost, though the cost of consumables such as toner and the drum or belt is still high. Another approach of this type is to use an electrostatic copier drum along with a line of dot-sized light-emitting diodes which will print a line of dots under software control, building up to characters as each line is printed. This approach has been used by Agfa.

The large mainframe machines can make effective use of line printers, which as the name suggests print a complete line of text at a time. A typical line printer would use a wide page of 132 characters, so that the printer contains 132 printwheels. Each wheel is positioned to the character that is to be printed in that position, and the whole line of printwheels is then hammered against the paper, with an inked ribbon between the printwheels and the paper to make the marks. The action is so rapid that it is impossible to see the printwheels stop moving, and the printing speed is considerably faster than any other printer type, ten wide pages per minute or more.

Exercise 1

A dot-matrix printer uses nine pins in a vertical line. Show, using graph paper, how the pins would be activated as the printhead is moved across the paper to produce the letters H, L and K.

Plotters

Another type of machine for making hard copy is the plotter or graphics printer. This is a mechanism which uses four or more miniature ball pens to mark the paper direct, with no ribbon. It can be used for graphics work, and when it is used as a printer, the letters are drawn rather than printed. Because several pens are used, the markings can be in several different colours. The type described as graphics printers are not expensive and can be very useful, particularly if graphics output in colour is required, though the action is very slow. The true plotters, which are considerably more expensive, operate with a more precise pen mechanism and usually feature a flat bed for the paper, rather like the surface of a drawing-board. These machines are intended for very high resolution graphics drawing, particularly architectural and machine drawings, and they are used particularly in conjunction with computer-aided design (CAD) programs.

Paper handling

For some purposes, paper can be handled in single sheets just as it is for a typewriter. If a computer is being used mainly as a word-processor for letters, then the use of a daisywheel, laser or 24-pin dot-matrix printer along with single sheets of paper is the preferred method, but for other work it is more usual to require some form of automation of the paper handling. For the daisywheel and laser types of printer this often takes the form of a sheet feeder, which can be single or twin bin. The blank sheets of paper are stored in one container (or bin) and fed into the printer as required by an arm. The mechanism is almost identical to the feeder mechanism of the old rotary ink duplicators. The twin-bin types provide an additional feeder bin for alternative sheets so that, for example, A4 sheets can be fed from one bin and C5 envelopes from the other. Software commands to the printer can be used to select which bin is chosen. Sheet feeders are reliable if the paper is dry and the sheets have been separated after cutting, but unless the paper has been prepared to some extent there is a possibility of faulty feeding, either taking no paper at times, feeding the paper at an angle, or feeding more than one sheet at a time. The use of dry, good quality, paper which is well shuffled before loading can reduce problems to almost zero.

The other very common method of feeding paper is the tractor (also called pin) feed. The paper is in the form of sheets that are joined at a perforated edge, and the sides of the paper are punched at 0.5 in intervals (Figure 5.3). This allows the printer to use a pair of sprockets mounted on top of the printer to grip the paper in place of the usual friction grip between two rollers, and it avoids any possibility of the paper slipping or twisting. Tractor feed is essential for continuous lengths of forms on which printing must be placed precisely, and it provides better for very fast paper feeding. The usual form of paper is **fanfold**, with the sheets folded in alternate directions at each perforation. Paper can also be supplied in *microperforated* form, allowing the tractor edges to be torn off after printing, at the same time when the paper is 'burst' into individual pages. Automatic bursting machine are available when the amount of paper being handled is very large.

When tractor feed is used, it is important that when printing starts the first sheet of paper is in a position that allows the top line to be used – this is called the **top of form** position. If this is not correctly set then there is a chance that this sheet will be printed at or below the perforation line so that when the sheets are burst, some text has overlapped, and the space that should have appeared between sheets is placed on a sheet. Different designs of printers make different provision for setting the top of form position, and in some

Figure 5.3 *The form of the paper for a tractor-feed printer. This allows a printer to work unattended with, typically,* 2000 *sheets in a single print run*

cases this means using the first sheet for this purpose, measuring the correct distance from the perforation and placing this mark in line with a mark on the tractor mechanism of the printer. The position is then set in the controller mechanism of the printer by pressing a button or in some cases by switching the printer on when the position has been set.

More recent printer designs make better provision for setting the top of the form. Instead of locating the tractor feed sprockets on top of the printer and pulling the paper through, they place the sprockets inside the printer so that the paper is pushed to the printing position. This allows the top of the form position to be set on the first page rather than on the second, avoiding waste and making the setting much easier, since the paper edge need only be lined up with a mark on the printer. Such printers also allow mixed use of single sheets and tractor feed continuous paper, using a different paper path for the single sheets so that one single page can be fed through without even removing the continuous paper or the tractor feed mechanism.

An older form of continuous paper is the teleprinter roll, which uses a roll of paper with no perforations. This had the disadvantage that the paper could move sideways in the rollers of the printer, but was convenient for some purposes. It is now seldom used for computer printers, and the old teletype machines for which it was originally intended have in the main now been replaced by fax machines, which use a different form of paper.

The keyboard, mouse and graphics pad

The keyboard is the main device by which data is entered into the computer. Though the essential keys are the alphabetical keys that a typewriter would use, some fifty-three keys, most keyboards in use today possess a considerably greater number, typically 102. The extra keys are used to control computer functions, making it possible for a whole series of actions to be carried out by pressing a single key. The keys that are termed **function keys** and labelled as F1, F2, up to F10 or F12 are of this type and are found arranged either at the left-hand side of the keyboard or as the top line of keys above the normal set. In addition, it is customary now to place an additional set of number keys at the right-hand side of the keyboard (where they are almost useless to left-handed operators), and these keys are also used for controlling the place on the screen where a character will be placed. This dual action is controlled by another key, the number lock. The most useful of the added keys for computing functions are the keys that are labelled **Ctrl** (control), **Alt** (alternate) and **Esc** (escape). The Esc key is normally used as its name suggests to escape from a course of action in a program, and the Ctrl and Alt keys are used along with the normal character key to achieve other effects.

The operating system of a computer can use several different ways to respond to the keyboard. Keyboards are generally connected so that each key makes a single electrical contact, and the contacts are arranged in a matrix pattern (Figure 5.4) rather than with each pair of contacts requiring a pair of wires to the computer. Each key can therefore cause a connection to be made between a row and a column on the matrix, and in some cases it is possible to make false connections so that, for example, pressing the **O** and **M** keys together will produce **OM7**, the 7 being produced because the pressing of O and M together creates a new path, the path for the digit 7. The first generation of small microcomputers used the CPU to control the keyboard, detecting which row was connected to which column when a key was pressed and using this information to place an ASCII code into the memory of the computer. It is more common now for the keyboard to have its own controller chip so that less of a burden is placed on the main CPU.

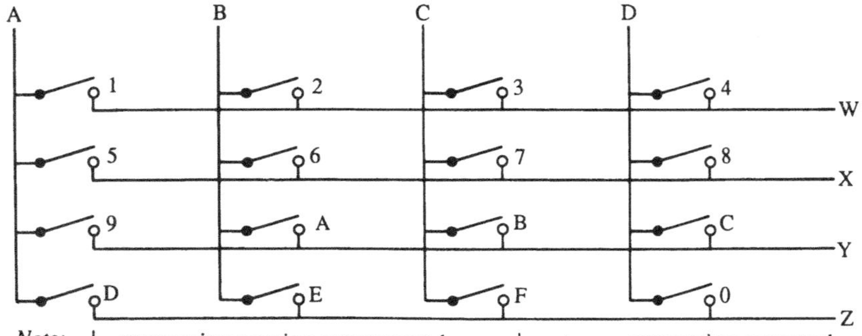

Note: ―┼― means wires crossing, not connected ⊢ ⊥ means wires connected

Example

Pressing key 6 joins line B with line X. The computer (either the main CPU or a secondary unit on the keyboard) sends a pulse to line A, and checks lines W to Z in sequence for the pulse. If nothing is found, the pulse is applied to B, and the same search action carried out. If a key is pressed, than at some stage, a pulse will be found on one of the lines W to Z, otherwise no key is pressed

Figure 5.4 *The matrix form of wiring to the keys – illustrated here by a simple sixteen-key set which uses eight wire connections rather than sixteen*

There are two main ways in which a computer can deal with a keyboard, polling and interrupting. In a polling system, the computer runs in a cycle which continually tests for a key being pressed. This means that when the computer is programmed to expect an input from the keyboard, nothing else can be done because the computer is doing nothing else but test the keyboard. It also makes it possible to disable the keyboard when the computer is engaged on some action that requires no input from the keyboard. A polling system was often used for the early microcomputer keyboard systems, but the interrupt system became more frequently used in later designs. In the interrupt system, the computer is normally engaged on work other than testing the keyboard, and only when a key is pressed does the computer run a piece of program that test to find the key and its corresponding ASCII code. This method is much less wasteful of CPU time, and also allows the keyboard to be disabled when no input is required.

The difficulty in either system is how to deal with an emergency stop. It is sometimes necessary to break off a program action, perhaps because the program is engaged on some lengthy calculation which the operator realizes is not needed, or is about to make changes to data on the disk which should not be altered. This calls for a **Break** key which can be pressed to interrupt the program, and such an action is relatively easy to program in either the polling system or the interrupt system of working. The problem, however, is that some actions, like reading from disk or writing to disk, ought not to be interrupted, since interruption can cause corruption of data. The key that is used to break into a program must not be one that could be hit by accident, and in some cases, it should be completely disabled.

The solution that is used on many modern machines is to have a Break key which will interrupt some programs when it is pressed along with the Ctrl key. This avoids the problem of pressing the key by accident, as used to happen often on one early design of microcomputer in which a single Break key was located close to the Return key that is used to enter each item of data. Programs can disable this Break key, which is tested on a form of polling system some fifty or sixty times per second. Where the Break key action has been disabled and it is essential to stop an action, a combination of keys can be struck which will cause the computer to reset. This is a drastic action which will clear the memory and reload the operating system, an action called **rebooting**. Whereas the use of the Break key simply stops a program running, leaving the program and (usually) its data still in the memory, the reboot action stops all activity, removing all programs and data from the memory, and starting all over again. The reboot action is so drastic that it requires more than one key to be pressed, and on the PC type of machine it needs the Alt, Ctrl and Del keys to be pressed simultaneously.

Even a reboot can sometimes be insufficient. If a faulty program causes the CPU to **crash** and go into a closed cycle of meaningless instructions, then even the reboot keys may have no effect because the keyboard interrupt program can no longer be used. When this happens, only switching off and then switching on again after a short interval can regain control. This also will cause a complete loss of any programs or data in the memory, but this type of reboot (a hard restart) should never be necessary other than when a new program is being tested in its pre-release form. The commercial user of a computer is most unlikely to be in possession of such programs.

The mouse, a small trolley which can be moved over the desk and which is connected to the computer, is not an alternative to the keyboard, but an enhancement of keyboard action. Many programs are **menu-driven**, meaning that the user is asked at frequent intervals to select from a number of possible choices which are displayed on the screen. The older style of program would number these choices and ask the user to type the number, then press the Return key to confirm the choice. When a mouse menu is used, an arrow or other pointer appears on the screen and can be moved by moving the mouse on the desk. When the arrow is over the item to be selected, a button on the mouse can be pressed to confirm the choice.

The mouse is used normally when two other programming devices, windows and icons, are also present. A window is a section of screen which is processed separately from the rest of the screen. One window might, for example, permanently display a set of menu choices, which the main part of the screen showed the results of the computing activity so far. Icons are images used in place of words, such as a picture of a disk to mean the use of the disk drive, or a picture of an office file to mean a file of recorded data. In a full WIMP (window, icon, mouse program) environment, all choices are made in a reserved window by using the mouse to point at icons, a form of control pioneered by Xerox and taken up by the Apple Macintosh computer.

The mouse, however, cannot compete with the keyboard for entering data, and its use on some programs, notably word-processing programs, can be to slow down the user considerably. The merit of mouse operation is that it allows error-free menu selection to be made by users who are not familiar with a keyboard or with the commands that have to be typed for disk filing and other activities. Some users see this as an essential programming method to encourage the use of computers by people who dislike having to learn typing or the forms of commands. The use of a mouse can make an unfamiliar program very simple to use and easy to learn; on the other hand, using a mouse on a familiar program can often be much more tiring than the typing of commands which have been committed to memory.

Graphics pads (or tablets) are another enhancement of a keyboard that are of considerable use in manipulating graphics. A graphics pad looks like a small drawing board, with the difference that it can control the screen when a suitable **driver** program is running. This allows you to 'draw' with a pen on the graphics pad and see your drawing appear on the screen. Many systems allow for pre-drawn shapes (squares, circles, arrows, etc.) to be selected and moved around the screen also, saving time when a drawing can be built up from such elements. The operating software will usually provide for saving the images as a file on disk, printing the images, and (usually) incorporating them into other programs, notably desktop publishing programs. Some makers of graphics pads also provide disks of preset images, such as architectural, electronic or mathematical symbols.

Scanners and OCRs

Another recent addition to the peripherals that can be used with computers are scanners and optical character readers (OCRs). The scanner allows text or graphics on paper to be read and converted into digital form. The principle is illustrated in Figure 5.5, with a row of LEDs (light-emitting diodes), each of which is pulsed in sequence by the computer so as to emit a flash of light. This light is reflected on the paper and picked up by a detector, but the amount of signal picked up will vary according to whether the light

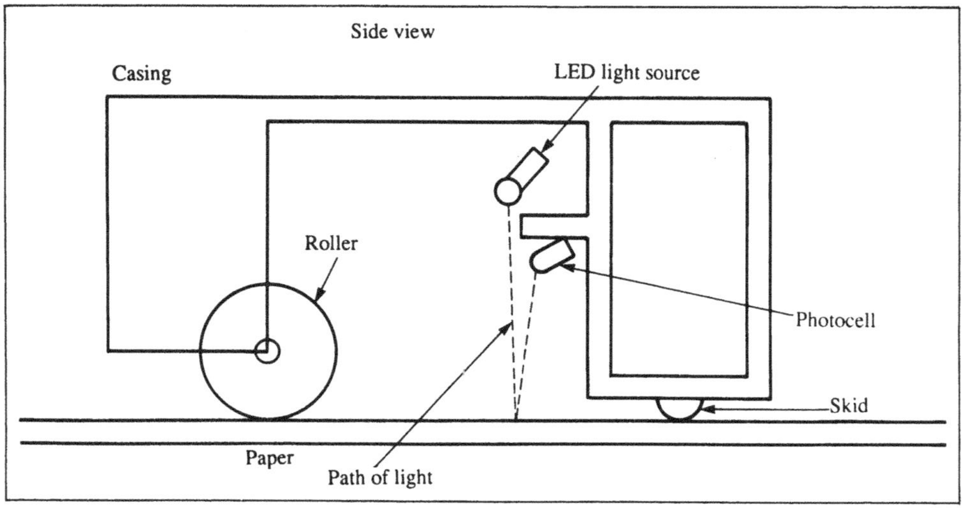

Figure 5.5 *The principles of a scanner, which uses miniature photocells to detect the light reflected from paper which is illuminated from miniature LEDs. The LEDs are pulsed by the computer so that the signals from the photocells can be used as digital outputs.*

has been reflected from blank paper or from ink. The signals from the detectors are then processed so as to provide digital bits than can be stored as a representation of the image.

Scanners can provide conversion of images into digital form using typically 200 to 400 dots per inch, so that considerable storage space is needed. For example, an A4 size image will require up to 3.9 million dots at 200 dots per inch, and if one dot corresponds to one bit, the storage required is about 500 K. Small scanners for microcomputers permit 4 in wide pictures to be scanned, moving the scanner by hand over the picture and using a graphics program to edit the results. Larger scanners move the paper mechanically and scan to A4 width.

Optical character readers allow the scanning of text to produce a text file rather than a set of graphics dots, with each character being converted into its ASCII code. This is much more difficult and even the best OCRs will sometimes misinterpret a character, but the output requires very little memory space as compared to a graphics image, and the text can be processed by a word-processor.

Exercise 2

List the types of data whose input is best dealt with by using;
(a) A keyboard.
(b) A mouse.
(c) A graphics pad.
(d) A scanner.
(e) An OCR.

The VDU

The visual display unit (VDU), or display screen, was not a normal part of a computer system until comparatively recently, and became so mainly when the first microcomputers appeared, since screen output was for these machines more important than printed output – some early machines did not even provide for the connection of a printer. The established use of mainframe computers in batch computing or in process control did not call for anything other than printed output, and even when VDUs were incorporated, they were used for conveying messages to the operator rather than as any part of the computing action.

The arrival first of minicomputers and then microcomputers firmly fixed the VDU as an essential, rather than optional, part of a computer system. This made it possible to develop programs that depended on the user being able to view the action of the program on screen, essential for the new types of programs that were being developed, such as word-processors and spreadsheets. The change has been so complete that it is difficult now to imagine a computer system without a VDU.

The majority of computers are designed to use either their own VDU or to connect a standard VDU unit. A VDU should be constructed to much higher display standards that can be attained by a TV receiver, allowing text and graphics to be displayed sharply and clearly. Many VDUs that are sold as part of a computer system operate on a system that differs considerably from that of the domestic TV receiver. The clarity of a domestic TV receiver is geared to the national TV system, which in Europe provides for a maximum of 600 horizontal lines on screen for monochrome pictures, with the equivalent of 300 lines for colour. This is only marginally acceptable for computer use, and though some VDUs that are sold as computer monitors are a little better, it is usually preferable for the sake of the operator's eyesight to provide for much better resolution (the ability to distinguish close-spaced lines from each other). This sometimes requires the VDU to operate with 1000 or more lines per screen height, using standards considerably better than those of TV. Such VDUs are costly, and in general it is difficult to carry out actions like word-processing with colour monitors that cost less than about £800 (at the time of writing), though much cheaper monochrome monitors are quite suitable. For a comparatively low-cost computer system, unless colour graphics are essential, the monochrome option is usually much more satisfactory.

Terminals

A terminal is a combined keyboard and VDU, and the name usually implies that the combination has no computing ability, and is simply an attachment to a mainframe or minicomputer. The use of terminals, however, allows several operators to have access to the machine simultaneously, timesharing the CPU and often making use of separate blocks of memory. Each terminal user logs on to the computer by typing a set of codes, and from then on the terminal behaves as if it were the only one connected. When the user logs off again, any memory that has been allocated for the use of that terminal is free for other uses, and only disk or tape files for that user are protected from re-use.

The distance between the computer and each terminal can be large – the Prestel computers are miles from terminals that use them – so that a serial connection is used between the computer and its terminals. This, as noted earlier in the section on serial connection of printers, allows for the use of simple cables with as few as two cores, but limits the speed at which information can be transferred. For most of the purposes for which terminals are used, however, speed of input or output is not important, and the speed of computing is that of the main computer, subject to any delays caused by timesharing.

Terminals are often classified as being *dumb* or *intelligent*. A dumb terminal is simply an extension keyboard, depending entirely on the computer to which it is linked. An intelligent keyboard has some computing capabilities of its own, so that it is capable of actions independently of the main computer, and can prepare work even when the main computer is not available. In large mainframe installations, desktop PC machines are often used as intelligent terminals.

Punch-hole codes

Before the development of reliable magnetic recording methods for computer data, computer input often made use of punched paper tape or cards. The tape was 1 in wide and was usually held in reels of one thousand feet length. The data was coded on the tape in ASCII, using the position of a hole across the tape to represent each 1 bit in a byte. A set of sprocket holes was pre-punched into the tape, so that for a seven-bit ASCII code there were three bit positions on one side of the sprocket holes and four on the other. For eight-hole ASCII (using a parity bit), the division was three and five. The spacing between sprocket holes was 0.1 in, so that each linear inch of tape stored ten bytes of code, requiring about 8.5 ft of tape per kilobyte.

An even earlier method used punched cards. The cards allowed eighty columns of data, one byte to each column, but the coding was not ASCII but more like a decimal coding. Row positions 0 to 9 were used for coding digits, and two other rows used along with the digit rows were used for letters of the alphabet. The punching was of rectangles rather than the round holes used with paper tape. Since each card held at most eighty bytes, the number of cards required for feeding in data could be large. The advantage of the system was that when each card held data for a database, one person's data could be held on one card, and it was possible to read the card by eye to check the contents.

Both paper tape and cards were read by machine, using either metal contacts or lightbeams to detect the hole positions. Tape could be read more rapidly because it could be wound past the reader, whereas each card had to be fed into place, read, and then moved on. The preparation of either form was by punches attached to keyboards which were often part of teletype machines. A notable advantage of both tape and card was that the data could be prepared to feed into the computer well in advance, while the computer was running another form of program. Paper tape could be run through a teleprinter to give a printout of the data on the tape, quite separately from its use in the computer. Another notable advantage was the both card and tape were **archival**, meaning that nothing short of burning or shredding was likely to destroy the data, which could be held in the form of tape or cards for very long periods. Neither method, however, was ever used for microcomputers.

Bar-codes

The modern equivalent of paper tape and card encoding is the bar-code (Figure 5.6). This uses a pattern of thick and thin bars to carry data in binary form, with the considerable advantage that bar-codes can be photocopied and printed, like any other piece of printed material. Bar-code printers can be connected to a computer in place of or as well as a conventional printer,

Figure 5.6 *A typical piece of bar-coding which can be used to place computer data in coded form on paper. Dot-matrix printers can reproduce bar-codes, and light-pens can be used to read the codes*

and it is also possible, using a controlling program, to print bar codes with an ordinary dot-matrix printer. One very common use of bar codes is to identify stock items, and their use for this purpose is common in shops.

The reading of bar codes was originally carried out by a form of light-pen which was moved across the coded bars. By detecting the reflected light, the presence and width of each bar can be detected, so allowing the code to be read when the reader is controlled by a program. Readers can be 'intelligent' in the sense that they operate separately from the computer, or the reader may consist of the light-pen only, completely controlled by the computer. For reading bar codes on paper sheets or tapes, the light-pen is held stationary and the paper moved at an even rate past it. The reading of bar-codes by moving the light-pen by hand is not reliable, and a later method uses a miniature laser beam which is scanned automatically (by a rotating mirror or prism) across the bar-code. This latter system is now used in point-of-sale readers for supermarkets, and has completely replaced the older light-pen type of reader. Bar-codes can be printed by specialized machines, or by dot-matrix or laser printers using suitable software. Unlike punched tape and cards, bar codes have briefly been used as an input method for microcomputers, and at one time magazines carried short programs in bar-code form. This, however, was at a time before disk drives became generally available on microcomputers and the arrival of low-cost disk drives made the use of bar-codes for this purpose unnecessary. They are used, however, to a much greater extent on larger machines.

Exercise 3

Data recorded on paper as punched tape or bar-codes is said to be 'archival'. Why can data recorded on magnetic tape or disk not be classed as archival?

Transmitting data

Transmitting data, as far as computing is concerned, means transferring information from one computer to another without involving the laborious task of typing all the information over again. The information could be text, meaning that it consists entirely of letter and number characters as you would generate in a text editor or a word-processor, or it could be program data such as would be obtained from a spreadsheet or a database program, or it could consist of programs themselves. The simplest, safest and most obvious way of sending data from one computer to another is by recording the data on a disk and posting it to the user of the other computer. Like so many things that seem simple and obvious, however, there are snags. One is that a disk created by one make of machine may not be readable by another. In earlier days, when all computers could use paper tape punches and readers, the punched hole format for the paper tape was standardized and any computer could communicate with any other by sending a paper tape through the post. The same interchangeability existed when 8 in floppy disks arrived, but when machines started to use 5.25 in disks, each manufacturer of computers decided that its own system had some unique merit, and interchangeability vanished. The problem of lack of standardization has haunted computer communications ever since, and we now have some machines of the PC type using 3.5 in disks and unable to read information from the older 5.25 in disks, though recent models allow for the external connection of other disk drives.

Connections between computers can be made using either parallel or serial connectors. A parallel connection means that a large number of separate wires will be used, at least one for each data bit in the byte or word, so that parallel connectors often use twenty-four or more cable strands. Parallel connections allow very fast communication, but unless booster amplifiers are used the distance that can be bridged by a parallel connection is short, up to about 2 metres. Serial connections use a minimum of two wires (or one wire and an earth return) to convey the signals, and therefore must work with one bit at a time. This slows down the possible rate of exchange of signals, but makes it possible to transmit data over almost any distance.

The serial connection will use some version of the RS-232 system. When RS-232 was originally specified, two types of device were used and were classed as data terminal equipment (DTE) and as data communications equipment (DCE). A DTE device can send out or receive serial signals, and is a terminal in the sense that the signals are not routed elsewhere. A DCE device is a half-way house for signals, like a modem (see later in this chapter) which converts serial data signals into tones for communication over telephone lines or converts received tones into digital signals. The original conception of RS-232 was that a DTE device would always be connected to a DCE device, but with the development of microcomputers and their associated printers it is now just as common to require to connect two DTE devices to each other. This means that the connections in the cable must be changed, as we shall see. The original specification also stipulated that DTE equipment would use a male connector (plug) and the DCE equipment would use a female (socket), but you are likely to find either gender of connector on either type of device nowadays. What started as a simple and standardized system has now grown into total confusion, and this sort of problem occurs all the way along the communications trail, not least in the use of words.

The original cable specification of RS-232 was for a connecting cable of twenty-five leads, as shown in Figure 5.7. Many of these connections reflect

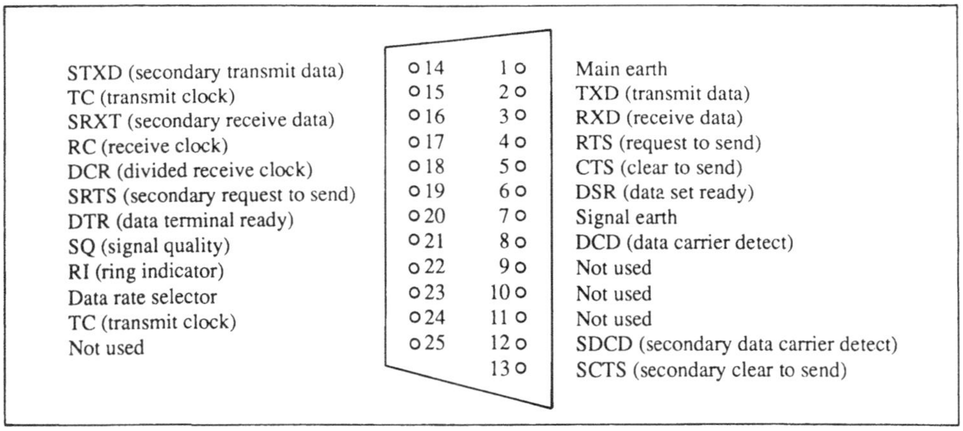

Figure 5.7 *The original specification of the RS-232 connector for serial input or output, along with typical modern specifications*

the use of old-fashioned telephone equipment and teleprinters, and very few applications of RS-232 now make use of more than eight lines. The standard connector is the D-type 25 pin, but even in this respect standards are widely ignored and some manufacturers use quite different connectors. Worse still, some equipment makes use of the full 25 pin system, but uses the 'spare' pins to carry other signals or even DC supply lines. The advantages of using serial connections, however, outweigh the problems, because when a modem is connected by the RS-232 cable to your computer it is possible to use a simple single line (telephone or radio link), and distance is no problem – wherever telephone or radio messages can be sent in the world you can transfer computer data providing that both transmitter and receiver operated to the same standards.

When data is sent one bit at a time, some method has to be used to allow the receiving computer to distinguish one group of eight bits (a byte) from its neighbour. This problem does not exist for a parallel system, because in the instant when a character is transmitted, all of its bits exist together as signals on the eight separate lines. For a serial transmission there is just one line for the bits of data, and the eight data bits must be sent in turn and assembled into a byte by storing them at the receiving end. The problem is that since one bit looks like any other, how does the receiving machine recognize the first bit of a byte? The way round the problem is to precede each transmitted byte of eight bits by a start bit (a zero) and end it by either one or two stop bits (each a 1) – notice that once again there is no standardization of the number of stop bits, though one stop bit is slowly becoming the more common practice. Ten (or eleven) bits must therefore be transmitted for each byte of data, and both transmitter and receiver must use the same number of stop bits. The transmitting computer will send out its bytes of data, and at the receiving computer, the arrival of a start bit will start the machine counting in the bits of data, storing them into its memory until it has a set of eight, and then checking that it gets the correct number of stop bits after the last data bit. If the pattern of a zero, then eight bits (0 or 1), then a 1, is not found (assuming eight data bits and one stop bit), then the receiving computer can be programmed to register a mistake in the data, and start counting again, looking back at the stored data and starting with the next 0 bit that could be a start bit. The recounting is fast, and can be carried out in the time between the arrival of one bit and the next, so that it would be unusual to miss more than one character in this way. All of this is the task of the communications software that you use with each computer and is carried out automatically if, and only if, you have programmed the software to work with the correct protocols. This type of data transmission is called **asynchronous** to distinguish it from another method in which both computers are synchronized to the same rate and data is sent continually, using dummy data when no real data is being sent. The advantage of synchronous transmission is that no start or stop bits are needed once synchronization has been established, but the asynchronous method is much more commonly used.

Good software can make use of methods of adding data so as to provide for better checking and can even provide for correction of errors to some extent. The checking methods can range from the simple checksum to the very complicated Reed-Solomon system (also used in compact discs), but they all have one factor in common: redundancy. All checking involves sending more bits or bytes than the bytes of the data, with the extra bits or bytes carrying checking and error-correcting signals. Some of these can work on individual bytes, even on individual bits; others are intended to work on complete blocks of 128 bytes or more. The checksum, for example, works by adding the number values of all of the ASCII codes in a set number of bytes, often 128. This sum is transmitted as a separate byte, and at the receiver the codes are again summed and the total compared with the transmitted checksum. Only if the two match will the set of bytes be accepted. Because these checking methods all involve the transmission of extra bytes, they slow down the rate of communication of useful data. For text transmissions, the use of elaborate checking is often unnecessary because an occasional mistyped character in text is often not important compared to the need for a high speed of transmission. For sending programs, however, one false byte is usually enough to ensure that the program does not run correctly, so that much better checking methods must be used even if this means taking longer to transmit the data. The user has to select, by way of the communications software, different methods for transmitting different types of data.

Given that the transmitter and the receiver are set up to the correct protocols, meaning that the baud rate, the number of stop bits and the use of parity will be identical, some method of handshaking is required to ensure that signals are transferred only when both transmitter and receiver are ready. You might, for example, be recording data on your disk as it arrived, so that there would have to be a pause in the reception of signals while the disk system got into action. Another possibility is that you are printing out the data as it is transmitted, and your printer operates at a speed slower than the baud rate of the transmission. Whatever the reason, just to have transmitter and receiver working at the same rate is not enough, because you also have to ensure that the bits are in step at all times, and you have to make it possible to pause now and again without any loss of data. A serial link to a printer can make use of **hardware handshaking** meaning that the handshaking can be implemented by using electrical signals over another set of lines, but this option is not open to most communications applications because extra telephone lines are not available for this use.

The handshaking is therefore implemented in software by using the XON/XOFF system. This uses the ASCII code numbers 17 and 19, which are not used for characters, sent between one computer and the other. Data can be sent out from a computer following the ASCII 17 code, and disabled following the ASCII 19. Since these codes are sent over the normal data lines, no additional electrical connections are needed. The rate of data transfer is slower because of the time that is needed to send the XON/XOFF signals, so that if a system is organized in such a way that the least use of handshaking occurs, both transmission and reception will be faster. The use of XON/XOFF is by far the most common method of software handshaking that is used in communications (another system is called EIA).

The modem

Two computers that are reasonably close to each other can be linked by a serial cable of the non-modem type, but a much more common requirement is to link computers for which the only connecting link is a telephone line. This calls for the use of a **modem**. The telephone system is intended to transmit the electrical signals that are obtained from a microphone operated by the human voice. Like any other waves, the waves of sound of the voice cover a range of frequencies, meaning the number of vibrations per second. In honour of the pioneer of radio, Heinrich Hertz, the unit of one vibration per second is called the hertz, abbreviated to Hz. The range of frequencies that is needed for intelligible (as distinct from high-quality) speech transmission is quite small, of the order of 300 to 3000 vibrations per second, usually written as 300–3000 Hz. By contrast, the transmission of music of the quality that we get on a good recording demands (but seldom gets) a range of frequencies from about 30 Hz to 18,000 Hz, and television pictures require a range from 0 Hz to 5.5 million Hz because of their complicated pattern. The equally spiky signals from a computer also, even if they are slowed down to a low speed of 300 per second or lower, simply cannot be transmitted through a telephone circuit.

What we need is a device that detects a computer on signal and turns it into one tone and will similarly turn an off signal into another tone, or a tone that is different from the first in some way, like being out of step. The action of converting the computer signals into tones is called **modulation**, and we must be able also to carry out the opposite action which is called **demodulation**. The combining of the words modulation and demodulation gives us the word modem, which is the name of the device that carries out this transformation. The modem is connected to the computer by a serial link, using normal hardware handshaking, but the lead out from the modem to the outside world is a single lead, suitable for telephone connection, using XON/XOFF handshaking.

For most purposes, it is necessary to use a modem that will work in both directions at the same time (full duplex) so that just altering one tone is not enough, and you need to be able to work with two. For low baud rates, it is possible to have four different tones in use, two for transmitting and two for receiving, with the actual frequency of the tones carefully chosen so as not to cause problems with the telephone system itself. Most telephone systems around the world use different tones to represent the different dialled numbers, and even in the UK where the old pulse system (one pulse for one, two pulses for two and so on) is still used for domestic telephones, the tone system is used between exchanges.

For the higher baud rates the use of separate tones is not possible. You cannot carry a signal of 2000 baud with a frequency that is lower than 2000 Hz, and because the higher baud rates are much too close to the upper limit of frequency that the telephone lines can cope with there is no possibility of using four tones each higher than the baud rate and each separable from the other. The faster modems therefore use a system of phase shifting, meaning that the frequency is unchanged but a change is represented by a shift (called a phase-shift) of the signal, as illustrated in Figure 5.8. This allows a signal of comparatively low frequency to carry several thousand changes per second, so that a rate of 2000 bits per second can be carried with a signal that need be sampled only 600 times per second. This is where baud rate and bits per second become different, and the established practice as far as computer communications are concerned is to refer to the rate in bits per second as the baud rate. As a computer user, the number of bits per second is the important figure for you, the baud rate is the figure of importance to the telephone line engineer. The more modern telephone exchanges which are being installed all over the country will cope with these phase-shift signals, but where the old fashioned 1910 style (that is,

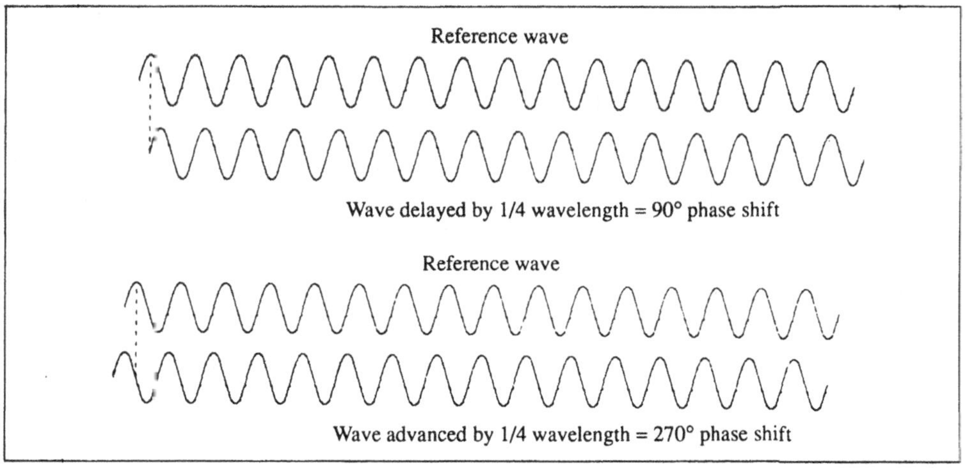

Figure 5.8 *Conveying digital information by phase-shifts in a signal; part of the action of a modern modem. This permits the rate of data communication in bits per second to be greater than the baud rate, the number of cycles of signal per second*

the date of invention, not the type number) of automatic exchange is still in use, you can use only the slower baud rates.

> ***Exercise 4***
>
> Two computers are connected together by a serial line. The two are set to use the same baud rate of 4800 bits per second, but data typed on one keyboard produces only gibberish on the screen of the second. What else might need to be changed?

Networking

Serial connections are extensively used for networking, the connection of several computers together so that they can share files and peripherals like printers, disk drives, etc. A local area network (LAN) means the connection of computers that are physically comparatively close, in the same room or the same building. A long-haul network (LHN) means the connection into a network of computers that are distant, so that the connection has to be made over telephone lines or by satellite links. LAN connections can be made using serial cables based on comparatively inexpensive cable, such as TV coaxial downlead cable or simple twisted insulated cable, and the main complications of the system reside in the software. LHN connections require the use of modems, usually high-speed types, and also require software of a very high standard. The main problems of all forms of networking are to ensure that there are not undue waiting times for equipment, and that files will not be compromised when several users have access to them.

Preparation of data

When only small amounts of data need to be supplied to a computer, any preparation of the data is confined to ensuring that the data is in the order in which it needs to be entered, such as surname, forename, age, reference number. For such applications, data entry will be by way of the keyboard directly, with the data handling program running. This is by far the most common method of initial data entry for microcomputers, and for many applications of minicomputers. It can also be used for mainframe machines which have terminals fitted at which data can be entered.

Manual data entry like this, however, is not always necessary. When a shop sends its daily summary of activity to be processed by a central computer, it is not necessary to read each till-roll and type the numbers and items into a terminal, because the tills can encode the transactions as bar-codes or as punched tape, or as magnetic tape. These forms of recorded information can then be collected and fed to a reader connected to the main computer for batch processing. Even data that consists of text need not be typed again, because an optical character reader (OCR) can be used to scan the printed or typed material and convert each character to ASCII code to be fed into the computer. Readers of this type are available now for microcomputers, and cheaper versions, called **scanners** exist (see earlier in this chapter) which will make a copy of printed material to the VDU, though elaborate software is needed in order to convert this to the form of ASCII codes suitable for processing.

One very common and simple method, where typing has to be used, is to have a data gathering program running in a microcomputer, preparing a disk for use in a mini- or mainframe machine. This has the advantage that the data is prepared away from the main computer, and is delivered in the form of a floppy disk which can contain a large amount of data as compared to a paper tape. The use of paper tape and card is rather unusual nowadays, though bar-codes are extensively used for small amounts of data.

Suggestions for practical work

1 Type a few lines of text, and compare the printing speed and quality from a daisywheel printer, a dot-matrix printer and a laser printer.
2 Use a program that employs a mouse to make menu selections and compare this with a program that relies on typing for selection.
3 Use a computer which is connected to another by way of a serial link.
4 Use a scanner, OCR or bar-code reader to input suitable data.

Multiple-choice test questions

1 A document contains several sizes and styles of print. It is best printed using:
(a) a daisywheel printer
(b) a dot-matrix printer
(c) a line printer
(d) a plotter

2 One important advantage of using tractor-feed paper with a printer is that:
(a) the printing is faster
(b) the paper feeds through faster
(c) the positioning of print can be more precise
(d) the paper stays gathered up

3 A logo has to be copied from an artist's drawing to a set of computer-produced forms. The preferred method is to use the combination of:
(a) a scanner and a laser printer
(b) a keyboard and dot-matrix printer

(c) an OCR device and thermal printer
(d) a mouse and daisywheel printer

4 Data is being transmitted by a modem to a remote computer using telephone lines. The rate of transmission:
(a) can be as fast as the transmitting computer can operate
(b) is unlikely to exceed 9600 bits per second
(c) can be as fast as the receiving computer can operate
(d) must be less than 300 bits per second

5 When data is to be transmitted between two computers, using modems, an essential requirement is that:
(a) the computers should be of identical make and model
(b) the disk system must be of the same capacity
(c) the serial protocols must be identical
(d) the keyboards must be used at the same rate

6 Text data which is being gathered for transmission from one machine to another by way of a modem:
(a) must be typed
(b) must be bar-coded
(c) must be in English
(d) must be in ASCII codes

6 Introduction to files and filing

Objectives

- Describe how data is physically organized and accessed on serial, sequential and randomly-organized files and databases (8).
- Define field, record, file and block (8.1).
- Compare file and record processing on different types of media (8.2).
- Describe typical file labels and explain their use (8.3).
- Describe the organization and accessing of serial, sequential and indexed sequential files (8.4).

A file is a collection of data that exists in the backing store of the computer in the form of recorded number codes. The recording method will normally be magnetic, using tape or disk, though some files on paper tape are still used, and bar-coded files also exist. The computer file is usually of a large amount of information and not necessarily on one topic exclusively. For example, if you were creating files for classification of steam rail locomotives, you would not devote one computer file to each single locomotive. It is more likely that you would have one file for the UK, one for the USA, one for Europe and so on, or you might have one file for very early types, up to 1860, one for 1860 to 1920, a third file for 1920 to 1975. In ordinary office terms a file often means a collection of information about one subject or person, but the ability of the computer to carry out rapid searches through recorded data make it possible and more useful for the files to be much more extensive.

In a filing or **database** program, data will be handled in the form of **records**. Each record is a collection of information that consists of individual **fields**. For example, if the data consisted of employment details, one record would be concerned with one person and would carry all the information on that one person. One of the fields would be used for surname, another for forenames. There would be a field for age, one for number of years worked, one for present salary. Other fields would be use for education, previous experience, qualifications; using a field for each type of relevant data.

In a file that dealt with all the employees in a factory, one record would concern one person. In a file of fighter aircraft of the Second World War, one record would deal with the Spitfire, another with the Messerschmitt 109. A record in a file is what we often mean by a *file* in office terms, and we can think of it as one page in a whole set of pages that make up the complete file. One important difference is that a paper file can often be of any size we like – if we want to devote three folders to one record we can do so. Computer files often impose a size restriction on each record and though you are free to specify what this size is when you design the file you cannot from then on alter the allocated size.

Each record of a file is further subdivided into fields. A record might consist of just a few fields, such as surname, forename and telephone number, or it might have a very large number of fields, particularly if it dealt with a lot of details. A file held on paper could, once again, devote as much space as was necessary to each field, but a computer file often has a limited space available, and if the content of the field has to be used in calculations (such as dimensions that can be used to calculate area, volume, rate of flow etc.) then the field will have to be a number field rather than a string field. The design of the fields and records is a matter for the user of the file, however, and in this book we are more concerned at this point with how the file is maintained and used by the computer.

Each file, to be recorded on disk, requires a file name to be allocated. This is not necessarily true of files held on the older media (paper tape and cards) because whereas one paper tape held one file, and one card held one record, a disk can often hold several files, particularly if the disk is a hard disk. A mainframe mechine using data on magnetic tape will often use a reel of tape for each file, so that again there is no need to have to identify the file other than by labelling the tape (including the header and trailer records, see later). The use of hard disks by machines of all sizes has made the use of file names familiar to all computer users, however, and the operating system of a machine will often impose restrictions on the file names. Figure 6.1 shows the specification of a file name for the PC type of machine, a pattern that is used for a large number of other machines of various sizes.

When the number of characters that can be used for a file name is restricted, as it normally is, then there is always a risk that a file will be

The file name can use three portions: a disk drive or path designator; a main name; and an optional extension. The main name can be of up to eight characters, and the extension can be of up to three characters in length. If a drive letter is used, it must be separated form the main name by a colon. If a path name is used, it must be separated by a backslash. The extension is separated from the main name by a point. If the drive or path portion is omitted, the current drive or path is assumed. Examples of valid names are:

A:MYPROG.BAS **CURRENT.TYP** **B:INSTR.DOC**

\WSTAR\TXT\OLD\CHAP.027 **C:\TEXT\TITLE.TXT**

Figure 6.1 *The specification of a file name for a PC type of computer using the MS-DOS operating system* recorded using the name of an existing file. If the software does not intervene, the effect will be to record the new file over the older one, completely replacing the older file. If good file maintenance procedures are used, there will probably be two other copies of the deleted file on other disks, but these are probably older versions of the file which may have had data added since these backup copies were made. A better way of dealing with the problem is for the software to compare any suggested file name with the names that already exist on the disk, and to remind the user if there is a possible conflict of file names. This does not prevent the user from recording one file over another, but it does stop the process and ask for confirmation that this action is intended, which is a useful safeguard. Some file-creating programs do not allow a file to be recorded at all if there is an existing file of that same name. This is more of a safeguard, but it can lead to difficulties if you frequently want to update a file but keep the same file name, rather than using successive version numbers in names such as DATFIL1, DATFIL2 and so on. It is also wasteful of disk space if several versions of the same file exist, and there is a risk when you delete earlier versions that the current version could be deleted by mistake.

A few types of program that create files will also create file names, identifying files by serial number. This, though convenient in some ways, makes it very much more difficult for the user to associate the file name with the contents of the file. Using names like STAFFDAT, STEAMDAT or FIGHTERS has the merit that the user can tell from the name of the file what the subject matter is, whereas file names like F0000001 and F0000023 carry no such associations. These numbered file names can, however, be useful as part of a file system in which a program is used to search for files.

File labels

Each file consists of a set of records, and in addition to the records of data there will be at least one record, often two, that are used for identification and organization. These records are called **file labels**. A disk file will usually have one file label, a header, but a tape file often has two labels, a header and a trailer. Each of these records must start with one field, which can be of one single bit only, which will identify the record as being a label and not a data record. For a header, the record will also contain the file name, the date on which the file was created or last updated and, for a disk header, a list of sector numbers to show where the records are stored. Other information, such as an end-of-use (purge) date can be included if needed.

The trailer label is used only for tape files to identify the end of the records, and will contain the identification field, the number of records (which for disk files can be put into the header) and, for very large files, the reel number if the records take up more than one reel of tape. Many disk systems will use no real trailer, only a single end-of-file (EOF) ASCII character.

Some database programs for PC machines make very little use of labels, relying on the labels that are automatically created by the operating system itself. For larger machines using manufacturer's operating systems, it is more likely that the header and/or trailer will be created by the database program, and the basic information listed above may be supplemented by other data according to the requirements of the program.

> ***Exercise 1***
>
> Plan out a file for storing examination and test results for a period of three years, showing the fields and record structure.

Serial files

The physical organization of the bytes of a file determines very considerably how a file can be used, and the simplest form of organization is serial. A serial file stores the bytes of a file in the order in which they are output from the computer, and must retrieve them in the same order. The order of the bytes of the file is very often the order in which data is entered into the file from the keyboard, though the data-gathering program may re-arrange the information before recording it. Some forms of backing stores are such that only serial filing is possible (any form of tape, for example), others permit the user to opt for serial or to use other forms (magnetic disks or drums). The use of serial filing is best illustrated with reference to a tape storage system, such as a magnetic tape cartridge or cassette.

A tape storage system operates on the principle of winding the magnetic tape at a constant speed past a recording/replay head. Each bit of signal will magnetize the tape, with a 0 bit magnetizing the tape in the opposite direction from a 1 bit. Because of the movement of the tape, the bits are recorded on separate parts of the tape, though it is possible to use multi-track recorders so that the unit is one byte or word rather than one bit, with one bit of the byte or word on each track. Whichever method is used, the distance between bytes is set by the speed of movement of the tape and the rate at which bits are recorded, and the bytes are recorded in strict sequence, the order in which they are sent from the computer to the tapehead. Each byte occupies its own piece of tape, and when the tape is replayed, the bytes will also be retrieved in this same order.

This action of tape forces any file stored on tape to be in serial form, so that if the 274th record is required, then either the whole tape has to be replayed or the correct piece of tape has to be located by other methods. Unlike the audio use of tape, digital tape is reeled at a very high speed for normal reading or writing, so that reading the whole tape from the start is not necessarily such a prolonged matter as it would be for audio tape running at its slow playing speed. The retrieval, carried out in this way, can use one of two methods for locating the correct record:

1 To read all of the records into the memory, and then find the wanted record in the memory.

2 To count the records as the tape replays and read only the required record into the memory.

Either of these methods can be used with an optional method of recognizing the wanted record, comparing a keyword (surname, works number, type name etc.) with the keyword that can be read from the first field of the record.

The first method can be very effective if several records from a file will be wanted, because with the records all stored in the memory of the computer access is very much faster than it would be from tape or even from disk. The objection is that a large amount of memory may be required and it would clearly be out of the question, for example, to read several million names and addresses into memory in this way. For a reasonable amount of data, the contents of a single floppy disk, for example, this method is feasible for many computers.

The second method is better if only one record is required, because the amount of computer memory required for storage is only that needed for the one record. The time required will in general be less than is required for the first method, because unless the required record is the last one to be recorded on the tape, it will be found before all of the records have been read. The snag with this method is that if another record is then needed subsequently, the whole reel of tape has to be rewound and the search process repeated.

Serial files can also be used on disks and drums. The organization of a disk is into tracks and sectors (see Chapter 4); and the corresponding magnetic drum names are cylinders and sectors. The sectors are numbered from track 0 onwards, so that a serial file can be recorded with one record per sector, a very common arrangement if the size of record permits. This makes it very easy to record and replay at high speeds, because the head of the disk or drum drive need only move by one track (cylinder) distance as each track is read. The speed of hard disks in this respect is not always as fast as might be thought from the quoted access time, because many hard disk systems require the disk track to pass the head twice or three times in order to pick up all of the information on the track – this is termed a 1:2 or 1:3 interleave, and only disk drives with 1:1 interleave are operating with the access time that is quoted. The way that most computer operating systems organize disks, however, usually means that a serial file recorded on a hard disk will not necessarily be recorded on a set of adjacent tracks, and this can be true also of a floppy disk unless the floppy has newly been formatted or has had all previous files deleted. The speed is usually, however, superior to that of tape systems, and this makes it easier to use the second method of retrieval for a single record.

The main advantage of using serial files is that each record can be of a different length, since the only effect of this will be to make the record take up more tape or more disk sectors. There need be no fixed record length nor even a fixed field length, so that serial filing is particularly useful when the amounts of information in each record can be very different (Figure 6.2). The main disadvantage is the need to read a large number of records so as to be able to obtain one specified record, and also the problem of maintaining a sorted list. It is possible to read all of a set of records into the memory of the

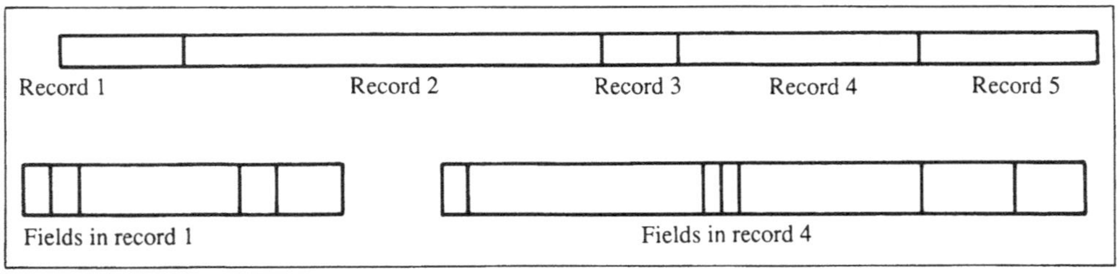

Figure 6.2 *Serial filing allows for large differences in the size of fields and records, even for different records having different numbers of fields*

computer, and rearrange them into alphabetical order, using the first name in the record on which to base the order. It is possible also, if the number of records is too large for the memory, to carry out this reorganization on two disks. You then have the problem, however, that when you enter another record it will almost inevitably be in the wrong place, at the end of the list, so that the sorting will have to be carried out all over again. This problem is elegantly dealt with by using a sequential rather than a strictly serial file.

Sequential filing

There is a fine division between sequential filing and serial filing, and many users make no distinction between the two. Strictly speaking, a sequential file is like a serial file in the way that the records are recorded, but with the difference that the records are linked, so that each record contains data that will allow the next record in a sequence to be retrieved. Filing of this type is pointless on tape unless the tape system is under software control that allows data to be read from one record and used to wind the tape in either direction to locate another record, so that sequential recording and replay applies mainly to disk and drum recording. A tape file can, however, be described as being sequential as well as serial if the records are in some order, like alphabetical order of first field.

Suppose, for example, that the records are stored on the disk with one record to each sector, and with each record carrying its sector number as part of the record. Now if each record can also carry another sector number, that of the record which follows it, then records can be read in a sequence which is not the sequence of writing. One very common sequence would be alphabetical, so that the last record whose first field starts with **A** will carry a 'next-record' number for the next record whose first field starts with **B**, taking a very simple example. This type of system allows for a record to be read, and then the following record quickly located and read. If the number for the previous record is also recorded, then it is equally possible to read records in reverse order, and the order of reading can be quite different to the order of writing. This is particularly suitable if the organization of the records has to be serial but the reading should be in some order such as alphabetical. A set of records in which each record carried a location number for another record or records is called a **linked list** (Figure 6.3).

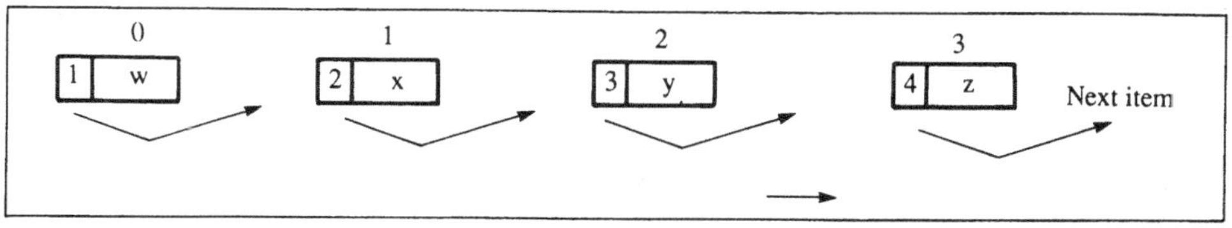

Figure 6.3 *The form of a linked list, which allows each record to carry a number that can locate the next record in the sequence*

Linked lists are an elegant solution to the problem of keeping a serial file so that records can be printed or worked on in alphabetical order. The program which inserts the sector numbers can ensure that when a new record is added, the numbers are rearranged so that the new record will be placed into the correct order when read. This, however, requires altering the numbers in two other records, the one that will precede the new record and the one that will follow it, and another way of implementing a sequential file is often preferred, the use of an index file along with the use of a random-access main file.

An index file (or inverted file) contains keys to the main file. For example, if the main file contains records that pertain to aircraft, holding details of wing span, length, unladen weight, wing area, engine type and so on, the index file would contain only the names, along with a sector number from which the main record could be located. This index file can be maintained, since it is essentially a small file, in alphabetical order, and can be re-arranged each time a file is added.

The enormous advantage of using the indexed-sequential filing system is that searching for a specific file is very simple, because the index file can be searched first, using a binary search. This is possible only if the index file is always maintained in alphabetical order. The basis of the binary search is as follows, assuming that some name has been typed into the computer and the corresponding record is required:

1 A point half-way down the index file is selected, the name read and compared with the typed name.
2 If the names are identical, the corresponding file is retrieved.
3 If the index name starts with a letter that comes later in the alphabet (a lower-order name), then the first half of the index is selected.
4 If the index name starts with a letter that comes earlier in the alphabet (a higher order name), then the second half of the index is selected.
5 The half-index is now used in a second set of comparisons, using an entry half-way down the list, and this process of halving the list and then comparing with the middle item is repeated until a perfect match is found, otherwise the program reports that no match exists.

This process, illustrated in Figure 6.4, can obtain a match, if one exists, in remarkably few steps, even for a very large index list. In fact, the larger the index file, the more efficient the method is as compared to a search through all of the list in order. A binary search (or binary chop) method can be applied only when the list is maintained in order, however. The number of

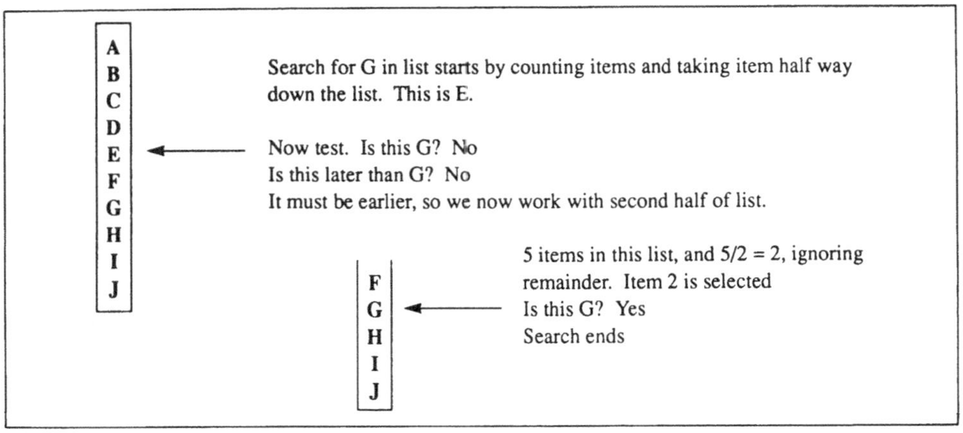

Figure 6.4 *The action of a binary search (binary chop) to find an item in a list that has been placed into order*

comparisons that must be made in a binary search is at most only ten for a list of 1024 items, as distinct from an average of 512 for a one-by-one comparison, and in general the maximum number of comparisons n is such that 2^n is equal to or just greater than the number of key items (so that the number of key items is less than 2^{n+1}). Once the key has been located from the index file, the sector number can be obtained and the record copied from the main file. This form of keying, however, is more often applied to random-access filing.

Note that serial or sequential filing can be implemented on disks or drums as well as on tape, but random-access filing (see following section) can be implemented only on disks or drums.

> ***Exercise 2***
>
> Draw up a program plan to show how you could change one field of a record in a serial file.

Random-access filing

Random-access filing, as the name suggests, means that it should be possible to get at any record (or set of records) on the disk without having to read all of the earlier records as well. This does not mean that it is necessary to create a random-access file by scattering bytes all over the disk (though this could be done), simply that it should be possible to locate and read any byte on the disk. As you might by now expect, this is not done by reading one selected byte but by reading one complete sector into memory and working on it there. In general, a file will initially be created in the memory of the computer and then recorded, using much the same general techniques as we have used for serial filing. The user can then add to the file, replace items, change items, and select items at random, all using random-access techniques. The important point about such random-access filing is that it is possible to extend a file so that the file length is much greater than could be held in the memory of the computer. As an alternative, of course, the random-access filing methods that are used for extending a file can be used to create the file in the first place. Using a random-access file, it is possible to extract single items or groups as we please, amend or delete or replace items, all without the need to read the whole file as would be necessary with serial files. For most purposes, all that ever has to be read or written for one record is one sector of the disk. This freedom, however, is bought at a price, and that price is more restrictive organization.

Random-access filing is possible only if each record in the file consists of the same number of fields, and each field in the record is of a specified size. There is nothing magical about random-access filing. The name of the file is stored on the disk directory, and the directory also contains the starting position of the file. From then on, it is easy. If each record is 100 characters (bytes) long, for example, then it is easy to find the fourth record (numbering from 1) because it will start at the 300th byte in the file, and the seventeenth record will start at byte 1600. Similarly, if the 100 byte record consists of four names each of twenty-five characters, then it is easy to find the third name in a record by getting to byte 75. Without these fixed lengths, random-access filing is not possible, certainly not in this comparatively simple form (Figure 6.5). A filing program for random access must have some form of instruction that will to allow you to specify each field, its name in the file, and its length in number of characters/bytes.

With each record of fixed length, the storage on the disk can be allocated accordingly. The usual method is to allocate a fixed number of disk sectors to each record, often one sector per record. This means that each record can be assigned with a unique 'address' number from which the program can locate the correct disk sector – if each record takes more than one sector the starting sector can be located. This makes location of records very easy, but only if allocation by number is used. You can, for example, easily locate record number 17, but there is no simple way of finding the record whose first field is the string "SINCLAIR". For this reason, random-access filing is usually associated with a serial index file as described above.

Since each field in a random-access file must be of a fixed length, what has to be done if the information does not fit? To start with, we ensure that any

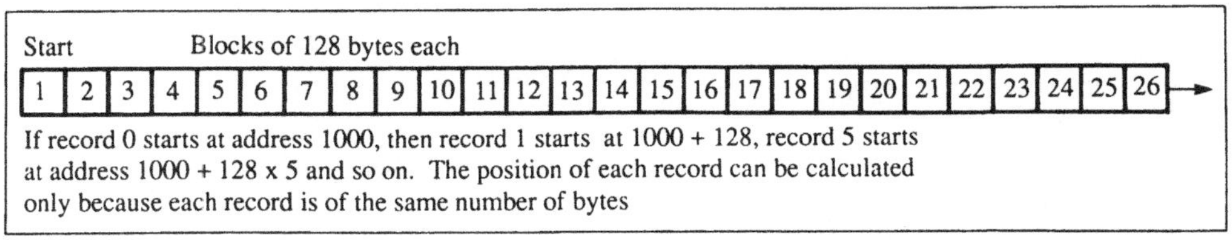

Figure 6.5 *Random-access filing normally assumes that each record is of the same fixed size, so that its position from the start of the file can be found easily*

number information will fit, by methods that we can look at later. The awkward items are strings like names and addresses. These will be chopped if they are too long and padded out with blanks if they are too short, and a random-access filing program will carry out this work automatically.

Numbers are treated in a rather special way. Since each item that is stored in a random-access file must be a string, the obvious thing to do is to convert each number into a string. This could be done by converting each digit of a number into ASCII code, and recording these ASCII codes as a string, but this is a slow action, and for large files with a lot of numbers it can noticeably increase the time that has to be spent just waiting. In addition, the conversions that are made in this way can be to quite long strings and the fields have to be made long enough to hold all the characters. The alternative is to make string characters out of the code numbers that are used for the compressed form of numbers. The principle is to convert into string form not the number itself, but the code that is used to store the number. The result of this will be strings that are often of very weird characters, if you try to print the result, certainly not recognizable as numbers. The advantage is that each type of number always provides a predictable string length. If, for example, the computer codes integers in two bytes, then the string for any integer is of just two bytes. If a floating point number is coded in five bytes, then its string is five bytes long, and so on. The use of these codes means that some of the string characters are unprintable (such as the characters below thirty-two) and others may not print either on screen or on paper (such as 128 to 255), but since these strings will never in the normal course of events be printed, this is not really important. If, incidentally, printing out a complete record as it exists on the disk results in odd-looking characters, it is likely that this is due to the contents of a number field being printed as a string.

For a two-byte integer, it is fairly easy to see how the scheme works. The number 65 is character A in ASCII code, so when the string version of 65 is printed, you get an A printed. Taking another example, the number 16706, is more of a surprise, because it gives BA. The ASCII code for B is 66, with A being 65, and 16706 is 66 + 256*65. This corresponds with the way that larger integers are stored as two bytes. The strings that correspond to floating point numbers are considerably more complicated unless you have a taste for mathematics.

Exercise 2

How could a form of random access be used for records of greatly varying lengths (*hint* – indexing).

File organization and access

Whatever form of programming language is used, the handling of files demands that commands be used in the correct sequence, whether for reading or for writing. Since the serial form of file is by far the easier, we can concentrate first on what has to be done in order to create such a file, using a straightforward example of a file of names. The actions that are described are carried out as part of the filing program, and the operator will not necessarily be aware of what the program is doing. As far as the operator is concerned, questions appear on the screen, and answers are typed on the keyboard, and the disk or drum drives operate intermittently.

The first action is to open the file for writing, and for this purpose the command word will usually be OPEN. Following this command word will be a name for the file, and a reference number. The name is the file name under which the file will appear on the disk or tape, and the reference number (also called **handle** or **channel number**) is one that the computer uses in order to allow it to work with more than one open file – it allows the computer to reserve part of its memory to gather bytes up for writing to a disk sector or reading a complete disk sector. Where the language permits both serial and random-access filing, letters such as S or R may be used also in the command to specify what type of file is being opened. For a serial file it is usually necessary also to specify by using letters whether the file is being opened for reading, writing or appending. The choice of appending allows new data to be placed at the end of a serial disk file, but for a tape file it may be necessary to locate the end of the file in some other way, and appending may not be possible in any simple way.

Opening the file establishes the file name and the memory store (the buffer) which will be used as an intermediary, but it does not necessarily cause anything to be recorded. Some filing programs working on disk will record the file name at this stage, others record the file name along with the first batch of data. Once the file has been opened, in any case, data can be gathered into the buffer memory. The program will use the screen to place questions, and the answers, each of which will be one field of the record, are gathered together in the buffer memory. The program will need some method of separating one field from another, and the symbol that is used for this purpose is called a **delimiter**. Very often the carriage return can be used as a delimiter, because it has been pressed in order to enter each field item, but for some files the comma is also an acceptable delimiter, so that an entry such as FIELDING, JOSEPH, TOM JONES would count as being three fields.

Data is recorded on to the disk or drum only when the buffer is filled (Figure 6.6), since it would be immensely time-wasting to record each byte separately as it is typed. This use of a buffer also makes it easy to correct an entry before it is committed to the disk, and some programs display the total content of each record on the screen for the operator to check before the buffer is copied to the disk. Once the contents of the buffer have been copied to the disk, and the disk sector verified by reading it again and comparing it with the buffer contents, the buffer is cleared (flushed) so that the next collection of data can be entered.

There is an important difference between writing to a serial file and appending. When a write action is selected, then the file that is written will replace any existing file of that same name. When appending is chosen, the file name must be the same as that of an existing file, and the data is added to the end of that file. Serial filing programs normally allow a write action only

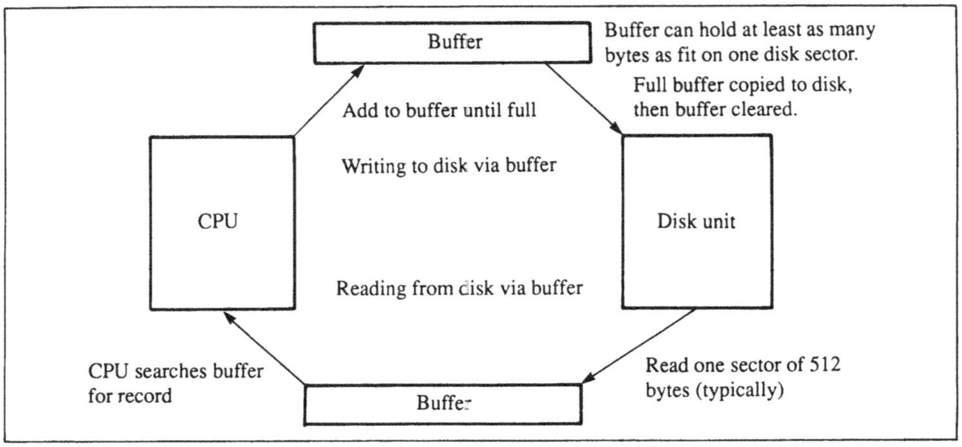

Figure 6.6 *The use of the buffer ensures that disk read and write actions are carried out only as and when needed to fill or clear a buffer. It is never necessary to read or write single bytes*

for the purpose of creating a new file, and any attempt to use an existing file name will be prevented or, at least, queried. The program will normally be written so that a new file name implies that a file should be created and written to, an old file name implies that data is to be appended or read.

At the end of data entry, whether appending to an existing file or starting a new file, the file must be closed, using a CLOSE command. This has the effect of recording the file length on to the disk so that the disk keeps a tally of file name, starting location and finishing location for that file. Some disk systems will spread such a file around the disk, using whatever locations are free, and in such a case, each change of location also has to be held in this tally, the file allocation table (FAT), which is maintained automatically by the operating system. If the file is not closed, no length number is recorded, and the file cannot subsequently be used, because the disk operating system will not accept a file which is of unspecified length. It is therefore vitally important to close a file after writing, and a filing program must contain not only means of closing the file in normal circumstances, but of closing the file even if the user presses the Break key or tries to leave the writing action other than by the normal menu path.

When a serial file is to be read, it has to be opened for reading, specifying the file name, allocating a number, and using a letter R or the word **Read** to indicate that reading is required. The use of the R or Read ensures that the operating system will open the file and find the start of the file, because the reading of a serial file always starts from the first byte in the file. Once the file has been opened for reading, the program can contain commands that read a record from the file, and these commands can be repeated (the program contains a **loop**) so that all of the records are read into memory, or until a record that starts with a specified field is found. Once again, the action is to place the record or records into a buffer part of memory, reading in one sector of disk or drum to this buffer, and then transferring bytes as required.

The use of the buffer is the factor that makes it easy to locate any field of a record, since memory can be searched much more quickly than bytes can be read from the disk. If all of the records are to be stored in memory, they will usually be stored as a string array or some similar form of complex variable like an array of records or structures.

A file should be closed after reading as a matter of habit, but closing a file after reading is not so vital as closing a file after writing. Failure to close after reading might cause unwanted reading at some other stage in the program, but it cannot result in the file becoming unusable, because the writing action has ensured that the file is correctly entered into the file allocation table on the disk. A well-written program will, however, ensure that files are open only when they need to be, avoiding any risk of a file being left open. If, incidentally, a disk file is unreadable due to a failure to close the file after writing, the data can often be recovered by a program which allows bytes to be placed directly into the FAT. This requires considerable knowledge of the disk operating system, and there are a few specialists who will undertake data recovery from disks that have suffered calamities considerably more serious than a simple failure to close a file.

The use of random-access files introduces rather more complications. To simplify the description, we shall assume that each record on a random-access file has been placed on a different sector of the disk. This is, in fact, a very common method. The essence of random access is that a record can be placed on any sector of the disk that has been allocated for it, and the method by which this is done is to allocate a number to each record, and use that number to locate the disk sector – the number could, in this example, simply be the sector number itself, allowing for the difference between the usual numbering of sectors from 0 up to the maximum, and records starting at 1 rather than 0.

The OPEN command for a random-access file must therefore cause rather more organization to take place than that of a serial file. The file name will have to be specified, and the fact that this is a random-access file. A file reference number will be allocated and in addition, the size of the record which in this particular example will be the same as the size of the disk sector. If the record size is small, the data will be organized so as to pack a whole number of records on each sector – a record is never split across sectors unless the record size is fixed as being of more than one sector. Some random-access data programs go further than this opening process, and follow it by recording blank data on a fixed number of sectors, so that the size of the file is fixed in advance, with the disk space reserved. This makes the initial creation of a random-access file slower, but can greatly speed up the actions of reading and writing later.

Once a random-access file has been opened, it can be used for reading or for writing; there is no need to have separate opening command versions for read and write, and appending is meaningless – a new record can be placed in an unused sector or in one that already contains data, replacing that data. The data must, however, be prepared for writing. The size of the record has already been fixed, and the fields of the record must, at the time of entry be padded or chopped to their specified size so that the record length is achieved. If this were not done, then replacing one record by another could leave fragments of the original record if the replacement record were shorter. The command that is then used to write the record on to the disk must contain a sector number so that the record can be correctly positioned. If there is more than one record per sector, the number has the effect of placing the record into the correct part of the buffer before writing.

The reading of records from a random-access file follows the same pattern. A record number has to be specified, and this allows the disk sector to be identified, the record read into the buffer, and so made available to the program. If there is more than one record per sector, then the number is used first to locate the sector (remember that there will be a whole number of records per sector) and then to locate the record within the buffer. The snag of any simple random-access system is that the operator needs to know the number of a record in order to read it or write it, and there is no obvious connection between this number and the contents of the record.

This makes the use of a key (index) file almost essential for random-access filing. A key file will, as usual, contain a name or other reference that the operator can use, along with the random-access record number for that item. The key file, being reasonably short, can be a serial file (Figure 6.7) that is read into memory and which can then be alphabetically sorted and searched

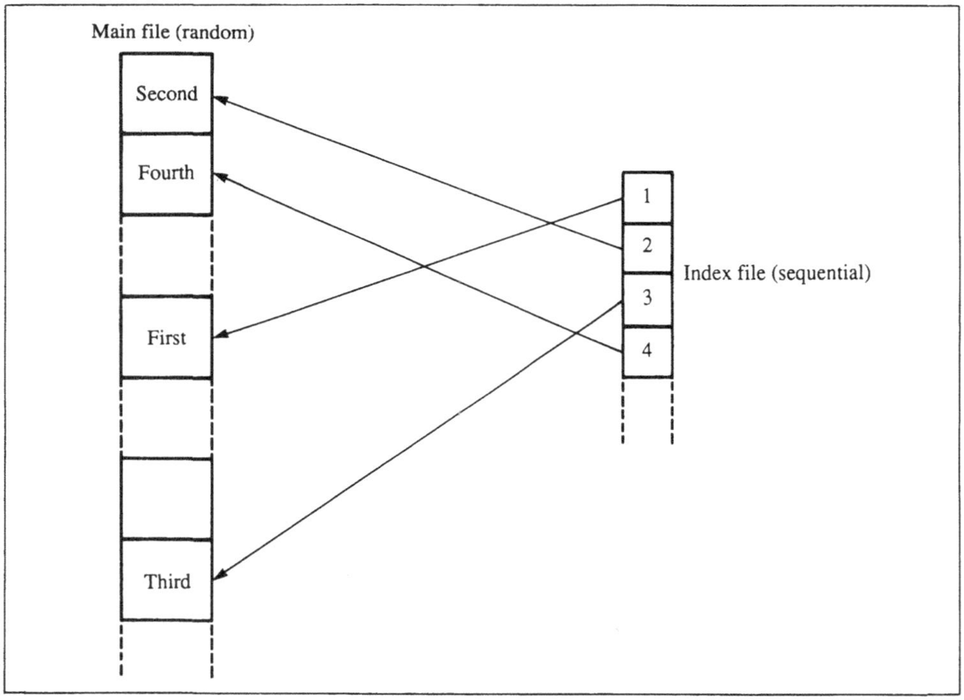

Figure 6.7 *The relationship between the key file and the main file in a keyed access system. When a change is made in the main file, the key file must also be amended and then re-sorted if necessary. Since the key file is small, it can be re-sorted quickly*

by a binary search method. Once the key item is found, the random-access record number can be obtained and the record copied from the random-access file (or written to the random-access file). The use of a key/index file along with a random-access file is standard practice for a data processing program that uses random access, and more than one index file can be created and used for a single main random-access file. As we shall see in the following chapter, however, there are other methods of obtaining a record number from a name or other field of a record.

As for a serial file, the random-access file must be closed after use for reading or writing, but particularly for writing. The type of program that allocates file space by writing a dummy file at the time of opening can also ensure that this file has been closed again before it is re-opened for reading or writing, and this makes for greater security. Failure to close the file correctly after reading or writing is not quite so serious if the complete file size has already been established, though it can result in the corruption of some records unless the program can sense that the file has not been closed. If the dummy file method has not been used, the random-access file must be closed after any write operation, because there is a possibility that any write will extend the size of the file.

Once again, all of these actions should be built into the database program, and should be concealed from the operator. At one time, it would have been regarded as normal for the operator to specify disk sectors, and allocate space for a file, but modern programs are arranged so that as much of the action as possible is **transparent** to the operator. This confines the operator's responsibility to the entry of data in correct format, in response to messages on the screen, and this process should never be interrupted by any type of technical data such as record numbers. The program should carry out all of the checking actions that are needed, such as allocating disk space, finding records, warning when a disk is full and should be changed, closing files in the event of the Break key being pressed. Everything must be done to ensure that an operator action, deliberate or accidental, should not corrupt data by leaving a file open after writing, replacing a valuable record by a less useful one, or any other action that can make a file useless.

Exercise 3

Why is the use of disk considered superior to the use of tape for filing purposes?

Other file actions

The maintenance of file demands actions other than simply writing and reading, though these are the actions which are needed to keep individual records up to date. Other file actions concern the file as a whole, and are not necessarily part of the database program. File actions are always provided as part of the disk operating system of a computer, and the older database programs often require the operator to leave the program and make use of the operating system directly in order to carry out these file actions. Modern database programs, however, are written so as to avoid this requirement, so that the user of the program need not necessarily have much knowledge of the operating system.

File deletion is one such process. The form of command uses a word such as DEL or ERASE followed by a space and then the name of the file – the full name, including any extension, may be required. When this command is used from the operating system there are no safeguards, and the file is deleted whenever the Return key is pressed. When File Delete is made part of the menu of a database program, the operating system command will be used, but the program can incorporate safeguards such as placing details of the file on the screen and asking the operator to confirm that this file is to be deleted.

Another action of the operating system is file renaming, which allows the name of a file to be changed without altering the contents of the file. This can be a useful action if a program does not permit a new file to be opened with the same name as an old one. If, for example, the file name is STEAM.DAT, and a new version is to be written, the old version can be renamed to STEAM.OLD or STEAM.BAK, so preserving the data intact, but allowing the new file to be recorded and used in preference to the old one. Some database programs carry out this renaming action automatically when a new file is given the same name as an old one.

The standard operating system commands will also include the comparison of two files. This is not quite so useful as it might appear, because the resulting report will specify only whether the files are identical or not, and will not necessarily show the differences. Once again, this operating system command can be used from within a program to check whether a new version of a file differs from an old one. This information can be important, because when a file has been changed, it ought to be backed up. This leads to the other file utility, the COPY action. Once again, it should be possible to copy a file from one disk to another without leaving the program, and it should be possible either to leave the file name unchanged or to specify a new file name (as well as a different disk drive), whichever is required.

Suggestions for practical work

1. Create a simple serial file and use a disk-sector reader to show how the file is arranged on the disk.
2. Create a random-access file and use a disk-sector reader to show how the file is arranged.
3. Examine simple programs for changing a record in a serial and in a random-access file.
4. Use a disk-sector reader to examine the header of a file.

Multiple-choice test questions

1 An advantage of a serial file is that it:
(a) must use fixed length fields and records
(b) can use fixed length fields and variable length records
(c) can use both fields and records of variable lengths
(d) can use fixed length records with variable length fields

2 The main advantage of random-access filing is that it:
(a) can make use of tape more efficiently
(b) allows a single record to be read or written
(c) requires the memory to be filled from the disk
(d) allows records to be of any length

3 The use of an index file in association with a random-access main file allows:
(a) the main file to be kept in serial order
(b) the main file to be shorter
(c) the index file to be left unordered
(d) the index file to find records in the main file

4 A file kept on magnetic tape can be:
(a) serial, sequential or random
(b) serial or sequential only
(c) serial or random only
(d) sequential or random only

5 An index file for a random-access main file is kept in alphabetical order of the name in the first field. This means:
(a) a new entry is put into a specific disk sector
(b) a new entry is put into the index file only
(c) a new entry is put into the first available space in the main file
(d) a new entry always replaces an older entry

6 A system is designed so that when a file is altered, the previous version exists as a BAK file. This ensures:
(a) a mistaken change can be corrected before another change is made
(b) the file can never be deleted
(c) the older version of a file is never lost
(d) the BAK version is always the latest version of the file

7 File processing and management

Objectives

- Explain the concept of an addressing algorithm and its applications (8.5).
- Describe common file processing procedures (9): runs for batch file updating (9.1); updating a file on-line (9.2); an internal sorting algorithm and an external sort and merge method (9.3); a commercial sort/merge utility (9.4).
- Describe procedures for ensuring the security and integrity of files: data validation procedures; file and data control procedures; mechanisms for ensuring the security of files; recovery procedures; ensuring the privacy of files.

File addressing

In Chapter 6 we saw that a major problem of random-access filing is that the use of a record number does not necessarily make a record easy to find. In other words, if you are looking for the record for SINCLAIR, you do not immediately think of the number 472 because there is no obvious association between the two. Yet, unless this number can be obtained, the record can be recovered only by reading the records as if they were part of a serial file. The topic of **addressing** is concerned with ways in which a record and its location in a random-access file on the disk can be more readily connected. All of the methods that are described can be used directly on the records of a random-access file, or on a set of keys that are held in order to make access to a random-access file quicker. Some programming languages make random-access files available only in keyed form.

One obvious and simple way is direct addressing. If the file is concerned with employees of a firm, and each employee has a works number, this number can be made the record number (Figure 7.1), or the record number

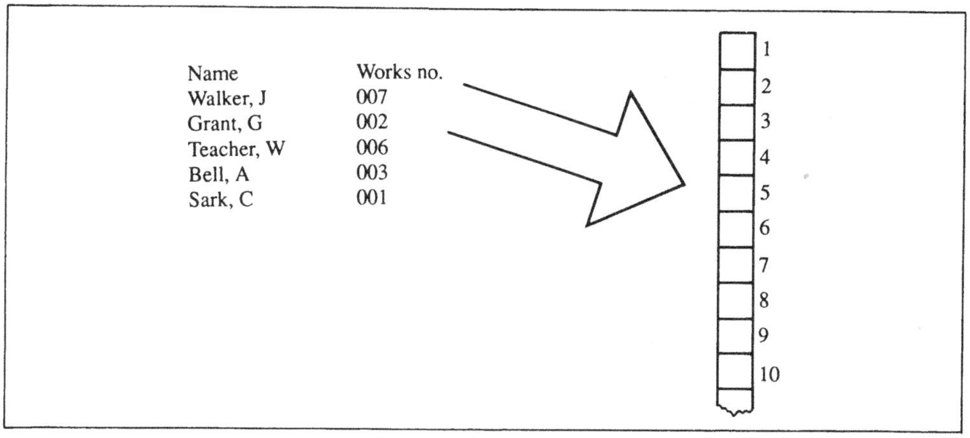

Figure 7.1 *Using a works number as a record number so as to make access easy in a random-access file*

can be calculated (within the program) from this employee number. This scheme can work well if the employee numbers follow a simple pattern such as 001 to 247, but if the numbers are scattered, so that there are only fifty employees but the numbers range from 1002 to 7063, then to use these numbers as record numbers would cause considerable wastage of disk space, because the program would normally create space for all the numbers in the range numbers 1 to 7063. The logical response would be to use a range of 1 to 50 for employee numbers, but the purpose of using a computer to assist the work of a firm is to adapt the computer to the work rather than the work to the computer. It would be a different matter for a small firm which is just about to start using works numbers for its staff.

When no simple connection between a record number and the nature of the record can be established, some form of **addressing algorithm** must be used. An algorithm is a procedure or formula for carrying out a task, so that an addressing algorithm is a method of obtaining a record number from the contents of a record. The four main algorithms for locating a record are linear search, binary search, hashing or Btree search. Of these, all can be used on data in the memory or in a file, but the Btree method is useful only when the data is stored on the disk and is to be retrieved directly rather than by a search through records stored in the memory. The easiest method of showing how these algorithms work is to describe the action, using a structured English description, and go through an example for the less familiar methods.

The linear search is simply the method that we have already described for a serial file. Each record is retrieved in order of record number, and examined to find if it matches the requirement. If it does not, it is abandoned (remember that the disk record remains in place, and the copy in the buffer is being examined by the computer), and if it does match, then the record is used. The algorithm is shown in Figure 7.2, and it consists of a set of repeating steps, a **loop** which is terminated either by the finding of the record or by reaching the last record without finding a match. As an

```
Array consists of items Name [1] to Name [n].
Item searched for is called Wanted

  Lower = 1
  Upper = n
  Found = FALSE
  DO UNTIL (Found = TRUE) OR
    (Lower = Upper + 1)
    IF Wanted = Name (Lower)
      Found = TRUE
    ELSE Lower: = Lower + 1
    LOOP
  END
```

Figure 7.2 *An algorithm for finding a record by reading through a list in sequence*

example, imagine that the first field of the required record bears the same SINCLAIR. Each record will be read into the buffer, and its first field compared with the typed name of SINCLAIR (most programs convert lowercase letters to uppercase before comparison). If there is no match, the next record is read; if there is a match then the computer will use the record in the buffer to display on screen, print, amend, or carry out whatever purpose was intended.

Spelling and typing is of major importance in a search of this type, because if the request is for SINVLAIR (one finger has slipped), the linear search will not find the name, nor will any of the other algorithms. Some algorithms can be adapted to seek out all the names that start in the same way (all the SI?????? names, for example, where the ? means any single character) and display them so that the user can pick the one that is wanted. Other algorithms, notably the hashing methods that will be mentioned later, do not adapt well to this type of use. There are now available algorithms which were developed for use with spelling checkers which are very useful for finding approximations to a name, but these are beyond the scope of this book.

The binary search has also been described in outline earlier. This hinges on having the records arranged in an order other than the order of the record number, such as alphabetical order of first field. If we imagine that the records are arranged so that the names in the first field are in alphabetical order, a typical search action is described in Figure 7.3. The algorithm would take the middle record in the sorted file, and find a name such as MORGAN. This points to SINCLAIR being in the second half of the list, and halving the list again gives the name SELLEY. This means that the required name is now in the last quarter, and half way down this gives UCKHAM. The section between SELLEY and UCKHAM is now halved, and this process of division and comparison is repeated until the name SINCLAIR is found. If the name is not found by the time that the remaining list consists of only one name the program must show a message to the effect that the name does not exist in the file. Another minor point is how halving of an odd number is treated, so that the list is then divided into sections that are not exactly equal.

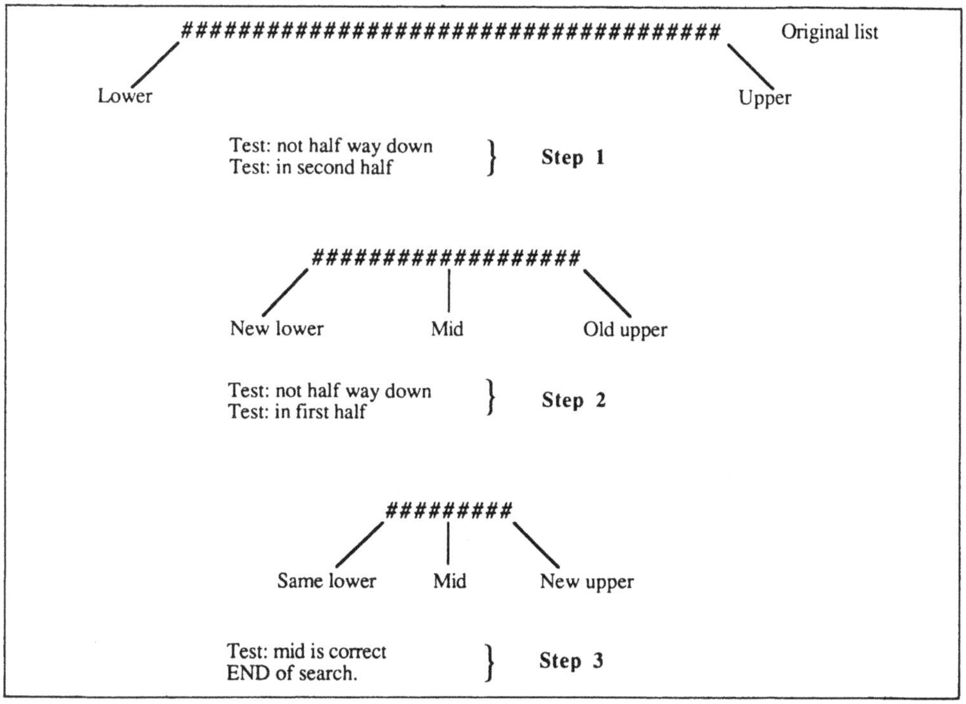

Figure 7.3 *A binary search used to find a record*

The algorithm in Figure 7.4 deals with the altering list size by using one variable for the number that is at the start of the list and another variable for the number that is at the end of the list. Each time a list is divided and there is no match between the first field name and the required name, these variables are assigned new values for the reduced section of list. This allows the same program steps to be applied, which is the essence of any repeating algorithm. The step **mid = (upper + lower)/2** implies that the answer is a whole number, with any 0.5 removed, so that an answer of 4.5 is converted to 4, and 76.5 to 76. The reduction of a list to one item is dealt with by the tests that start **IF MIDDLE = LOWER** and **IF MIDDLE = UPPER**, and in either case, the variable ABSENT is set to TRUE so that the program can report that the name is absent.

Hashing methods

Linear searching is slow, and a binary search is useful only if the records are arranged in order. The problem in each case is that the computer, unlike a human, cannot make any kind of intelligent guess about where to start looking for an entry, and must either start at the beginning (linear search) or in the middle (binary search). Either way, the computer must perform many data reads and comparisons, processes which are time-consuming. The most common method of dealing with these objections is hashing. In a hashing

```
Lower: = 1
Upper: = 1
DO UNTIL (Found = TRUE) OR (Absent = TRUE)
  Mid: = (Upper + Lower)/2                    * Get middle position
  IF Wanted = Name (Mid)                      *Is wanted name here?
    THEN Found: = TRUE                        * If so, end search
    BREAK
  IF Wanted < Name (Mid)                      * Is wanted name in lower half?
    IF Mid = Lower THEN Absent: = TRUE        * If nothing left, end search
        BREAK
    ELSE
    Upper: = Mid – 1                          * Shift upper mark to end of first half
  IF Wanted > Name (Mid)                      * Is wanted name in upper half?
    IF Mid = Upper THEN Absent: = True        * If nothing left, end search
        BREAK
    ELSE
    Lower: = Mid + 1                          *Shift lower mark to upper half
  LOOP                                        * Start search of new list
  END                                         * Item found, or search
(Note: BREAK means go to statement following LOOP)
```

Figure 7.4 *A binary search algorithm, showing how the changes in list size are dealt with by using variables*

algorithm, some formula is used to convert the data that is being searched for into a number, and this number is used as the record number. The principle is that the same process can be used on any name that is typed into the machine later, and by producing the correct record number allows the record to be recovered in a single fetch operation. Hashing is sometimes described as a **self-indexing** method of addressing files.

The main complication here is the chance that more than one item will yield the same number when the algorithm is used, and this has to be dealt with by a variation of the algorithm in which the next available number is used. The use of a hashing algorithm falls into two sections, the derivation of the hash number, and the method that is then used to locate the record once the hash number is found. The second part is comparatively simple, standardized, and brief, the first may be far from simple and can vary from program to program.

It is easier to start with an example of hashing, taking employee numbers first. Suppose that a department has five employees whose works numbers and names are as shown in Figure 7.5. The hashing algorithm is a very simple one, taking the last digit of the works number and adding 1 (so that if the last digit is a 0 we do not have to find a record whose number is zero). We might also have taken the first two digits and divided them by 2, ignoring any remainder. Another possibility is to take the sum of all the digits, and repeat until a single digit is left (so that 1746 gives $1 + 7 + 4 + 6 = 18$, then $1 + 8 = 9$). The results of these three methods are also shown in Figure 7.5. All of the methods give acceptably low numbers, but the third method has illustrated a problem that occurs in all hashing systems, a **collision**, meaning that two numbers have given rise to the same hash result. These

Name	No.	LD + 1	D1D2/2	Sum
Bell	1746	7	8	9
Teacher	2017	8	10	1
Haig	1124	5	6	8
Dewar	1515	6	7	3
Walker	1882	3	9	1

Hashing methods:
LD + 1 – last digit + 1
D1D2/2 – first pair of digits divided by 2
Sum – sum of all digits, repeated if necessary

Figure 7.5 *A set of names and works numbers, showing the effect of various hashing methods on the numbers*

two items, TEACHER and WALKER would be termed **synonyms** if this hashing method were being used.

Neglecting the problems of collisions for the moment, if we used the first method (last digit +1) then the five names would make use of record numbers 3 to 8, with only record number 4 remaining blank. This very simple algorithm is suitable only for these few items, because it can provide places only for records numbered 1 to 10. This illustrates that there can never be a totally general hashing method, because the method has to be tailored to provide a range of numbers that suits the number range of the data. The methods that are illustrated here can, however, be adapted to suit other examples. You could, for example, take the last two digits and add 1 in order to get a range of numbers that could be from 1 to 100, and the other suggested number algorithms can be similarly adapted to provide different ranges.

Hashing is most easily demonstrated on items such as works numbers which are already numbers, but the method is just as applicable to names. A name can be converted into a number by making use of the ASCII codes for the letters in the name. The simplest hashing method for a name is to add the ASCII codes for the name, so that SMITH becomes 83 + 77 + 73 + 84 + 72 = 389. This number might be used as it is, or hashed again using one of the methods illustrated previously. Using the last-digit +1 method would give 10, using the first two digits divided by 2 would give 19, and using the sum of digits would give 20 as the first sum, and 2 if this were repeated. Once again, the treatment that is applied depends on the number of records that will be used, so that if 100 records are to be used, the hashing must provide for at least this number, and preferably considerably more, since it would be undesirable to have to revise the hashing scheme completely just because one additional employee is taken on. Analysis shows that hashing becomes unsatisfactory when the number of items to be hashed is more than 80 per cent of the possible hash numbers, so that if your hashing scheme provides for 100 hash numbers to be generated, then performance (in terms of ease of locating a record) will deteriorate considerably by the time the number of records exceeds 80.

We can now look at how the problem of collisions is dealt with. The method is very simple – the colliding item is placed in the next available record position, advancing through the file. If the end of the file is reached before an empty position is found the file is searched starting at the beginning for an empty record. It is only if the file is not too full that there will be a reasonable chance of finding a vacant record close to a collision position, and this is one of the main factors that determines the rule-of-thumb that the number of used records should not exceed 80 per cent of the total number. The algorithm for placing a synonym is shown in Figure 7.6.

The important feature now is how to find an item. The first step is to apply the same hashing algorithm to the item that is to be found. This will result in a number, and we can use this number to recover a record. If a comparison of the name of the record (usually the first field) with the requested item shows that this is not the correct item, because of a collision when the item was written, the next record is selected, and so on until the correct record is found. If the end of the file is reached during this search, then the searching moves to the start of the file again. The algorithm is illustrated in Figure 7.7, and is essentially similar to the writing algorithm.

Hashing can be very fast because, for a majority of items, the record will be found at the first attempt, something that is very rare for either a linear search or a binary search. If the hashing method is unsuitable or the file is becoming filled more than one comparison may have to be made, but even then the time needed is never likely to be as much as is needed for a linear search, and often is less than is required for a binary search. An additional point to remember is that when a hashing method is used, the file does not

```
IF Filefull                              * Test file
  ERROR                                  * Out if full
Place = Hash (Data)                      * Find calculated place
  IF Place NOT Empty                     * Already occupied
    DO
      Place: = Place + 1                 * Next position
      IF Place > Max THEN Place: = 1     * If at end of file, go to start
    UNTIL Place = Empty                  * Test for empty place
WRITE Record TO Place                    * Found place, write record
```

Figure 7.6 *An algorithm that deals with a hashing collision, so that the data which gives the same hash number is placed later in the file, as close as possible to the calculated record number*

```
GET Hash (Request)                          * Calculate hash number
  Place: = Hash (Request)                   * Find corresponding place
    IF Record (Place) <> Record (Request)   * Not a match
      DO Place: = Place + 1                 * Try next place
    UNTIL Record (Place) = Record (Request)
  END
```

Figure 7.7 *The algorithm for finding a record by hashing*

have to be kept in any order; it can be a straightforward random-access file. Hashing methods generally have become the topic of intense study, and there are several books devoted entirely to the subject, though many of these are aimed at theorists rather than at programmers.

Btree methods

The Btree method is useful when a very large amount of data is held on a disk, and a record has to be retrieved in the least possible number of disk read actions. If a file can be held in memory and is sorted into order, the binary search is very much quicker, because the comparisons take very little time to perform, and no additional records or index items have to be fetched from the disk. If, however, the number of records or index items is very large, too large to fetch into memory, then a locating method which makes the least possible number of disk reads is preferable. If a binary search is conducted from disk, there will be an item read for each comparison. The Btree method uses each disk read to fetch a larger number of items, since a search through items, once read, will be much faster than the action of disk reading.

In a Btree of order 5, there will be a maximum of five items at each disk read, and these items will be sorted into order. The first set of items constitutes the root, and might contain only one number. The first comparison will determine whether the wanted item is equal to this number, in which case the data is fetched, or is greater than this number or less than this number. The decision will lead to another disk read, this time of up to five numbers in this example, and the comparison can be tried on all five. Once again, if a match is not found on any number, another fetch will result in a group of numbers from which comparisons can now be made. Because each read action produces a larger set of numbers, the amount of time spent on disk reading is much less than would be required for a binary search.

The algorithm for a Btree, however, can be very complex, and most programmers will prefer to buy the routine on disk rather than develop it single-handed. This requires the use of a modular programming language such as C, Pascal or Modula-2 or some of the most recent versions of BASIC, but this does not mean that a Btree routine will necessarily be available for programmers in other languages. In general, C and Pascal programmers are best served for libraries of these routines.

Exercise 1

Try a hashing algorithm for a list of twenty names, using a sum of ASCII codes. Any number that exceeds fifty should have fifty subtracted until the result is less than fifty. Are there any collisions in your list?

Sorting and merging

The two most important file operations that do not involve adding to or deleting from a file are sorting and merging. Sorting a file means putting it into order, either numerically or alphabetically. Merging means combining sorted files in such a way as to preserve their sorted order. The order can be ascending, such as ascending numbers 1, 3, 7, 15, 22, 36, or ascending alphabetical order of A to Z. Less common is descending order of number, and the inverse alphabetical order of Z to A. Number sorting is much easier, assuming that numbers are held in number form rather than in string form, but curious problems can arise with string sorting.

To illustrate the problems, consider what happens when numbers are held in string form. If we have the numbers 1, 2, 10, 101, 4, 5 held in string form, then these will be sorted into the order 1, 10, 101, 2, 4, 5 because of the use of ASCII codes for strings. The digit 1 is represented in a string as ASCII 49, and 2 as ASCII 50. Now when strings are sorted, the sort is made on the basis of first ASCII code, and only if the first codes are equal will the decision on the second codes have to be made. The string form of numbers 1, 10, and 101 will all have the starting ASCII code of 49, so that their order depends on the second digit, 0 and then any third, causing the arrangement of 1, 10, and 101. Each of these is placed before the 2 because the digit 2 in ASCII has code 50, greater than the code for 1. The string form of a number, in other words, contains no information on the place value of a digit, so that the 1 in 101, the 1 in 10 and the 1 in 1 all have equal weighting as far as a string sort is concerned.

The other problem of string sorts is also tied up with ASCII codes. Unless the letters of a string are all converted to uppercase (or all to lowercase) before sorting, some curious anomalies will arise because the uppercase letters have lower ASCII codes and will therefore be placed before their lowercase counterparts. For example, in the list able, middle, Zero, a simple ASCII sort will result in the order Zero, able, middle because the ASCII code for Z is 90 and the code for a is 97. Using a conversion to one case removes this problem, but it leaves one that affects accurate book indexing among other uses. Take, for example, the entries:

Flange, 22
Flange use, 116

which are in the order in which they would appear in an index, with the main topic first and a subsidiary later. Most sort programs would result in the reverse order because the space following Flange in the phrase Flange use has an ASCII code of 32 whereas the comma that follows Flange in the first entry has an ASCII code of 44. This can be overcome by replacing spaces in the file by other codes, such as ASCII 127, then sorting, and then replacing each ASCII 127 by a space again. The important point is that sorting is not necessarily a matter of arranging items into the order of the ASCII codes.

We will assume, for the sake of reasonable simplicity that we can work with numbers in correct integer or floating point form, and with strings which are converted to uppercase for the purpose of sorting. Several programming languages allow commands such as UPPER to be used to compare strings, so that uppercase versions are compared even if the version in the memory is in lowercase or a mixture of uppercase and lowercase. We will assume also that the files to be sorted are either held on disk, or are held in memory in the form of an array. There are two forms of sorting, internal sorting which is carried out on the array in memory, which can then be written back to disk as a sorted file, and external sorting, which is carried out on a file which exists on the disk. Of the two, internal sorting is faster but may not be possible for large files which cannot be fitted into the memory.

The simplest type of internal sort is the selection sort. The array is searched, using a linear search, for the smallest item (the smallest number, the word beginning with the letter of the alphabet closest to A), and this item, when found, is exchanged with the first item in the array. The search is then repeated, only this time starting with the second item, and the process continues in this way, incrementing the starting position each time. The algorithm is illustrated in Figure 7.8, and Figure 7.9 shows each step of a sort action on a set of numbers. The time required is governed by the number of times that one item has to be compared with another. On the first run, the first item has to be compared with n − 1 others, on the second run the second item is compared with n − 2 others and so on, until only one comparison is used in the final run. The total number of comparisons is

```
List is of items 1 to n

FOR item: = 1 TO n-1                          * Main loop start
  Min: = item                                 * Mark start of testing
    FOR Select: = item + 1 TO n               * Inner loop
      IF array [Select] < array [Min] THEN    * Test
      Min: = Select                           * New smaller item
      End FOR                                 * End of inner loop
  SWAP array [item] WITH array [Min]          * Put smaller item to start
End FOR                                       * End of main loop
```

Figure 7.8 *The algorithm for a selection sort routine*

	After run number							
Original	1	2	3	4	5	6	7	8
30	2	2	2	2	2	2	2	2
19	19	7	7	7	7	7	7	7
7	7	19	10	10	10	10	10	10
16	16	16	16	12	12	12	12	12
2	30	30	30	30	16	16	16	16
12	12	12	12	16	30	18	18	18
18	18	18	18	18	18	19	19	19
20	10	10	19	19	19	30	30	20
27	20	20	20	20	20	20	20	30

Figure 7.9 *The steps in a selection sort of a few items*

n(n − 1)/2, so that a sort of nine items requires 9 * 8/2 = 36 comparisons. For a large number of items, the number of comparisons that is required makes the time required for this type of sort unacceptable. For 1000 items, for example, the number of comparisons is around half a million.

A very familiar, but equally slow type of sort is the bubble sort. In this type of sort, the elements of the array are examined one at a time, comparing each element with the next in sequence, and interchanging the elements if they are out of order. Each time an exchange is made, a variable is set as a marker and when a search reveals that no exchanges have been made, the sort is complete. The merit of this method is that several exchanges can be made on each run, and if only a few items are out of place then the sort can be very fast. If, however, the array is large and completely random then the bubble sort is slow, using $n^2/2$ comparisons. The algorithm is shown in Figure 7.10, and the results of a typical run on a small amount of data are shown in Figure 7.11.

Sorts for large amounts of items cannot use the selection sort or the bubble sort, though some very fast sorting methods make use of a bubble sort once the list has been partially sorted. Fast sorts make use of comparisons between parts of the array that are not close to each other. The popular Shell-Metzner sort, for example, starts by halving the list and comparing the first item in the first half with the first item in the second half, then the second item in the first half with the second item in the second half, and so on until each item in each half has been compared and swapped if necessary so that the smaller items are in the first half. When this has been done, each element is then compared with one that is one quarter of the list length away, and any interchanges are done as required. The distance between the compared items is halved on each run until it is equal to one item, so that the last run is the same as a bubble sort.

Another very fast sort is the quick sort, whose algorithm is considerably more complicated than that of the Shell-Metzner sort, though it follows the same general principle of splitting the list into sections and comparing items from pairs of segments. The quick sort can be slower than a bubble sort for small numbers of items (for the last few passes it performs the same action as the bubble sort) but it is very efficient indeed for large amounts of data in the

```
Max: n-1                                          * End of list
DO                                                * Start loop
  Sorted: = TRUE                                  * Test condition
    FOR item: = 1 TO Max                          * Go through list
      IF array [item] > array [item + 1] THEN     * Test
        SWAP array [item] WITH array [item + 1]   * Exchange
        Sorted: = FALSE                           * Out of order, keep going
      ENDFOR
    IF Max = 1 THEN Sorted: = TRUE                * End of list test
      ELSE Max: = Max - 1                         * If not end, shorten list
UNTIL Sorted = TRUE                               * Test for no more exchanges
```

Figure 7.10 *The algorithm for a bubble sort, a type often illustrated in texts but very seldom used because of its low speed*

	After run number					
Original	1	2	3	4	5	6
30	19	7	7	2	2	2
19	7	16	2	7	7	7
7	16	2	12	12	10	10
16	2	12	16	10	12	12
2	12	18	10	16	16	16
12	18	10	18	18	18	18
18	10	19	19	19	19	19
10	27	27	27	27	27	27
27	30	30	30	30	30	30
						↑ No exchanges in this run, therefore ended

Figure 7.11 *The actions that are carried out in the process of a bubble sort of a small number of items*

memory. Many commercial sorts are quick sorts, and the routine is widely used in data-handling programs of all types. One of these is the SORT program which exists as a utility in the MS-DOS operating system (another fast sort is incorporated in the UNIX system). To use the MSDOS SORT utility, a command of the form:

SORT < UNSRT.FIL > SRT.FIL

is used. The file UNSRT.FIL is an unsorted file which can be string or numeric, and the file SRT.FIL does not exist until the SORT utility creates it. After SORT has run, the file SRT.FIL contains the sorted version of UNSRT.FIL, and the original version is still obtainable as UNSRT.FIL. If no destination file is specified, the result of SORT is displayed on the screen. SORT is fast, though several sort routines that are available in programmers' libraries (particularly for the C language) are even faster.

Exercise 2

Make a list of names in random order, and show how the list would change in each step of a bubble sort.

External sorting and merging

For very large files that exist on disk and are too large to be held in memory, external sorting must be used. The time that will be required for an external sort depends on the number of times that the disk must be read, so that reasonably fast sorting depends on doing as much of the sorting internally as the available memory permits. A typical algorithm is as follows.

Part of the file, starting at the beginning, is read into memory as an array and sorted. The size of this portion of the file depends on the amount of memory available, typically 250 K or so. The sorted array is then written as a new file, File A. The next portion of the main file is then read, sorted, and stored as File B in the same way, and the process is repeated until the whole file has been sorted and several sorted files are on the disk. The sorted files are then merged into one single file. The first n items are read from each file, with the number n depending on the memory size, and these items are sorted, then written to a file. The next n items are read, sorted and added to the file, with the process continuing until a complete sorted file has been written. The process is illustrated in Figure 7.12.

The problem with this method is that it is not easy to apportion the amount of memory required, and an older method makes use of merging, but uses many more disk reading and writing steps. In this method (Figure 7.13) the original file is file A, and files B, C and D will be required. The records are read from File A in pairs, and each pair is put into order. The first pair is then placed in file C and the next in file D, and so on, alternating between files C and D for writing. When all of the items from file A have been used, the files C and D are then merged back into A and B. This time, groups of four records are read, two from C and two from D, sorted, and then written to A. Another group is taken from C and D in the same way, sorted, and then written to B. This continues until all the records in C and D have been read. On the next run, groups of eight are used, four from A and four from B, writing to C and D again. The process continues until the group size is such that it can only be written to one file, the A file, and when this happens the file will be completely sorted. The use of pairs of files like this requires more work to be done, and commercial programs use a larger number of files, and larger groupings of records.

```
File A: = Start                              * Allocate first file
File B: = Start + 1                          * Allocate second file
REPEAT                                       * Start loop
  Read File A                                * Read and sort
  Sort File B                                * The files
  Read file B                                * Of both sets
  Sort File B                                *

  MERGE File A, File B TO File A             * Merge files, save as A
  File B: = File B + 1                       * Pick new File B
UNTIL File B > Max                           * All dealt with.

(Note: File opening steps not shown)

        Groupset: = 2
```

Figure 7.12 *Sorting items from files into an output file, using routines that will sort the items after reading them into memory*

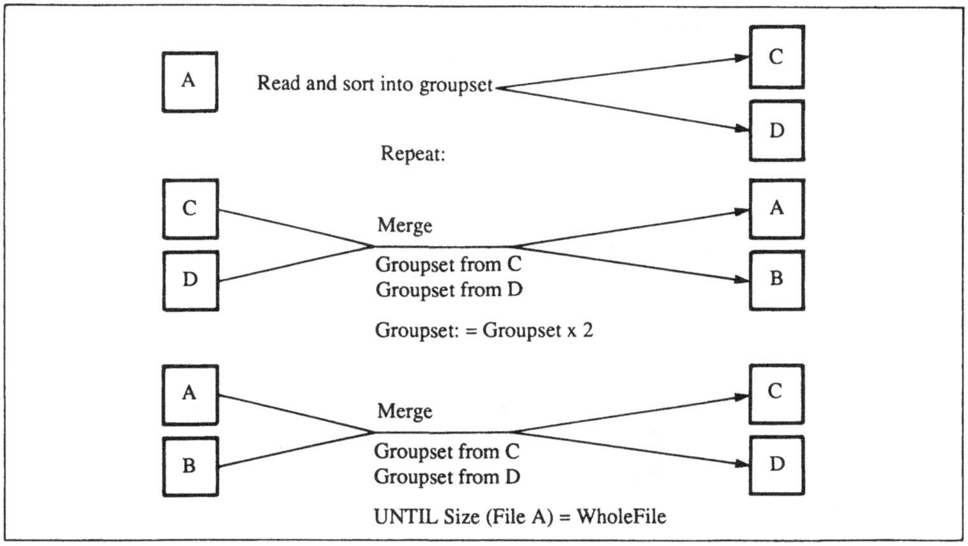

Figure 7.13 *Sorting items from disk files by merging. In this form, a large number of disk read and write actions will be required*

When a utility program for file sorting and merging is used, the operator is, as usual, unaware of the details of what files are opened or closed. The only intervention that is needed from the operator is to state the file name(s) of the file(s) of unsorted data and a file name for the sorted data, which can be the same as one of the files of unsorted data. For example, if we imagine a utility called MERGE, then it might require a command line such as:

MERGE FILE1, FILE2, FILE3 FILE1

with commas being used as delimiters to separate the names of the input files, and a space used as delimiter before the name of the output file which in this example is the same as the name of one of the unsorted files. When the operator presses the Return key to start this action, the MERGE program will be read (assuming that it is present on the current drive) and the files will be sorted and merged. This will involve opening new files and subsequently deleting them, checking how much memeory is available in the machine and on the disk, and then carrying out the merge action to make the best possible use of memory, minimizing the number of disk read and write actions. At the end of the process, the unwanted temporary files will be deleted. If the process is interrupted, these files can sometimes be found on the disk, and they are usually distinguished by having names that consist of characters like the $ sign, or with extensions that consist of $ signs. All that the operator is aware of is a notice on the screen which requests him/her to wait, and a lot of activity from the disk drive(s). When a screen notice appears to the effect that action is complete, the file that is left on the disk is a sorted and merged version. Note, incidentally, the important difference between **merge** and **append**. A merge action implies that items are inserted from one file into another in such a way as to preserve the existing order of the second file (alphabetical, ascending number, etc.), whereas an append action simply adds all the items in a file to the end of another file, as the **COPY** command of MS-DOS can do.

Updating a batch file

The principle of batch use of a computer is that a complete batch of records will be processed in a run which is made at some time later than the arrival of the data. A typical example is the processing of sales invoices after closing hours, and we need to look now at what the operator of the computer has to do in order to process a batch of invoices or other documents for this purpose. One very important aspect of this type of input is that it will alter the main files because each document that is processed will update a record, perhaps adding to the debt of a customer, altering the number of items in stock, adding to the total amount of money or credit transacted on that day. It is very important, therefore, to ensure that the identification of the record is correct. The correct customer must be debited with the correct amount, because if the action is to modify a record, there is no guarantee that in the event of a query later, the older version of the record will be available. Where the number of transactions is small, it is possible to make each document in a batch create a new record, and these records can then be processed to find totals. In a system of this type, it is possible to find the record that was entered and later correct any mistakes, but if the information that is entered simply modifies an existing record, tracing back in the event of a problem can be very difficult. Even for a very large system, then it is better to have a daily transactions disk which can be subsequently processed rather than adding in the details from each batch to a master file. No matter which method is used, however, correct identification of each record is important.

The identification methods include customer identification numbers for credit customers, departmental numbers, goods identification numbers, document (invoice) numbers and the date (Figure 7.14). The reason for using so many methods of identification is that it makes cross-checking by the program much easier, and this in turn makes it much less likely that a mistake by the operator will go through. There are two types of mistakes that can affect the files: operator mistakes (typing an incorrect identification or amount); and raw-data mistakes (where the original document contains an error that the computer operator will copy). A good set of identification numbers can reduce the possibility of error, though never eliminate them.

Customer name	Holmes, S. T.
Customer ID number	42151690
Department number	72D
Goods number	80162733
Invoice number	30512
Date	12/12/89

Figure 7.14 *The form of a typical data record for a store, using several identification codes for cross-checking*

Taking a simple example, the departmental number should tally with the goods number, so that it should be possible to detect that an invoice for goods PX70152 should not have been issued by Department X8. At the time of entry, the program can compare these numbers and refuse the entry, with a notice on the screen to the operator. The operator can then check that the keyboard entry corresponded to the document, and correct any mistyping error. If the error is in the document, then the document can be returned for checking and no incorrect data enters the files. It is not always easy to incorporate this type of checking into a program, but it is usually much easier than trying to make a correction once a record has been changed.

The program that controls batch entry should check that dates are feasible – it should not be possible to make an entry for the 29th February except in a leap year, there is never a 31st September, and any transaction recorded on a Sunday should be treated with suspicion (unless the Sunday trading laws are changed). These types of checks of data are elementary, but offer important safeguards. It is sometimes possible also to include range checks. A range check compares an amount with a maximum, and warns of the entry of a quantity that appears to be invalid. If, for example, the batch contains invoices from the haberdashery department in which no item is priced at more than £3.50, then an item cost of £25.00 should certainly be queried. The extent to which this can be done is limited, and it demands a good standard of programming and equally good standards of maintenance, particularly when inflation is rampant. The aim, as before, is to try to detect oddities in the data so that further checking can be carried out before a record is altered.

The program will require a way of signalling that a document has been processed, and this often requires the use of the Return key. Another means has to be used to signal that no more data requires to be processed. Some programs use the Return key for this purpose also, so that pressing the Return key without having entered data ends the session. A more modern trend is to use the Esc key, or one of the function keys, for this purpose, so that pressing return without entering data simply creates a blank entry which is ignored.

Exercise 3

List and describe the checks that would be made on data for a batch entry into a file in which each record contains name, address, age, social security number, income-tax code and date of birth.

On-line files

Many stores now operate an on-line system, in which the details of a transaction are entered into a file at the time and point of sale. This requires much more computing power, because the computer will be time-shared to a large number of users who might be entering data simultaneously. The entry method will be to use an 'intelligent till' which transmits data to the computer as well as printing a receipt, and everything that appears on the receipt will also appear on the computer record. The till is really a terminal, often described as being a point-of-sale (POS) terminal.

The use of the computer on-line means that items such as departmental number need not be entered by the till-user, since each till can send its identification to the computer automatically when the till is used. The till user will enter the usual item code, and cash tendered quantities, perhaps also with a user identity code. These, along with the other details of the transaction, are entered into the main program files, and much less checking is used. Since the operator has been removed from the entry process, there is no possibility of copying errors, but there is also much less chance of checking data. The success of the method depends greatly on correct use of the tills, and the amount of processing that each till carries out. Some tills can be programmed to do a limited amount of data checking, but there is a limit to the amount that can be done at the point of sale. Stores which have introduced on-line methods have, in general, found the method better than batch working. There is no possibility, for example, of a date being wrong unless a till is faulty, and information is always up to date, so that a manager can look at a screen printout of the business of the day knowing that it is correct to the instant when the printout was requested.

File integrity

File integrity is a phrase which covers all aspects of keeping files that are safe and free from errors. The first line of file integrity is the use of reliable programs. Programs which have been in use for a considerable time have been subjected to the best of all possible testing, use by a large range of operators, and often these programs, though they may have faults, can be used without problems because the faults are known and can be avoided. By contrast, some new programs appear which are brilliant in concept but not necessarily safe to use. It is unlikely that any program would be sold that did not close files correctly, but there have been instances of programs which corrupted files when power was restored after a power-cut. Until a program has been in use for some time, it is impossible to predict what may happen in circumstances that the programmer did not allow for. Programs for main-frame machines may have been in use for many years and are thoroughly proven. By contrast, programs for microcomputers are seldom old; though they may be an updated version of a program that originated up to some ten years earlier. A wise precaution is to assume that anything untoward is likely to cause file corruption, and to use thorough backing up of all files at all times.

This is easier to advise than to carry out. If a file is held on a hard disk, there is little point in making two more copies on the same hard disk, since a disk fault could make all three copies equally inaccessible. Microcomputer users can often make a backup copy of a data file on floppy disks, particularly when the high-density 1.2 Mb disks are used. Larger machines often have provision for using a hard disk or drum memory for data that is being processed, with tape as the backup medium, and tape is also used as the medium for 'streamers' which will back up the entire contents of the hard disk of a microcomputer. A particularly good system for microcomputers is a combination of hardware and software which allows a domestic videocassette recorder to be used to back up the entire contents of any size of hard disk.

Backing up can be done in two ways. One way is to take a copy, usually on tape, of the entire contents of a hard disk. This has to be done at regular intervals, perhaps each Friday afternoon. The time that is needed for this can be a problem, because it can range from minutes to hours, depending on the methods that are used. In general, if backing up takes too long, there is a considerable risk that it will not be done. A much better method is to back up data as it is entered, a method that is particularly useful for microcomputer users who can copy data to a floppy disk at much the same time as it is placed on to the hard disk. My own word-processing system, for example, is arranged so that any new text files placed on the hard disk are copied to floppy disks at the end of a session. The backing up of data is usually more important than the backing up of programs, because programs are seldom altered and can be backed up at intervals in case earlier backups suffer demagnetization. Very few systems now will have facilities to make archive copies on paper tape, but this still remains as one of the few methods of making really secure backups which do not need to be replaced at intervals. When a computer makes use of a program or set of programs that have been written specially for the user's applications, then at least one copy of the program should be held at another site, preferably in a fireproof safe. A chilling statistic is that 80 per cent of businesses who have had computer files destroyed by fire are unable to resume trading.

Another aspect of file integrity is the validation of data added to the file and contained in the files. Some aspects of data validation have already been examined in connection with entry into batch files, using the principle that anything that can be done to check data as it is entered is preferable to trying to correct a record once it is in place in the file. Numerical data often lends itself better to validation methods than string data. Accounting systems, for example, can use two separate methods of finding the overall total of transactions in a day, and these totals should match. This type of check can expose either errors in the entry of an amount, or a possible attempt at fraud, and the best method is one in which the accounts manager obtains one total from the paperwork in the system and the other from the computer.

Validation of string data is always a problem. There is, for example, no sure way of knowing whether a name is correct, or if the spelling of a name is correct, other than referring to the owner of the name. Mistakes were most frequent in the early days of mainframes when the operator who typed names and addresses did not see these appear on a screen at the time of typing. The use of the VDU has made the entry of names less liable to error, but it can still be a potent source of problems. For example, if there is an existing customer called IAN SINCLAIR, what should happen when the name IAIN SINCLAIR is entered? Does the program question this entry, or is it accepted as a new account? Since either is possible, the only form of validation that can be carried out is to show both names on the screen and ask the operator to check that this is not a misspelling. This type of validation is more commonly associated with word-processors than with database programs, but because of the amount of work being carried out on artificial intelligence (AI), better data validation, even for strings, is being steadily introduced to database systems.

One of the main risks to file integrity is unauthorized or unnotified alterations to files, whether this is done maliciously or not. File alteration is a particular problem where a large database is held, because the alteration of a record can affect many users of the data, many of whom may not be aware of the alteration. Any user of a database has to decide who among the staff will be allowed to make alterations to files other than normal updating. The greater the amount of restriction, the better, and one of the benefits of the extensive use of microcomputers is that it has encouraged senior management to make more effort to control computing activities directly. On the other hand, if access to files for the purpose of alteration is made too restricted, a customer can find that the incorrect addressing on parcels is used for nearly a year after the correction was notified.

As so often happens, the best way to control file alteration involves some common sense. It makes sense to allow anyone who can do so to correct errors in the spelling of a name or address, but only a few to alter credit limits. It should not be difficult to classify fields of any record as being unrestricted, restricted, or highly restricted according to the type of data held, and to use some form of protection for the most restricted areas. Password use is the main form of protection, but it should be done by using random 'words' that are produced by the computer and changed at intervals. It is very unwise to allow anyone who is to have access to files to make up his/her own password, because this usually produces something based on initials or date of birth, and is usually easy to guess. By using random nonsense mixtures of letters and digits, changed at least monthly, passwording becomes a reasonable way of protecting the data from users.

The most difficult task is protection against anyone with programming skills and fraudulent intent. I have emphasized programming skills, because computer fraud is certainly not practised exclusively by those who program the machine. The spread of microcomputers has meant that a considerable number of people who are not working as programmers have programming skills, sometimes of a very high order and totally unknown to their employer. In some cases, fraud is carried out simply as a way of drawing attention to unrecognized skills, sometimes even to show how vulnerable a system is. The main forms of computer fraud involve altering data files or altering programs, and though both actions require some skill, it is skill that can be easily acquired by anyone at any age.

Taking just one example, a file can be modified to insert the name of a bogus supplier. The record is then updated at intervals to show equally imaginary goods being sent and invoiced, and the computer will, in the normal course of events, arrange for payment to be made. Unless the address to which cheques are sent is verified, this type of fraud can persist for years until someone notices a huge quantity of items stated to be accumulating in stores, but not physically present. By that time, it is possible that the originator of the record will have left the firm, and the bogus account will have been closed. This type of fraud is most easily carried out when a large database is in use, because it is then easier to make sure that the fraudulent record is used in such a way as to look genuine. When separate files are used, there is a chance of someone picking up a discrepancy when data is copied over from one file to another. The only countermove is to make regular checks on any account which seems to pay out sums with no evidence of any verifiable items appearing in a stock list and subsequently sold.

Modification of a program is another fruitful way of using a computer system for fraud, and is more difficult to detect. The old favourite is to skim fractions of a penny from accounts, so that there is no way of checking against paper records. These fractions arise as a result of interest calculations and VAT calculations, and though each amount is small, the accumulated total taken over a large number of accounts can be very substantial. Program modification can be used to operate fraudulent records in such a way that money is sent out to a dummy account for years after the programmer who changed the program has left the firm. These actions are best dealt with by replacing the operating program at intervals. Large systems will generally use a custom-designed program which exists in two forms, the **source-code** and the **machine-code**, and it is the machine-code version which is used to operate the computer. The source-code is used to produce a machine-code by way of a program called a **compiler** (see Chapter 8). When a program is tampered with, it will virtually always be the machine-code which is altered, because alterations in this code are almost impossible to detect, unlike alterations to the source-code. Putting the source-code through the compiler again will result in a new machine-code version which can be compared byte-by-byte with the older one to see if a change has been made. The source-code for an important program should be kept away from the computer operations room, held securely to be used only in emergencies, along with a machine-code version that has never been run and which is guaranteed to be free from any alteration.

Microcomputers and to some extent minicomputers will generally make use of off-the-peg programs for which the source-code is not available, and a master copy of any such programs should be held. This makes it very important not to use off-the-shelf programs which are copy-protected, because if only one copy can be used there is no backup and no possibility of comparing this with another copy. Some programs are also deliberately made with serial numbers incorporated in the code, so that buying several disks will result in having versions with different serial numbers so that comparisons always show that differences exist, masking changes made for fraudulent purposes. The likelihood of changes being made successfully to such programs, however, is rather less than of making changes to a custom-designed program. One obvious point is that the programmer in charge of a mainframe may have designed the program, and knows very well how to alter it, but where microcomputers are used then no one may have such experience of any of the programs that are in use.

Suggestions for practical work

1 Use a hashing program to generate hash numbers from names and numbers and check the effects of collisions.
2 Compare the search time needed by a hashing algorithm as compared to a linear search, both working on the same long file of names.
3 Use Prestel to find information such as times of flights to Paris, and comment on the number of selection steps needed to retrieve the information.
4 Use a commercial accounts package and list the data validation methods that are used.

Multiple-choice test questions

1 The fastest method of retrieving a record from a random-access file is by using:
 (a) linear search
 (b) hashing
 (c) binary search
 (d) Btree

2 A file of names is being sorted into alphabetical order, and is first converted into uppercase. This is done because:
 (a) only uppercase names can be sorted
 (b) names never start with lowercase letters
 (c) uppercase names are easier to sort
 (d) it allows the use of ASCII codes for sorting order

3 The fastest types of sorting algorithm for large files depend on:
 (a) inserting items into the correct position in a new file
 (b) repeatedly going through the list interchanging items that are in the wrong order
 (c) dividing the list into sections and comparing items in two sections
 (d) comparing the last item in the list with the first

4 A customer gives an address as 37 Fairway Ave. The computer can query this if one of its files contains the entry:
 (a) Fairway Ave < 31
 (b) Fairway Ave > 31
 (c) Fairway Ave
 (d) 37

5 To ensure integrity of a file you should:
 (a) make another copy on the same disk
 (b) make another copy on tape

(c) keep two other copies on other media
(d) make a printout of the data

6 The greatest risk, from the aspect of data security, comes from:
(a) hackers working over the telephone lines
(b) other computer users
(c) maintenance staff
(d) burglars

8 Programming introduction

Objectives

- Explain programming language concepts (11): levels of languages (11.1); functions of assemblers, interpreters and compilers (11.2).
- Explain concepts and functions of operating systems (12): loading, running and logging of programs in a multi-programming environment (12.1); purposes of a job-control language (12.2).
- Describe common utilities and packages (13): use of a standard media transfer package (13.1); selection and use of a commercial applications package (13.2).

Languages and levels

A programming language is a way of creating a program for a computer, usually by typing instructions which can then be converted into the number-codes that control the actions of the machine. These number-codes are called **machine-code**, and all of the actions of any program are carried out by machine-code. The machine-code is placed into a specified part of the memory of the computer and, by placing the address of the start of the machine-code into the program counter register of the CPU (see Chapter 4), the program is started. A working computer is *always* under the control of a program, whether this is the boot program that reads in the operating system, the operating system itself, or some applications program which carries out the task of word processing, data processing, spreadsheet creation, or whatever the computer is being used for. Without a program, no computing activity is possible.

The main hazards in this process are poor planning, which will have the result that the program does not do what is intended, and poor implementation, which causes bugs. A bug is a program fault which might be minor (so that a message appears on the screen only momentarily) or major (the program ceases to operate when requested to print a file, for example). The process of removing bugs is called debugging, and the source of all bugs is, of course, the programmer. Bugs are most likely to appear when the programmer has to plan every detail of a program, because in a program of more than trivial length, there is simply too much detail for planning to be 100 per cent effective; there is too much to remember and too much to take account of.

The most obvious method of programming is to place into memory the number codes that are needed to carry out the action that we want. This is called machine-code programming, and it is tedious, error-prone, and liable to hold a bug in every byte. There are three main reasons for using it. One is that it is the only way to program a completely new microprocessor for which nothing is written. Another is its speed, and the third is to achieve tighter control over the computer. The first reason applies only for those who design and write language compilers for new microprocessors, but the other two are the reasons that keep machine-code programmers in business. Machine-code is fast; there is nothing faster, and for some types of programming, notably animated graphics, this speed is essential. The other reason is also important. There are always features of a machine that can be controlled only by machine-code. No language, and particularly languages intended for applications programming, can ever cope with every possibility that a programmer might want. If it is necessary to have the screen scrolling diagonally, or to read a disk that is abnormally formatted, or use a non-standard printer, then machine-code is needed to write the routines.

At this point, we encounter the idea of the **level** of a programming language. Machine-code comes at the bottom of this heap of levels, because it consists of direct instructions to the computer, and each code will have to be looked up in a table. Even the simplest action might require a few hundred codes to be looked up and placed in the memory, which is why machine code programming is so tedious. If you compared writing a program to building a shed, machine-code corresponds to starting by growing the trees, and doing all the carpentry with a blunt penknife.

There is such a continuing need for machine-code that we need a programming language, assembly language, for each CPU or microprocessor type in order to write machine-code with less tedium and fewer bugs. Assembly language, then, comes slightly higher up the scale as compared to machine-code because it is easier to write, but it still translates directly to machine-code. In an assembly language program, the programmer types a set of directions which the assembler program then converts into number codes. This eliminates the need to look up tables of codes, but it requires the same meticulous planning and intimate knowledge of the machine as direct machine-code does. The difference is that the steps of the programs are letter-symbols rather than numbers, and the program is easier to read and to write for that reason. If you know that you need to place into the accumulator register a number that represents a total, for example, then the line:

LDA, Total

is considerably clearer than a set of number codes would be.

What about the other end of the scale of levels? There is one old-established high-level language, Cobol, which, when you read a program written in this language, looks almost like a set of instructions in English. When you write programs in a language like this you do not expect to have to worry about the details of the machine that you are using. You are not interested in what microprocessor or CPU it uses (Cobol was in use long before microcomputers arrived) or how many bits make a byte or what address is used for the printer port. You do not need to know ASCII codes or routines in the ROM (if any) or any of the things that constantly occupy the minds of assembly language programmers. You simply write your program lines, run them into the machine, compile, and sit back like anyone else until the compilation fails. The language processor, invariably a compiler (see later in this chapter), converts the instructions of your program into machine-code, and the computer can then execute this machine-code.

The name *high-level* is a good one. You are so far above the ground level of machine-code that you hardly know there is a machine present. Needless to say, a language like this should be the same no matter on what computer the program is intended to run. The language is portable – but that does not mean that you can pick it up easily. Between the heights of Cobol and two other old-established languages, Fortran and Algol, and the depths of machine-code, there are languages at all sorts of intermediate levels.

The fundamental problem is that high-level languages are powerful but inefficient. They allow you to turn your problem-solving methods into programs that run smoothly but at a great cost in memory space. They can be cumbersome, using lines and lines of program which can take all day to compile even if the program runs fairly quickly once compiled. At the other end of the scale, machine-code is very compact, very fast and very efficient, but sheer hell to write and debug in any quantity. In addition, a program written in assembly language has to be very carefully documented if there is to be any chance of modifying it at a later date, or if anyone else might have to work with it.

The reason that we have such a large number of programming languages is that we are constantly trying to get a better balance of these different virtues. What we want is a high-level language that makes it easy to express our solutions to problems, is very compact both in statement length and its use of memory, and which translates into as few bytes of machine code as would be provided by an assembler. There is no such language, and probably never will be, but some languages come nearer to the ideal than others, and some are a better solution for some specific types of problems. For example, a lot of programming of the type used in robotics is well handled by the language Forth, but no one would set out to write a word-processor in Forth – and it is not a language for which there are many vacancies for programmers.

The history of computing, then, is littered with languages which seemed to be a good idea at the time or which looked like being a good solution to one type of need. The greatest computing languages are the ones which have incorporated ideas that have lasted and have passed into other languages in turn. For example, one of the first great languages (still in use) was Fortran, and its principles have been so absorbed into BASIC that a Fortran programmer can easily switch to BASIC without feeling that this is a radically different type of language. The other great language of the early computing days is Algol, and that has been the starting point for the invention of several other great languages, notably Pascal, Modula-2 and C.

At the time of writing, BASIC, once regarded as language purely for beginners, has evolved into forms which rival Fortran for general-purpose programming, and has taken on many features of other languages. It has also benefited from being the subject of a standard, the ANSI-BASIC standard, and one of its particularly strong points is its usefulness in handling both numbers and strings. Pascal started as a language for academic computer studies, and branched out into being a language for commercial applications, though a later language, Modula-2 (by the same author) has been launched as a way around some of the deficiencies of the original version of Pascal. C is greatly favoured by programmers who write operating systems and utilities; it is a language which allows great control over the computer, but which allows equally large mistakes to be made. Hesitating about which language to learn, however, is pointless. Once you know a structured computing language thoroughly you will find it easy to learn another, because it is the ideas of computing that are difficult to grasp, not how they are expressed in languages. Hesitating about languages is almost as bad as not buying a computer on the grounds that there will be a better model along next year. There will **always** be a better model along next year, but that's no reason for not buying now. If in doubt, learn Pascal, since this is the structured language which is most favoured for learning about structured languages. Of the versions that are widely available, Turbo-Pascal from Borland is by far the most widely used on PC machines.

Compilers and interpreters

Most languages, including our examples of BASIC, Pascal, Modula-2 and C, can be obtained in a compiled or an interpreted form. Whatever language you use to express your program ideas, it has to be converted into machine code before it can be used in the computer. Interpreting and compiling are two different methods of carrying out this conversion, and if you have used only early versions of BASIC on small microcomputers, you will probably be familiar only with interpreting. When a language is interpreted, each instruction is taken in turn as the interpreter comes to it. The instruction is checked to find if it is valid, and then it is executed by calling up a machine-code subroutine. In practical terms, this means that a complete set of machine-code subroutines must exist on disk, in the RAM, or in ROM, and each reserved word of the language will call up a routine or a set of routines. This takes time, because the actions of searching that are needed before an instruction can be executed take much longer than is required for the execution.

In a loop of repeated instructions, for example, each instruction in the loop will be interpreted, checked and run on each pass through the loop, and it is this need to interpret and check on each occasion that makes a BASIC interpreter so slow in action, though there are some very fast interpreters which are fast because their action is closer to that of a compiler. The important point about a program written in an interpreted language is that the language interpreter must be present in the memory before the program can be run. If you want to run a program in interpreted BASIC, you first have to load in the BASIC interpreter, and then the program.

A compiled language, by contrast, converts all of the instructions of a program into a large machine code program. At first sight, this looks like the same type of action as interpreting, but the difference is that the two steps of searching and using are separated. The searching action finds the codes that correspond to the instruction, but these are recorded, not executed. The recorded file is then a machine-code program which can be run by itself, without needing the compiler program to be present in the memory. The difference is most easily understood if we look at how each would deal with a loop in which a variable had to be read from a file and then printed, repeated one hundred times (Figure 8.1). An interpreter on the first run through this loop would find the code module for reading a byte, read the byte, find the code module for printing the byte and then print the byte. All of these actions, including finding the code modules, would then be repeated for another 99 times. A compiler, by contrast, would find the code modules for reading and printing and include them into a loop that would run one hundred times, then save this set of codes on to the disk. Running the code would carry out the actions of reading and printing, but without the need to find where the code was stored. When a compiler is used the validity of the instructions needs to be checked once, the machine-code modules for the

```
Program:

  FOR n: 1 TO 100
    READ array [n]
    PRINT array [n]
  ENDFOR

Interpreter:            REPEAT 100 TIMES
                          Find code for READ
                          Find position of array item
                          Read array item
                          Find code for PRINT
                          Print array item
                          END

Compiler:               DO ONCE
                          Find code for READ, store code
                          Find position of array item
                          Read array item, store code
                          Find code for PRINT, store code
                          Print array item, store code
                          Gather up stored code as a file
                          Put code into a loop which will repeat 100 times
```

Figure 8.1 *Interpreting and compiling compared for a simple loop program* loop action collected, and a machine-code loop set up. The finding and collecting of codes is done once only, not in each pass of the loop. The result of compiling is usually recorded on disk rather than being run at the time (though some compilers will compile to RAM and allow you to run the result).

Once a program has been compiled, it consists of a set of machine-code routines, and these have then to be linked together and into the routines of the operating system, which for PC machines means MS-DOS or PC-DOS. If the compiler is a good one the machine-code may be reasonably compact, but it can never be as compact as it would have been if it had been created by an assembler (referred to as **native machine-code**). As a comparison, a machine-code utility which I wrote to send codes to the printer takes up 140 bytes when written in assembler; the compiled code from a high-level language requires 8 K of code. This order of discrepancy is for a short routine, and for longer and more elaborate programs the difference in the number of bytes is not so great. What is great is the difference in the time that is required to create the program, and on this basis the high-level compiled language wins comfortably.

Nothing is perfect, and both interpreters and compilers have merits and faults. The main merit of an interpreter is easy debugging. When an interpreted program stops with an error message it takes very little time to change the program text and try again. For a compiled program, this would mean loading in the text, compiling it, linking it and then running again, which is inevitably a slower process. The disadvantage of the interpreter is low speed, because the process of finding the machine-code routines can be a lengthy one, and it has to be done each time an instruction is obeyed, and along with this is the need to have the interpreter present in order to run the program. The ease of use of the interpreter is paid for by slow running, and the high speed of the compiler is at the expense of easy checking and changing. A few compilers permit **incremental compiling**, meaning that if a small section of the source-code is changed, only that section is re-compiled, not the whole code. This makes an incremental compiler of very considerable value to anyone whose programs are likely to undergo a lot of refinement over the years.

For most purposes, however, the use of a compiler is a considerable advantage. Even if you write programs only for your own uses, it is a nuisance to have to load in an interpreter before you can run a program. If you write programs for sale to others or for use by a firm the use of a compiler is essential. For one thing, it is usually easier to protect machine-code programs against copying if you feel that you must do so. More important is that you retain some control. Since you keep the source code, the text that was compiled to create the machine-code, you can alter the text, recompile, and issue new versions. Others, lacking your source code, cannot modify your program so easily. The main advantage, however, is that a compiler allows you to write programs in a high-level language but operate with fast-running machine-code. For learning a language an interpreter is very useful, but for writing serious programs, a good compiler is essential. Another essential is a language that is **structured** and **modular** (see Chapter 9).

> ***Exercise 1***
>
> Write a simple routine (such as the addition of two integers) in assembly language and also in a high-level language. Compare the number of bytes required for each version.

Operating systems

An operating system, often described as DOS (disk operating system) is a way of taking some of the burden from programmers and users of computers by supplying a set of standard routines. Every program that makes use of a computer will require routines to be written to accept input from the keyboard, and also output to the screen and printer. Every program will need to be able to make efficient use of the memory, and also the disk system. At a higher level of computer use, it might be necessary to be able to partition the memory so that more than one program is contained, allowing the user to switch from one to another, even to leave one program working while another is used.

It would be a considerable burden to programmers if each and every routine had to be written afresh for each program, and it would result in different programmers using different routines, making the machine more difficult to use. An operating system provides for all these 'housekeeping' actions with routines that a programmer can call on. When a program has data to write to disk, there is no need to write a routine which will find space on the disk, write the data and fill in the information in the file allocation table. With an operating system in use, the programmer writes a routine that places the address at which the data starts into a register, and then calls one of the operating system routines (by placing its address into the PC register).

This approach has several major benefits. One is that much of the drudgery of programming in assembly language can be removed, because the routines that the operating system supplies are the types that are most needed within assembly-language programs. Another is that programs do not have to be written with a particular computer in view, so long as that computer uses the same operating system. The differences between machines are taken care of by the operating system rather than by the programmer. The other benefit is to the user who can make use of a set of standardized commands like DIR (to print a disk directory) knowing that this will work on any machine that uses the same (or a similar) operating system. This removes much of the effort of changing from one machine type to another that uses or can use the same operating system, and the correct use of the operating system by programmers also ensures that programs will run on any machine that uses the operating system, subject to the hardware being compatible. Since the operating system will be loaded in each time the machine is used, it can contain a set of utilities, commands which the user, as distinct from the programmer, will find useful. Examples of utilities are the copying of files, the protection of files against replacement, formatting of disks and parking the heads of a hard-disk drive.

There are, of course, drawbacks. Programmers complain that some operating system routines, particularly from screen use, are too slow, or that the use of the routines restricts some types of program action. There may be a flaw or a bug in an operating system that will affect every program that uses the system (though usually only under unusual circumstances). The operating system may require so much of the memory that it leaves very little space for programs, or its user commands may be obscure and difficult to learn (user-unfriendly) for non-programmers. The advantages, however, outweigh the disadvantages, particularly for computer users who have suffered in the past from incompatible machines and operating systems.

Advanced OS actions

Any operating system should provide the basic actions of controlling inputs and outputs, disk operations and memory management, and must go considerably further than this. Most of the commonly-used operating systems have developed and grown in size over the years, and have added actions that were not considered necessary earlier. This has applied particularly to the operating systems for microcomputers as the capability of these machines has increased over the years. There are still textbooks in use which describe microcomputers as machines with a limit of 64 K of memory, but at the time of writing it would be difficult to sell any microcomputer which did not have at least 512 K and preferably more.

Multiprogramming is an action that a modern operating system is expected to provide. At its simplest level, multiprogramming means that more than one program can be loaded into different parts of the memory, and run independently. These programs are then **co-resident**, allowing the user to switch from one program to the other without the need to read in from the disk. The operating system can provide for one program to be a 'background' program, meaning that it runs only when required, usually by pressing a function key or a Ctrl key combination. This allows effects such as displaying a calendar over other work on the screen, and removing it shortly afterwards, restoring the original screen. Programs of this background type are sometimes referred to as TSR (terminate and stay resident) programs.

The simplest type of multiprogramming requires that the user shall switch from one program to the other, and often makes only one program a 'foreground' one. This implies that one program will be more permanent, and the others transient. For example, if a word-processor were the foreground program and a small name-and-address datafile the background, you could expect to interrupt your word-processing to bring up the name and address file, then later resume word processing exactly where you had left off when you started the background. What is more important here is what you cannot do at this simple level. You cannot necessarily transfer a name and address that you have fetched from the filing program into your word-processor document, and you cannot expect that the next time you switch to the filer program, it will be at exactly the state in which you left it.

The next higher level of multiprogramming allows a background program to remain running even while it remains in the background. One example might be a program which is needed to perform a long and elaborate calculation. This is set running by calling up the background program and running it, then the program is put back into the background and work on the foreground program is resumed. At some later stage, the background program is called up again, and the answer to the problem is ready, and is displayed. If this answer can then be transferred to the foreground program (without the need to retype it), then the operating system is of a higher level of multiprogramming capability than the simple scheme described earlier.

The highest level of multiprogramming allows more than one program to be run concurrently, timesharing the CPU, and displaying in separate 'windows' on the screen. This will provide for easy transfer of data from one window, and hence one program, to the other, and it may be possible to run several programs in this way. Full multiprogramming of this type can be very useful, but is very demanding of memory space and also of CPU time, so that an operating system which was written for a machine with limited memory and a comparatively slow CPU cannot be expected to provide this facility, and using a more advanced operating system on a machine which cannot provide the hardware essentials will result in, at best, very slow operation; at worst, continual 'out of memory' messages.

Multiprogramming has been a possibility in minicomputers for some time, and though it is also available on microcomputers, it is not necessarily available at the highest level. This is not always an operating system problem, because even if the memory size and CPU speed are both suitable, some machines are more capable of full multiprogramming than others because the CPU has been designed with this use in view. The unfortunate snag is that some of the most capable microcomputers from this point of view are those which are totally incompatible with the general run of business machines. Minicomputers are much more likely to be designed for full multi-programming capabilities.

Exercise 2

Determine what level of multiprogramming is possible with the machines available to you. Can multiprogramming be achieved by using an add-on program?

Networks

Networking is another action that can be incorporated into the more advanced operating systems. A network, in computing terms, is a connection between machines that allows data to be passed, and resources such as printers and disk drives shared (Figure 8.2). One very obvious early application of networking was to educational computing, where ten or more

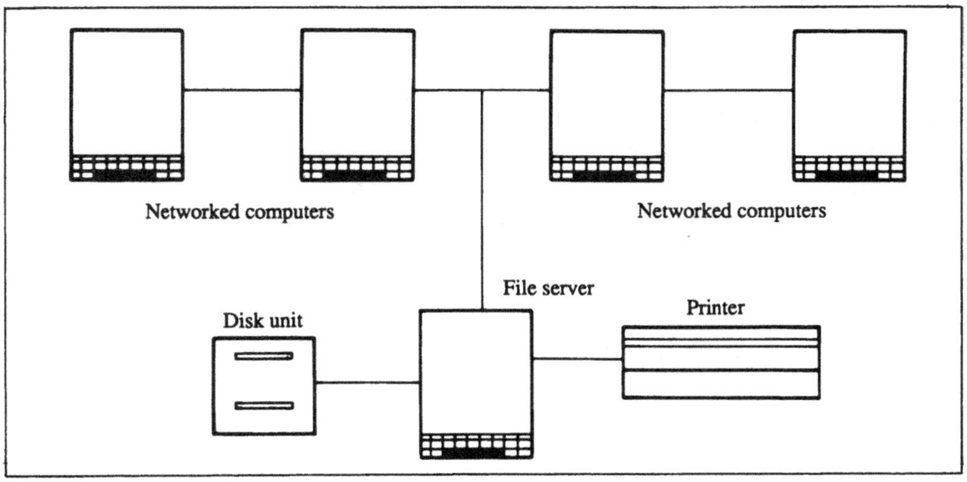

Figure 8.2 *The principle of networking, which allows resources to be shared among computers*

users may be working on the same program such as a word-processor, each creating a disk file and requiring the use of a printer at times. One solution is to have each student at a complete workstation, comprising a microcomputer with a disk drive and a printer, but this is very wasteful of resources. The network solution is to have one large machine, the **fileserver** with a hard disk drive and a printer connected to a set of machines which have no disk drives or printers. The fileserver sends a copy of the program to each station on the network, and each student can then make use of the program. When printing is required, a student will type the printing command, and unless another user is printing at the time, the document will be printed at the fileserver. If the printer is in use, the data is held over until the printer is free, so that the operating system implements a queuing system for data. As far as each user is concerned, the program works in the usual way, with no indication that there is no local disk drive or printer.

Networking commands in an operating system may, like multiprogramming provision, be at various levels of complexity. The simplest level provides for a program to be read from the disk and made available at each workstation, with data passed back to the disk drive or the printer. Each workstation has to be identified by a code so that disk files can be organized for each workstation. In this way, workstation 2 does not gain access to the files of workstation 5 even when both are using the same programs, and possibly the same file names. At a higher level, a networking system can cope with each workstation using a different program and being able to specify that files can be interchanged, or to request priority in access to the printer. As with multiprogramming, networking demands some timesharing of the CPU, but not to the same extent, since each workstation is using its own program in its own memory, and data is being passed to and from the fileserver only at intervals. This means that delays in the system are noticeable only when several users want to use the disk or the printer at the same time.

Networking has been in use for some time, and several different incompatible standards exist. One important point for anyone specifiying a networked system is to ensure that the system is not going to be used at the limits of its capabilities. If there are to be twenty workstations, then it is most unwise to specify a system which allows twenty workstations as a maximum. In the past, manufacturers have made exaggerated claims for networking systems, leading to the work 'notworking' being applied by users. Many networking systems are well established and have given trouble-free use over a long period, but this requires a good overall knowledge of the complete system on the part of the operator, along with a good choice of fileserver machine. One incidental point about networking is that suppliers of software often demand a higher price for a version of a program that will be used networked, on the grounds that without the network, each workstation would need a separate program disk.

If networking is not provided for by the operating system, then it can usually be provided by independent software. Some types of networking software will allow existing programs (used on a single workstation) to run networked, others require special network versions of the programs.

Spooling

Spooling is a topic that is closely related to multiprogramming and networking. Spooling involves holding data in a queue in memory so that it can be fed to its destination as and when possible. A printer spooler, for example, will hold text for delivery to the printer at the rate which the printer can cope with, while allowing the computer to work on a timesharing basis. Without a spooling system, a computer can be tied up for hours at a time simply because text is being printed. Since printing demands very little computing effort, particularly if the printer uses a memory buffer of its own, it is better to timeshare the printing action and use most of the time of the CPU for normal computing.

Print spoolers can be used along with or instead of printer buffers. A printer buffer consists of memory contained inside the printer or in a buffer box connected to the printer. The action is to hold most, if not all, of the text in memory and feed it to the printer. The computer is free to be used for other purposes as soon as the buffer has been supplied. The advantage of spooling is that it requires no other hardware, and makes use of the existing computer memory, combined with disk drives. A large document, for example can be spooled by saving it on disk (many word processors do this in any case) and feeding data from the disk to the printer at intervals, between which the computer carries out its other activities. The print spooler can be incorporated in the operating system, like the background PRINT command of MS-DOS, or it can be bought as a separate software package, or it can be part of another program, such as a word-processor.

Printing is the main action for which spooling is required, since it is one of the slowest peripheral actions, but spooling can also be used for serial communications. A document to be sent along telephone lines (uploaded) can be dealt with by a program that runs in the background with a multiprogramming operating system in use, while another program is used in the foreground. Since serial communications are notoriously slow, this saves a considerable amount of computer time.

Timesharing

All of the applications such as multiprogramming, networking and spooling make some use of timesharing of the CPU, since in the conventional serial processor design, one instruction is executed at a time. This timesharing of the CPU is automatically allocated by some operating systems, but is controllable by the user in others. The Digital Research DOS-Plus operating system, for example, has a SLICE command which can be used to adjust the fraction of time that the processor spends on a foreground task as distinct from a background task. The standard allocation is 16:1, and the command:

SLICE n

will make the allocation of time as n parts foreground to 1 part background. If, for example, you wanted the processor to spend 10 per cent of its time on background work, then the ratio of foreground to background must be 9:1, and this would be achieved by using SLICE 9.

Having the ability to control the ratio of foreground to background time is important in this particular operating system, because up to three background programs can be run along with one foreground program. In general, if an operating system allows more than one background task to run, some command will usually be available for altering the fraction of the time that is allocated to the background task. Note that using SLICE 1 in a DOS-Plus command would make the foreground and background time shares equal, halving the rate of foreground processing but considerably speeding up background work.

Timesharing *does not necessarily* result in programs running noticeably slower. If, for example, a program is input/output bound, meaning that it spends a lot of time waiting for keys to be pressed or a printer to finish, then timesharing will make very little difference, since the processor is idle for a large part of the program. If, on the other hand, the program is processor-bound, like a numerical analysis or CAD program, timesharing will make the speed even slower and will be very noticeable. If the timesharing ratio can be controlled, processor-bound programs should be allocated most of the processing time, with input/output bound programs allocated least.

Virtual storage

Virtual storage is a method of making the most of restricted memory by using a disk as if it were part of the memory system. Virtual storage is very often applied to word-processor programs, because when text is being worked on, it is likely that the earlier text will not be needed urgently and can be left on the disk. A typical example is that a document of up to nine pages is held entirely in the memory, but when a tenth page is taken, some of the earlier pages are saved on the disk. If, for example, the twelfth page is being written and the user needs to refer to the first page, there will be a slight delay while this page is read from the disk. All of this is transparent to the user, who can proceed as if the whole of the document existed on memory.

Virtual storage is also a very useful software device for spreadsheets which always occupy a lot of memory. By using virtual storage, spreadsheets much larger than can be accommodated in the memory can be used, but at the expense of speed of usage. When virtual storage is used for a spreadsheet, the normal automatic recalculation (which recalculates the value of each part of the spreadsheet when any number is changed) should be turned off, since this would make the time between entries prohibitively long. If the recalculation is carried only on request, all of the disk access can be done in one set of operations, speeding up the use of the spreadsheet considerably.

Virtual storage can also be used as a way of handling very large arrays in any programming language. When this is done programs will run fairly quickly for array sizes up to the maximum permitted by memory size, and then will slow down very noticeably when this size is exceeded, because the virtual storage is now in use, and the time of disk access has to be added to each operation.

Job control languages

Operating systems generally use what are called job control languages in order to make the work of the computer user easier. Each system tends, however, to use a different name for its job control language, though the principle is the same – to write a file in ordinary ASCII codes that will control a set of actions. The CP/M system uses the name **submit** file for a job control file; MS-DOS uses the term **batch** files. The batch file system of MS-DOS is more convenient to use and is more typical of modern job-control languages.

An MS-DOS batch file is a file of commands, each written in a separate line, using ASCII text, which can be produced by a suitable text-editor or word-processor. The commands allow for comments to appear on the screen, for other messages to be suppressed, for hard-disk directories to be selected and for programs to be run, as the main functions. For example, the file:

```
ECHO OFF
CD\WSTAR
WS
CD\
```

will carry out the following four actions:

1 Suppress unwanted screen messages (turning off screen echo).
2 Select the hard-disk directory called WSTAR.
3 Run the WS program (the WordStar word-processor).
4 Return to the main (root) directory *after* leaving WordStar.

This controls an entire session with the word-processor, avoiding the need to select the disk directory manually, to start the program running, or to revert to the root directory afterwards. All of these actions are carried out by the batch file. This batch file can be recorded on to the disk (the root directory of a hard disk) under a name such as WORD.BAT, and the command WORD will then start the batch file action. Note that the batch file is still active all the time that the word-processor is in use, and it takes command again when word-processing is completed. This makes it possible to run a whole set of programs in sequence, if this is a normal routine.

Using this job control language, the batch file, eliminates the need to type a set of commands, which might be quite lengthy. Any waste of time due to misspelling commands is also eliminated because once a batch file is correct it can be used from then on with no problems. In addition, there is provision for one particular batch file to be run immediately after the operating system has been read (after switching on or re-booting). This file must be named AUTOEXEC.BAT (in the MS-DOS system), and it can contain a complete list of setting-up commands which would otherwise take some time to type in and execute. This can include setting up a printer, ensuring that the keyboard is correctly defined, loading in the software to operate a mouse, and can end with an instruction to run a program if the same program is run each time the computer is used. My own AUTOEXEC.BAT file ends with the instruction:

DIR *.BAT

which gives a list of all the batch files on the disk, allowing me to select the program I want to run without the need to find where it resides on the hard disk.

> ***Exercise 3***
>
> List, with examples, the commands of the job control language that is used on the computers that are available to you.

Running programs

Running a program under most types of operating system requires you to type the program name and then press the Return key, or make use of a job control language that includes these actions. An outline of the use of a SORT utility has already been given in Chapter 7, so that other types of utilities will be used as examples here. One very commonly used type of disk utility is the COPY command which allows a file to be copied from one disk to another, or to a printer or the screen. Taking the MS-DOS version as a model:

COPY file1 file2

will cause the file called **file 1** to be copied, with the copy being called **file 2** and existing on the same disk. Note the space between the command word and the first filename and between the two filenames. By specifying the drive letter in the command, a file can be copied from one drive to another by using the command in the form:

COPY A: file1 B: file2

assuming that there is a formatted disk in the B: drive. If there is not, the COPY action stops and an error message appears on the screen. The COPY actions can be used to print out the contents of a file to the screen with:

COPY A: file1 CON

or to print to paper using:

COPY A: file1 PRN

The COPY command acts as a form of media transfer command, because it allows a file to be transferred from one disk to another. This can include hard disk to floppy, or 5.25 in floppy to 3.5 in floppy, or in the opposite direction. More extensive transfers can be achieved by using specialized programs, and some form of communications package will be needed if a file is to be transmitted by way of the serial port to another computer. The serial port can also be used to connect other forms of storage devices, such as bar code printers and even paper tape punches. If several files are specified in the first part of a COPY command, they will be appended one following the other into the output file.

The use of a communications package will involve setting up the correct serial protocols (see Chapter 5), and this can often be accomplished by using a file of a type similar to a job control file. Once this has been done, the program menu allows the choice of transmitting or receiving a file, and selecting transmission allows a filename to be specified. This can be done by typing the name, but a modern alternative is to select from the list of the files on a selected disk. Once the file has been selected, the transfer can start, and a screen message will appear to notify when the transfer is complete. Some programs of this type (notably the MIRROR-2 program running on IBM PC machines) can be placed in the background while a file is being transferred so that other computing can be done as a foreground activity.

An applications package

An applications package means a program, or more likely a suite of programs, that are designed to automate some actions such as payroll calculations and printing, accounts or stock control. If we take just one of these as an illustration, what is involved in the selection and use of a commercial program package, such as a payroll package? If we assume that the computer is already installed the choice of program is limited to the programs that can be run on that type of computer. If the computer is a PC type, then the choice is immense because more applications packages has been written for this type of machine than for any other.

The selection has to start with a careful survey of the requirements. How many employees will be covered by this package, and how many might be added in the next five years? A package that makes inadequate provision for growth is not particularly useful, and not all packages make it equally easy to add more names to the payroll. For a small number of employees, a very simple package might be thought more suitable, but it might require considerably more time to learn and need more effort to use. Whatever is selected must comply with legislation, such as Statutory Sick Pay, so that you cannot simply make use of a package that has originated in the USA and which has not been modified to fit the UK taxation system.

You will need to consider if the package caters for both weekly paid and monthly paid staff, if you are going to make such distinctions. This might also mean that you need to fix hourly rates and weekly rates. How many such rates are needed? A small firm might still have an astonishing variety of pay-scales, and even a modest package will cater for forty different rates of hourly and weekly pay. If the firm is small, there might be a considerable need for overtime, and you will need to consider how many overtime rates will be involved for night work, Saturday work and Sunday work – at least three overtime rates will be needed to cover these conditions. If any bonus payments are to be made, how many rates of bonus can be handled? Is there any allowance for other additions to pay, such as suggestions schemes, recruit-a-friend schemes, travel allowances, overnight lodging allowances and so on. At least ten such additions might be needed even for a comparatively small firm.

One vital feature of any payroll package is that it will make use of the tax and National Insurance tables which are issued by the Inland Revenue at least once a year. The program has to incorporate such a table, and it should be possible to print out the table and to amend it each year, usually for the first pay-day in June for an April Budget. Each employee will have been allocated a tax code by the local tax office, and this tax code must be entered into the program for each employee. The table then calculates the correct tax and National Insurance deductions that must be made.

Other features that you need to look for depend very much on how large your requirements are. You might, for example, have to make up payrolls for different departments of a firm – how many should the package cater for? The answer should always be substantially more than exists at the moment, because having to change to a new payroll program from an old one, because the old one was too limited in scope, can be a daunting process which, at worst, might require all the data you have entered to be entered again, since there is no guarantee that a new program would be able to read the data files of the old one. Do you intend to write cheques manually, or should the computer print the cheques? For a large organization, automatic cheque printing is preferable, and the capability to do so is useful even if the firm is small at present. The program should certainly be able to print the standard forms such as P11, P14 and P35, as well as the payslips. This will involve using pre-printed stationery, and a printer that can make use of it.

From this quite formidable list, you can see that selection of a package from perhaps some twenty or thirty possible candidates is far from easy. This is a general feature of computing, that the specification of what is required involves at least as much work as programming, and when a package is bought off the shelf, the specification comprises more than 95 per cent of the effort. One of the main benefits of changing over from manual to computer operation of a function such as payroll is that you are forced to think carefully about current practice. As a firm grows in size, many customs that seemed reasonable in earlier days start to make much less sense, and a complete reappraisal is called for. This seldom happens unless it is enforced, and a move to computer records is one such form of enforcement.

Using the chosen package will involve a fairly large amount of setting up work. The tax table must be prepared, though in most cases the table will be already incorporated and need only be amended for the most recent Budget changes. Some packages will make the amendment an easy task, others require that the table be altered using a separate editor or word-processor which is not supplied. Once the tax table is amended and thoroughly checked, details of the system can then be entered; the pay-rates that have to be used, the number of departments, the division into hourly and weekly rates and so on. The final entry is of names, work's reference numbers and tax codes. Once this has been done then the day-to-day action will be of entering hours worked for each member of the payroll. This is more likely to be an action that is done on one day per week, unless different departments are paid on different days.

One very useful principle is to make a 'dry run', with all the data entered, and produce a set of output for a previous week. This can be compared against the actual manual output of that week as a check that the program is doing what was intended, and any discrepancy must be fully investigated. For the sake of this dry run, blank paper can be used in place of the form paper that would be used for the various P-forms, and no cheques should be printed. After the dry run has been completed and analysed, all paper should be shredded to avoid confusing it with the valid results of later runs.

Suggestions for practical work

1 Write and test simple assembly-language routines using an assembler or a chip-development set.
2 Run a loop of about 20,000 steps using first an interpreter and then a compiler on the same computer.
3 Using a multiprogramming system such as Desqview 386 or Windows 386 on a suitable machine, use several programs running together.
4 List and use the ten most common commands of the operating system for your computer.
5 Write and use a simple job control file.

Multiple-choice test questions

1 Which of the following is most applicable to a high-level language:
(a) it contains a large number of commands
(b) it is a compiled language

(c) it can be used unchanged on almost any computer
(d) it is very compact in its use of memory

2 Which of the following statements about assemblers, compilers and interpreters is true:
(a) only assemblers generate machine-code
(b) an interpreter must be present to run an interpreted program
(c) a compiler must be present to run a compiled program
(d) each different type of CPU needs its own assembler program

3 When a computer runs several programs at the same time:
(a) only one program is really running
(b) only one program is loaded at a time
(c) the programs are running simultaneously
(d) the programs are being timeshared

4 One particular advantage of using a job control routine is that:
(a) it automates routine work, eliminating many mistakes
(b) it allows you to program in a simple language
(c) it does not require you to know the operating system commands
(d) it allows you to timeshare programs

5 One action that a media transfer package will *not* carry out is to:
(a) copy a file from one disk to another
(b) make a second copy of a file with the same name on the same disk or directory
(c) copy a file from disk to tape or paper
(d) copy a file from disk to VDU or to a modem

6 Most commercial packages need to be installed. This is so that the package can correctly use the:
(a) CPU
(b) disk system
(c) VDU and printer
(d) RAM memory

9 Programming methods

Objectives

- Describe on-line and off-line programming environments (14): tools for specification and design of programs (14.1); concepts of stepwise refinement; modular and structured programming (14.2).
- Use charts to plan overall design (14.3).
- Participate in design reviews and walkthroughs (14.4).
- Use an accepted documentation system to specify inputs, outputs and files (14.5).
- Given a complete program specification, code, test and document in the approved language (14.6).

Program design and techniques

Program design is much more concerned with planning than with writing lines of a program (coding). Beginners to programming tend to devote most of their attention to coding rather than to planning, which often seems to be an extension of common sense, mainly because it seems unfamiliar, and this bias to coding is emphasized by practice with short program examples which require much more attention to coding than to planning. Much of the problem about planning effectively arises from the fundamental differences between the way that the mind tackles problems and the way that the computer must handle them. The computer, as we have seen, operates in sequence, one action at a time, without the capacity to think ahead. The human mind often operates on several tasks at the same time, often working on more than one level, and looking ahead for possible obstacles or hidden connections. Effective planning of programs relies on the planner being able to think as a computer when looking at the plan, but to think as a human while designing the plan.

Planning becomes more important as the size of the program increases, which is why concentration on short programs, though effective for teaching coding methods, is not useful for teaching planning. A program of a hundred lines requires some planning; a program of ten lines may not. Going up the scale of complexity, a program of 1000 lines needs much more than ten times as much planning as one of 100 lines. Most applications programming deals with very complex programming, certainly more than one programmer is likely to be able to cope with single-handed, and the amount of detailed planning that is required demands considerably more time than the comparatively routine task of coding, particularly for a high-level language.

Much of the planning of a program takes place **off-line**, meaning that the work is done on paper, with the computer not involved. The coding will also be written off-line, so that the computer is not used, other than for testing ideas, until the completed code needs to be typed in. In most cases, only some of the code needs to be typed, because the remaining code will already exist in the form of routines on a disk.

Tools for specification and design

There are various methods that are available to make program design better organized, and these methods are described as tools. A simple example is a print layout chart, such as that in Figure 9.1, which shows the numbered columns of the screen or printer output, and is a useful guide to how text and numbers will appear. When a large amount of programming consists of laying out text or number results, the use of planning cards can save a considerable amount of time at the coding state, since the layout can be tried on the card, and once the acceptable layout is found the column numbers can be used when the code is written.

Also at the planning stage, the use of various other charts can be useful. The traditional programmer's aids were flowcharts (see later), but these are now out of favour because they are not ideally suited to modern programming methods. Warnier-Orr diagrams were used for some time, but the most accepted tool of program design nowadays is pseudocode. Along with pseudocode there are some very useful tools that make the code easier to write in particular situations.

Among these tools are the decision tree and the decision table. At some stage in planning a program we may find that there is a specification that might be of the form:

> For a client aged 56 or over, depositing £5000 or more, the interest rate will be 11 per cent, otherwise 10 per cent. The corresponding rates for clients of lesser age will be 10.5 per cent and 9.5 per cent.

A statement like this is often the cause of errors in programming, because of the difficulty in transferring a decision in this form into a set of program decisions. The task can be made very much easier by first splitting up the statement into a set of binary decisions, meaning that each decision can go either of two ways. The repeated splitting resembles the way that a growing tree branches out, so that the form of the layout is called a decision tree.

(only a section shown in detail)

	1	2	3	4	5	6	7	8	9	10	11	12 .... 80 132
1		P	r	i	n	t						
2			G	u	i	d	e					
3												
4												
5												
6												
7												
8												
9												
10												
11												
12												
... ...	At the usual print line spacing of six lines per inch, using 11 in fanfold paper, the number of lines will be 66											
66												

The number of columns can be 80 or 132 – the 80-column printers are used mainly for letter printing, and commercial forms generally use 132

Figure 9.1 *A print-layout chart which makes it easier to write the program lines that deal with the positioning of text or numbers on the VDU screen or on paper*

A decision tree for this statement is illustrated in Figure 9.2. The tree structure starts at the left-hand side of the diagram, using the age factor to make the first split in paths. Note that it is at this point that we can formulate the decision steps as age = >56 or age <56. This type of comparison is often a problem to novice programmers, who forget that if the decision steps are age >56 and age <56 then there is no provision to deal with the case of age = 56. A human operator could still take a decision (right or wrong), but a computer cannot do so.

The first level of branching therefore splits possible clients up into two groups, using age to make the decision. The next level of branching is determined by money, and the decision level is £5000. In each of the existing branches, the decision steps are cash = >£5000 and cash <5000, and the result in each case is an interest rate which appears in the action side of the tree.

The decision tree is particularly useful because it displays a statement which can be considerably more complicated than the example shown here, in a form which is well suited for converting into a program statement or set of statements, with simple yes/no branch at each level.

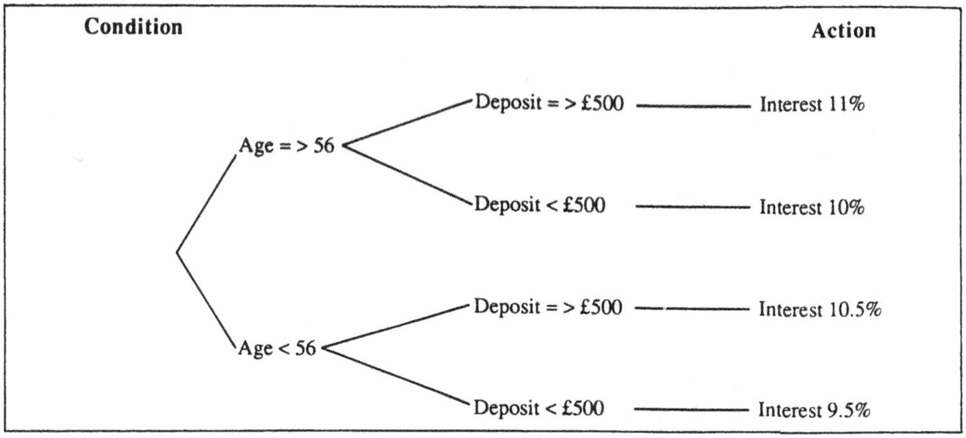

Figure 9.2 *A simple decision tree illustrated*

Another option is the decision table, which is often more useful for showing sets of conditions that may be too complicated to put into words. Figure 9.3 shows a decision table which has been made using the same example as was used above. The number of rules columns corresponds to the number of decisions that have to be made, and is 2^n where n is the number of conditions lines. For two conditions lines, as we have here, the number of rules columns will be $2^2 = 4$, but for three conditions we would need eight columns; for four conditions sixteen columns and so on. In the upper part of the table, the Y and N letters are used to show the combination of conditions that can be expected. These should be filled in like a binary count, with half of the columns filled with Y for the first condition.

The action part of the table contains a line for each possible action, and the columns to which each action corresponds is marked with a cross or a tick. The table is often easier to follow than the tree, but when the number of decisions is large the size of the table can be intimidating. Both tree and table, however, make the effort of programming decision steps considerably less and their use reduces the chance of errors in programming.

Conditions	Rules			
	1	2	3	4
Is age 56 or more	Y	Y	N	N
Is deposit £500 or more?	Y	N	Y	N
Actions				
Interest 11%	✓			
Interest 10.5%			✓	
Interest 10%		✓		
Interest 9.5%				✓

Figure 9.3 *A decision table drawn up from the previous example*

Exercise 1

Hotels in Turistica with more than twenty bedrooms are classified with up to four daggers. To qualify for one dagger, at least 80 per cent of rooms must have a private bathroom. Two daggers will be awarded if there is also a lounge with a bar, and three daggers if there is also a lift or escalator. The four dagger award requires, in addition to the above, either a swimming pool or a shopping arcade to be incorporated into the hotel. Set out these conditions into a decision tree and a decision table suitable for a program which determines the number of daggers awarded to a hotel.

Structure

The tools for program design hinge on the principles of structured programming and modularity. Modern programming languages are built around the principles of structured modular programming, so that we need to look at these principles in more detail. Of the two, structure is less easy to appreciate unless you have tried to program in an unstructured language such as early versions of BASIC. Structure, as applied to a program, means that the instructions of a program consist of steps, each of which has a start and finish, both clearly defined. A structured language will have a large number of instructions that control repetition, and such instructions show clearly what is to be repeated and under what conditions.

Figure 9.4 illustrates a repetition step programmed in two different languages and illustrating these differences. The structured language example (a) shows that a repetition step is going to be used and marks the start by using the word REPEAT. The conditions for repetition are shown at the end of the steps that will be repeated by using the word UNTIL. In this example, then, the steps that are shown between REPEAT and UNTIL are carried out until the test gives a TRUE result, which in this example will be when number N is equal to or greater than 70. The structure is emphasized by indenting (shifting to the right) the lines that will be repeated.

Contrast this with the unstructured example in (b). There is nothing to show where the start of the repetition occurs, and the only line that indicates a repetition is line 130. This contains the statement:

IF N < = 70 GOTO 110

(a) Structured
```
N: = 0
REPEAT
  N: = N + 1
  PRINT NAME [N]
UNTIL (N = > 70)
```

(b) Unstructured
```
100 N = 0
110 N = N + 1
120 PRINT NAME$ (N)
130 IF N < = 70 GOTO 110
```

Figure 9.4 *A repetition (loop) step programmed in two different languages to illustrate the principle of structuring* which contains a test and the instruction to go back to an earlier line if the test is TRUE (N less than 70). The start of the repetition is therefore line 110, but there is nothing in line 110 to mark this. If in the course of typing the program the line 130 were mistyped as:

IF N < = 70 GOTO 100

then the repeating section of program *could never end* because the value of N could never become 70 (it could never exceed unity). If the GOTO number were mistakenly typed as 1100 then there could be no repetition at all.

Lack of structure makes programming very difficult for programs of any reasonable length, and makes program steps very difficult to follow. A structured program is easier to design, easier to check and, most important of all, much more likely to be free of unsuspected bugs. Older computing languages are not particularly well structured, and their use is now discouraged except for maintenance of old programs. Modern structured languages such as Pascal, Modula-2 and C, along with more specialized languages, are replacing the older Fortran and Cobol for programming purposes.

Modularity

Modularity is the ability to work with sections of a program in the certainty that all of the sections will fit together when the programming is complete. This allows for easy team work, with each member of the team working on a small number of modules. It also makes life easier for an individual programmer who can work on a module without having to worry about how it will fit in with several dozen other modules. For individual or team, the most valuable feature of modular programming is that a module, once written, can be tested on its own and can be put into a **library**, allowing it to be copied into other programs. You will certainly, for example, need a good data-entering routine in all of your programs, so that a module that had proved to be reliable would be a major feature of your library and would be used in many programs.

Early programming languages used a form of module called a **subroutine**. The subroutine had to be placed beyond the end of the program, so that it could be used only by a specific instruction, a **call**. In BASIC, such a call uses the GOSUB instruction, so that the statement:

GOSUB 1000

means that the subroutine which starts at line 1000 must be run. The lines of the subroutine end with the instruction Return, which allows the program to resume action at the point just following the GOSUB statement.

This is a very primitive form of modularity. The lines of subroutine must be contained in the same program; there is no provision for reading the subroutine from a disk. The subroutine is referred to be a line number, so that the line number needs to be known at the time when the program is written. Worst of all, the subroutine can make use of all the variables that are contained in the program – these are referred to as **global variables**.

Modular languages use components called **procedures**. A procedure is called by using its name, and many languages allow procedures to be called up from the disk as an alternative to existing within the program. Even more important is the provision for using **local variables**, meaning that a procedure can use a variable of its own which is totally unconnected with any variable in the main program. Suppose, for example, that a procedure exists for displaying text on the screen by counting out twenty lines and holding them on the screen until the space bar is pressed. A procedure for carrying out this action could be used by a large number of different programs, and it might contain a variable called COUNT which is used to hold the number of a line, ranging in value from 1 to 25.

Now if this variable COUNT is local to the procedure, then it exists only within the procedure and has no connection with the program that calls the procedure. A program that called the procedure might itself use a variable called COUNT which was used to hold a money total, and which might have a value like 276.45 when the procedure was called. Running the procedure allows its local variable called COUNT to take its successive values of 1 to 20 without affecting the value of COUNT in the main program.

In addition to using local variables, procedures can have **parameters** passed to them. Taking the example above, a procedure for printing lines of text on to the screen would need to work on variables that contained the text; we need to pass this information to the procedure. Suppose, for example, that the procedure is called SCREENIT and we need to use it to print a set of array values OUTVAL. Modular languages allow the procedure to be called in a style like:

SCREENIT(OUTVAL)

so that the procedure will work with the values of OUTVAL. There are similar arrangements for a procedure to **return** a value to the main program if this is required.

The use of modules means that programming can be split up among a team with each member of a team working on a different part of the program, in the knowledge that the modules will eventually work together. In addition, modules that have been written previously or bought in the form of a library can be used in any part of the program. This makes programming more standardized and more reliable, and further steps in this direction have led to the development of object-orientated programming (OOP) in which the modules of a program are even more isolated from each other.

Exercise 2

How structured and modular is your chosen programming language? Are loops marked with words such as REPEAT, DO or WHILE? Does the procedure (or subroutine or function) allow the use of local variables, and for passing parameters? Can procedures be stored separately on disk or does each have to be compiled along with the main program?

Planning for structuring and modules

The accepted method of planning is called **top-down planning** (or **stepwise refinement**), and it deals with program design in very much the same way as a traditional artist dealt with a painting, starting with an outline and progressing later to the details. The important objective of top-down planning is to break up the overall problem into a set of smaller problems, then to break down each of those in turn until each problem unit is one that can be dealt with without further analysis. Each of these units can then be programmed as a module, which is why we have placed such emphasis on the use of a suitable modular language for programming. In all of this process of breaking down the problem, there is no attempt to describe how the problem is to be solved, only what amount of breaking down is needed. The breakdown of the problem can be made considerably easier if the planner considers at all times what the user will expect of the program.

For example, if the problem consists of the design of a word-processor (a ridiculous example, because no one would design a custom word-processor, but this allows us to look at ideas which should be familiar) then the first breakdown might be into sections:

1 Text editing.
2 Formatted printing.
3 File control.

Text editing will deal with the entry, correction and general manipulation of text on the screen, formatted printing will deal with the way that such text is output to the printer, with all the effects of paging, line length, emphasized print and so on, and file control contains the ability to save and load files, rename, copy, insert and so on. Division into these three sections might be reflected in the program by a preliminary menu or a permanent key layout that allows the user to choose which section to use.

Now in each of these sections, it is possible to add further detail. In the example, under the heading of text editing, we could put four subheadings of page layout, text entry, block work and search/replace, since these are four important tasks that come under the general heading of text editing. These can be shown in a hierarchy chart, or structure chart for this example, as shown in Figure 9.5 when a first layer of detail has been added. This type of chart can be expanded to show the breakup of each of these individual sections, but the chart can very easily become too detailed if this is done. The important point is to see how the pieces fit together and, in particular, the points at which a user will face a menu, or be able to carry out an action by, for example, pressing a function key. If WIMP programming is to be used, the whole program becomes a large loop in which each action, after completion, returns to the main menu even if the menu is not displayed unless a suitable key is pressed.

At this point, there need not be any relationship between the detail of the plan and the modules of program that will later be written. The emphasis at this point is on breaking down the problem, and we can worry later about the flow of action and the finer detail of programming. Once we know from what fundamental units the program can be constructed, we can decide how these will interact and how they should be coded. It is only too easy to become

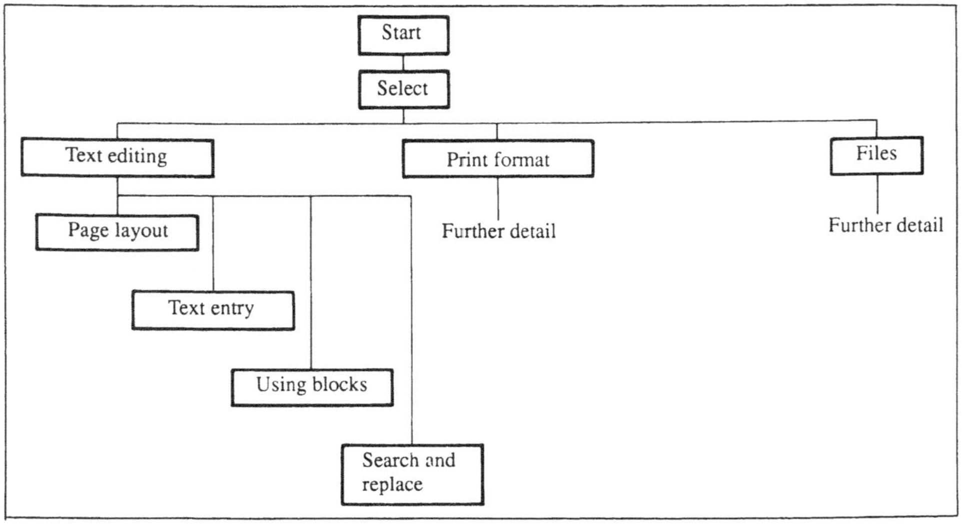

Figure 9.5 *The start of planning a program, at the point when the first layer of detail has been added*

totally bogged down in detail. We might, for example, start to worry now about what should happen if we want to save a file just after entering a piece of text. This is totally unnecessary, because it can be catered for later, but if the overall planning is neglected now, it might be impossible to have any of the actions running correctly later. Detail at this point is the enemy of progress, and one of the problems about planning at this stage is that it appears too easy, too obvious.

Planning in diagram form is not a method that appeals to everyone, and the main alternative is to use indented headings, as Figure 9.6 shows. The relative importance of sections is shown by their position on the page, most important to the left, and the relationships are also shown by placing actions under the actions that they in turn constitute. In the example, name is shown as one step down and one step right from files. This implies that naming a file

- Files
  - Name
    - Write
      - Overwrite
      - Copy from
      - Rename
    - Read
      - Copy to

Figure 9.6 *The indented-heading method of planning which can show more useful detail than the purely diagrammatic type* will immediately follow the selection of the files menu, and that a file must be named before it can be written or read; there can be no unnamed files. None of this makes any decision about how the detail will be performed, whether the files choice is achieved with a menu showing, with a **hot key** (a function key that executes the action at any point in the program), or by using the mouse to select an icon. That type of detail is done later, though an overall decision has to be taken at some stage about how all the menus are to be presented, since it would be ridiculous if each menu choice followed different methods. A few commercial programs exhibit this lack of consistency to some extent.

The difficult decision is to know how far to take this planning process of breaking the problem down. The beginner is often advised to take the breakdown as far as the module, but without stating how large the module shall be. In fact, it is quite likely that a section ready for programming will require more than one module, because unless very large and unwieldy modules are being used, breaking down to single module level is unsatisfactory. It introduces too much detail into the planning process, and it makes it very difficult to show how the modules interact. For example, it would make sense to break down the word-processor to a module for entry, but not to modules for insert, delete, overtype, and so on, because these are modules that belong inside the text entry module and should be kept with each other.

There is simply no hard-and-fast rule that can be used to decide how large a module should be for effective programming. Any rule based on the number of lines of listing is inappropriate, because ten lines of Modula-2 might be needed to achieve the same effect as one line of C (and it might take ten times as long to write and debug the C), and in any case so much depends on what the lines achieve. A module that consisted simply of messages to the programmer could consist of a large number of lines, one that involved a complex set of choices might be better broken up further. A good guide is that the module should carry out one minor but well-defined piece of the action, and that it should be possible to test the module independently of the main program. If the module requires more than two pages of listing, then perhaps it might benefit from being broken up, but only if this can be done in a logical way by making some part of the action into a separate module. The main criterion here is that if any action is likely to be needed at any other part of the program, then it should probably be a separate module. Note that **module** in this sense need not mean the unit that is called a module in the Modula-2 language, but a portion such as a procedure or function.

Exercise 3

Examine the planning of your own program that forms your project. Are menu choices presented in a consistent way? Have you taken full advantage of modularity of the chosen language?

Specifications

The process of design by breaking down a problem can be greatly assisted (or hindered) by the way that the problem is specified. It is not enough, for example, to request a data filing program, because this is far too loose for a specification. The planner needs to know what form the data will take, how it is to be entered, how it must be manipulated, the form of filing, what access is needed. Specification of a program is best tackled from the standpoint of the user, by showing what the user will expect to see on the screen and get on the printer, and by what entries the user is expected to make. The task of any computer user is to provide inputs and expect outputs, so that by concentrating on these, the outline of a specification can be drawn up. Once the outlines of the inputs and outputs have been decided, the main processing actions can be filled in.

The next layer of detail will deal with *how* the inputs and outputs are to be dealt with. If the user is accustomed to working with, for example, Lotus 1 – 2 – 3, then it might make sense that the menus and choices of the proposed program should follow on the same lines as those of 1 – 2 – 3. A user who has been recruited from a firm that made extensive use of Apple Macintosh computers might baulk at the conventional menus and wish to select from a set of icons, using a mouse. If this is to be done a choice of operating software must be made in order to provide these effects (why re-invent such a system). Concentration on the user aspect of a program at this stage helps considerably in making a program acceptable to the user, if not actually user-friendly, and it is easy to list several commercial programs which have obviously *not* been planned in this way. Others by contrast, are not so much friendly as positively servile, and this overemphasis on ease of use becomes profoundly irritating to the user after a short time.

A very important part of planning that must now be considered is the use of data types. Some programmers consider this part to be *the* most important part of any planning, because fixing what data type is used for each data item virtually fixes the form that the programming will take. The simpler items that are dealt with by string or number variables are not of such importance at this point as the collections of items. Would it, for example, be useful to treat a list of items as a simple array, as a **queue** (first into the list is first out, Figure 9.7), as a **stack** (last in is first out, Figure 9.8)? Would the use of a

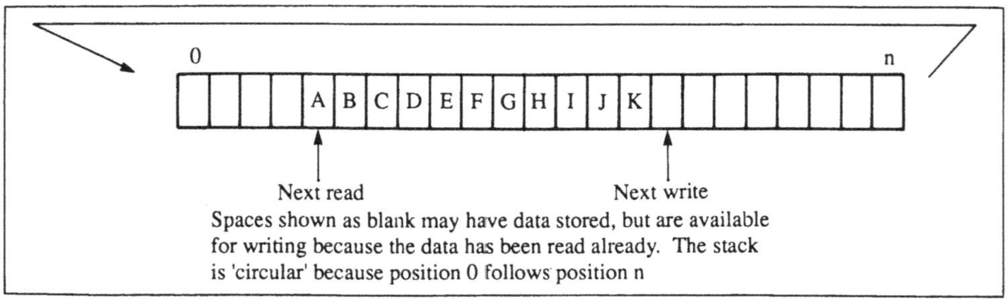

Figure 9.7 *A queue form of data list, in which items are read in exactly the same order as they were written*

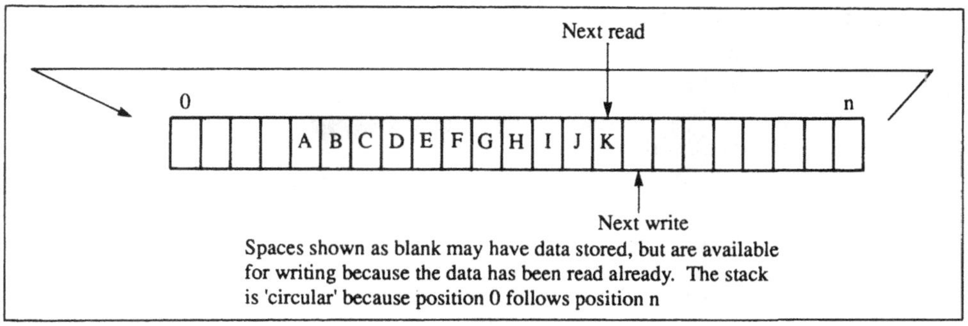

Figure 9.8 *A stack form of data list, in which the items are read in the reverse of the order of writing*

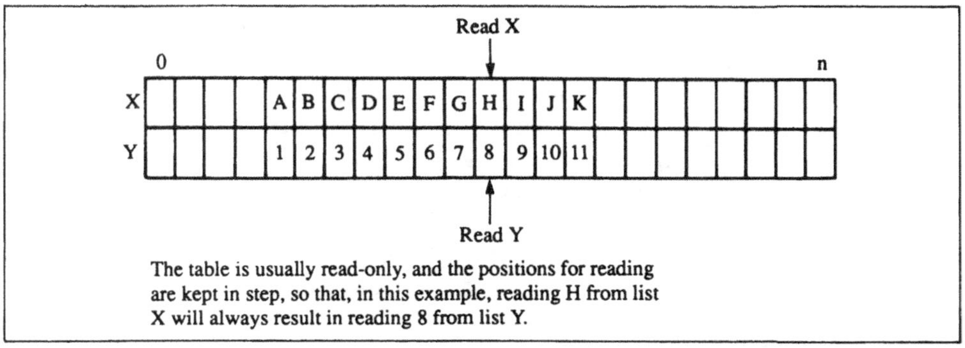

Figure 9.9 *A table, in which items are entered in pairs so that finding one item of a pair allows the other to be located*

table (a set of arrays, Figure 9.9) help? Can items be collected together into records (structures)? These decisions must be made before any attempt can be made to write the program modules, because it would be disastrous to have two separate modules written in which a list of items was treated as a different form of variable.

The overall plan along with the detailed specification should now make it possible to write programmers' specifications for the modules. The most important modules will be those that exercise menu choice, and it should be possible in many cases to write a single module that will carry out all of the menu work. This should be regarded as the key module, and all other modules as subordinates, lower-level modules. The general rules for defining a module are as follows:

1 It should be possible to enter a module at only one point, the beginning. This, note, is not true of conventional BASIC subroutines in which each line is numbered and a subroutine can be entered at any numbered line.
2 The module should always return control to the point in the program following the calling point. This implies that the module must contain no instructions of the GOTO variety which can take control elsewhere without automatically returning.

3 If a module has to make use of other modules, these should be of lesser importance, never of greater importance. In some case, a module may need to call **itself** (recursion) as, for example, in a data entry module in which data is tested and the module is called again to get the correct data after an incorrect entry.
4 Each module should use local variables as far as possible, and should affect variables in the main program only if this is an essential part of the action of the module.

These requirements are very difficult to meet if programming is to be carried out using early versions of BASIC but, by contrast, it would be very difficult *not* to meet these requirements when using a language such as Pascal. The requirement for a module to take control from the point where it is called and subsequently to return control to a position immediately following that point is a central concept in modular design. A program designed in this way makes it unnecessary to have to wade through several sheets of listing in order to find out what is happening. This independence can be assisted by giving each module a meaningful name. If, in the course of reading the listing of a module, you come across a procedure called GETKEY it is possible to gain some idea of what this procedure does without needing (at this stage) to examine the fine detail of this procedure. If, on the other hand, the procedure is called PROC001C then there is not much choice – you simply have to find where this occurs on the listing and read this portion. The aim in writing each module should be to make it possible to see what the module does without having to turn to the fine detail – a module should be as much a piece of top-down planning as the program that makes use of the module.

At one time, the planning of a module would be done using flowcharts or other graphics methods, but the trend now is to make use of the type of structured English or pseudocode that has been illustrated throughout this book. This has several advantages. One is in space, because a flowchart can occupy an amount of paper that is out of proportion to its importance, and requires drawing. Pseudocode is easier to write and to follow, and the indenting of statements reveals their relative importance. The most important aspect of pseudocode is that it makes the final step, to source-code, much easier, which is something that cannot be said of flowcharts.

A method that is extensively used as an intermediate to pseudocode is Jackson structured programming (JSP). This is particularly suited to data processing program design, and relies on diagrams which can be developed into pseudocode. The distinctive feature of JSP is that the diagrams are based on the type of data that a program will use, rather than on the steps of a program, and the use of JSP requires considerable practice before it can be really useful.

Documentation and planning

The act of planning requires paperwork, and all of the paperwork apart from the roughest of notes will eventually form the outline documentation for the program. The documentation that will finally be drawn up will consist of several parts:

1 The user documentation, which describes the normal working of the program. This can be outlined at an early stage, but must eventually describe accurately the current version of the program. There are a few commercial examples of manuals which describe earlier versions and are supplied with the manual. The documents should clearly show the limitations of the program, the hardware that is necessary (minimum memory size, type of printer, etc.) and details of any setting up steps. This section must also show clearly how to run the program.
2 The planner's documentation, outlining the planning stages. This should contain a section that will allow for detail of future modifications. This documentation will contain a statement of the problem, input and output requirements, data structures, and algorithms.
3 The programmer's documentation, which will consist mainly of the pseudocode listings of the modules with a few additional notes, and the final modules in the selected programming language. This is the document that will be consulted if the program has to be modified at any stage, and this particular set should be laid out in some standard manner. The programmer's documentation will also contain test data and test results which show that the program works and that the input and output steps are suited to the user.

The planner will specify what standards will be required for the listings, and much depends on the language that is used. Listings in C, for example, will generally require more comment lines than a corresponding listing in Modula-2. When Modula-2 is being used, it is possible for each module to be compiled independently, but other languages often require that all of the listing be typed and compiled in one piece. This can make the listing very long, and the testing much more difficult, and if the listing itself follows some accepted standards, it becomes much easier to carry out the testing and debugging stages.

The first point is that the modules should be clearly separated in the listing, unless the listing is printed out in the form of one page per module. This can be done by using blank lines between modules, or comment lines of asterisks, or the module names and reference numbers placed between blank lines. The precise method is not so important as that some uniform system should be used. Many structured languages are written so that the main program (often of a few lines only) is placed at the end of the listing, so that all of the procedures or functions are placed earlier. This can allow the modules to be put into alphabetical order of name, making them much easier to find.

In addition, the start of a module should contain several comment lines on the module itself. These lines should show what the module is expected to do, in terms of what inputs are expected to the module and what outputs will result from the action of the module. If the module is a straightforward one, then no more is needed, but if a complex piece of arithmetic or logic is to be performed there should be a note about the method. This need not be detailed; a sort module need only state which type of sort is being used rather than a description in detail, but it must be enough to allow a reader to understand the process.

Furthermore, the listing of the module itself can be laid out in a way that makes it easier to follow. The most important part of this is indentation of lines to indicate loops or decision steps, and another useful point is that the names of any procedures or functions that are called should reflect the purpose of the procedure or function. There can also be some further separation of subsections within the module itself, because most modules consist of groups of statements which should be separated by blank lines or by a combination of blank lines and comment lines. Individual statements may also require comments.

This detailed structure for the listing ensures ease of reading and ease of modification when the time comes to move from Version 1.0 to V. 1.1 and onwards. No program is ever finished in the sense that there is always likely to be some improvement that can be made. This makes it very important in a team effort to ensure that each programmer knows where the borderline between perfection and practicality is to be drawn. Messages that appear on the screen must be correctly spelled, no matter how illiterate the comments on the listing may be. Compared to spelling, screen layout of messages is less important, yet programmers fuss more about layout as a general rule. One point to avoid is having one message overlay another in such a way that part of the original message is visible. This does not inspire confidence in a user, nor does having to press a key more than once to escape from a menu (as a result of calling a procedure more than once in sequence).

Exercise 4

For the program which forms your project work, outline the user documentation. Assume that the user will know only the bare minimum about the use of the computer and the program, and indicate what information will have to be emphasized and in what order the information should be presented.

Coding

The production of the listing is the result of the work of the team of programmers, possibly one programmer for a small program, in producing the coding. If possible, these modules will have been compiled and tested independently, and the ability to achieve complete independence in this respect is a very formidable advantage of Modula-2. The coding will start as notes on paper which will result in outlines written in pseudocode, and finally in written listings. These listings must be written neatly, because they may be typed by someone other than the programmer. At this stage, lines should be indented where needed, and comments should be present so that the programmer has a reminder of what the module is intended to do.

Comments that are written later are often not helpful, because by that time the programmer may have forgotten what the original intentions were. By putting in the comment lines early, the objectives are put into view, and if the objectives change then the comment lines can be changed also. If the module size is such that it uses a couple of pages at most, then the labour of rewriting it is much less in the event of a re-think.

The actual use of the programming language varies from one programmer to another. There is a temptation in some languages to be clever for its own sake, to be looking always for short-cuts. This is an attitude that has resulted in some deplorable programs (often in C) which have required considerable modification in their short lives. The more straightforward the methods that are used, the less likely that something obscure will go wrong. The reason that Pascal and Modula-2 programs tend to cause fewer disasters at the testing stage is that the programmer gets considerably less latitude in these languages, particularly in the respect of the use of memory. C allows (and encourages) programmers to make use of the addresses at which variables are stored (pointers) and it is the incautious use of these pointers that is often the cause of program crashes in a C program. Use of addresses is often necessary in parts of a program that depend on the use of a particular disk-drive or VDU (hardware dependent programs), and when this is needed, these pieces should be in modules of their own which can be replaced if the hardware changes or if problems arise. Nothing that is hardware dependent should be embedded inside a main program.

One useful guide which can apply to programming is the principle of defensive programming. As a simple example, consider a routine in which a variable is incremented until its value becomes 100. Straightforward programming would halt this action by using a test such as:

IF (Count = 100)

so that the loop ends when the value of variable count reaches 100. The defensive programming equivalent is:

IF (Count = > 100)

so that the action is terminated when the value of count reaches 100, or has any value exceeding 100. The reasoning here is that if by some mischance the value of count became 101 or any other value higher than 100, the first test would not pick this up. This is a possibility if count is a global variable, or if its value is passed from another routine. If count were defined as an integer, the value would eventually cycle back to 100 again, but who knows what would have happened in the meantime. Defensive programming makes use of tests that are drawn up in the assumption that something is likely to go wrong at some stage, and ought to be detected. Another example in which defensive programming is needed is any routine in which the number of characters in a string is concerned, because there is always a chance that a string will contain no characters, so that if the program does not cater for that number being zero, trouble is inevitable.

One of the other weapons of defensive programming is the use of tests, such as for string length, variable size and so on. By placing a test of this type before any statement in which the quantity might be critical – a simple example is the specification of a filename – much trouble can be averted. The defensive programmer works on the assumption that when the user is asked to press any key, he/she might possibly press the Esc or Break key, that a user will sometimes type a letter O in place of digit zero, that the wrong data might be placed in a field, or that a global variable might have an unexpected value. Allowing for these probabilities (they are not just possibilities) can make a program much more user-proof and tolerant, and hence easier to use. There are programs in everyday use that pundits dismiss as unfriendly and old-fashioned, but they do not accidentally delete files nor accept nonsense commands and hence they are highly regarded by their users.

The writing of a program should always be followed by a desk check and a 'walk-through'. This is probably better done when a printed listing is obtained, but it should be done also on each module before compiling. The aim of a desk check is to ensure that the programming is valid, and it is often better when a team is working on a program to have the desk check done by a programmer other than the programmer who wrote the code. The aims of a desk check are to look for redundant or missing statements, inconsistent use of any global variables, correct use of local variables and the correct assignment of each variable before use. These are all things that a programmer can easily overlook, but which are noticeable at once to someone looking at the listing for the first time. This must always be done on a paper listing, because it is notoriously difficult to pick up errors when the lines are displayed on the screen.

The 'walk-through' is more tedious, and should be done module by module. A walk-through involves writing down the effect of each line, as if the computing work were being done by paper and pencil, so as to check what values variables have at various stages in the program. Though the work is tedious, it can often reveal some errors in assignment that other checks do not show, and it can also be a very useful way of checking that memory is being used correctly. The results of a walk-through should be retained as part of the documentation, because in the event of problems arising, a check of the actual values of variables and memory contents against those listed in the walk-through can be very useful.

The next version

All programs, other than the most trivial, contain bugs. A well-behaved program can have innocuous bugs which might result in such things as a corrupted screen display which sorts itself out when you press any key, or the need to press the Return key twice to get an input accepted. A poorly-tested program might contain more serious problems, such as file corruption which does not show up until the program has been in use for several months, or the inability to escape from a lock-up (when, for example, a print command has been issued when the printer was switched off). At some stage, then, the art of amending an existing program will have to be called on.

There are two opinions as to who should amend a program. The original programmer knows the program well, and should be the person best qualified to carry out the amendment, but there is a risk that over-familiarity makes it difficult for the original programmer to see the fault, or inclined to do more than tinker with the root of the problem. On the other hand, another programmer might spend too long getting to know the listing, but be more prepared to make a thorough effort of the amendments. If the original programmer has left the firm before the program comes up for amendment, of course, there is no option. Whichever course is followed, the listing will be the main piece of documentation that will be used, and the comments on the listing will at this stage be vitally important. If the comments have been put in at the correct stage, right at the start of the coding stage, then it is often possible on reading the listing to see a discrepancy between the stated objectives in the comments and the actual effect of the program lines. The worst nightmare of anyone charged with the responsibility for amending a faulty program is to find that the listing is uncommented, because trying to follow someone else's program is often more difficult than programming from the beginning for yourself.

In a modular program, it should not take long to find which module is causing the problems. If, for example, there is file corruption in a word-processor, it should arise from the file-handling modules, and is unlikely to be in the modules that simply read files. The process of tracking down the faulty module is not always as straightforward as this example, but it is always considerably easier for a modular language than for any other.

Corruption of memory is always more difficult to track down, but is much more likely to have its roots in any module that makes some direct access to memory than elsewhere. It is possible to have a compiler that puts in bugs, but these should be documented and comparatively easy to detect and rectify, so that the search for the source of trouble should normally be made on the program listings rather than elsewhere.

Once the fault is found, the module can be re-written. This might call for some paperwork planning, but as often or not needs only a line to be re-typed. When this has been done, the module should be retested if this is possible before the whole program is recompiled (or the recompiled module added, as can be done in Modula-2). The next obvious step is to retest, using the data or the sequence of actions which brought the problem to light in the first place. The testing should then extend to other data and the usual boundary testing, because there is always a chance that the change that has been made will have caused another problem. This is less likely when a modular language is being used, but the possibility cannot be discounted. The whole program should be retested thoroughly, and the version number changed – the convention is to change the version number by 0.1 for a minor amendment, and by 1.0 for a major rewrite.

The amendment of a program calls for changes in all of the documentation, particularly the user documentation if the change is obvious to the user. Most of the amendments under this heading are made in order to correct faults, and there is little point in referring in user-documentation to a fault which was not known earlier and which no longer exists. The all-important listing should be printed out, and the older listing labelled as such, but not scrapped at this stage. A comment line should be put into the amended module to show what was amended and when, and the planning documentation should carry a note about the change as well, showing what the problem was and which module was changed. The aim is to ensure that anyone who needs to know what has been changed can find the changes quickly and easily without having to wade through the entire listing.

Patching

Sometimes it is not possible to make changes to a program by recompiling the source code. This might be because the source code is no longer available, because it belonged to a consultant who wrote it, or because the program is a commercial one for which the source code is not available. In such cases, alterations are sometimes (certainly not always) available by way of **patching**.

Patching is the alteration of the machine-code, and it requires the use of specialized software (such as Norton's Utilities or PC Tools-Plus for the PC type of machine) which allows the contents of a disk or of the machine memory to be inspected and altered. The amount of alteration can never be large, because the absolute location of bytes and their number must not be changed. If, for example, you can change a single byte to another value, then this is permissible, but you cannot change a single byte number to a two-byte number quite so easily, and if a message requires twenty-five bytes, then you cannot change it to a thirty-byte message, though you *can* change it to a twenty-byte message with five spaces. You can, however, make some useful changes to your program or to your operating system in this way – the directory display of MS-DOS, for example, can be changed from single column to two-column by changing one byte in the COMMAND.COM file.

Patching, however, is not to be undertaken lightly, unless it is provided for by a custom-designed patching program, as it is in later versions of WordStar. When you patch a program, you are altering some parameter and, unless you know exactly what you are doing, there is no telling what bugs might be unleashed by such actions. Specialist computer magazines often publish lists of patches to well-known programs and operating systems, and these are generally reliable, but you have to be wary of a patch for a version 3.2 which does not apply to version 3.3 of the same program. When patching, observe these rules:

1 Always patch on a spare copy of a program, and on a spare disk.
2 Patch only where you are sure of correct information – never patch at an uncertain location.
3 Test the program thoroughly after patching, using **copies** of your data, never the originals.
4 Avoid any patching that will affect a hard disk. A floppy that has been mauled by bad patching can be taken out and re-formatted, a hard disk is not so easy to deal with.

Files can be patched as well as programs, but the need for patching files seldom arises unless there has been a change to the file-creating program which makes older files incompatible with later ones. This can sometimes be remedied by patching the older files if the location and nature of the patch can be worked out.

The documentation for a program should note in detail any patching that has been carried out, giving the date and the nature of the patch, along with the reason for patching. The date is important because if the patch has affected files, then the date shows from what point files will have been affected – most operating systems date their files at the time of saving them. It is important to remember, however, that patching is a drastic measure. It requires an excellent knowledge of the system, unless a well-documented routine patch is being undertaken, and if bungled it can have disastrous results.

Suggestions for practical work

At this stage, all practical work must be directed to the programming project. The planning, coding and documentation should be re-examined in the light of this chapter, with particular attention to documenting testing procedures. Lack of thorough testing is a perennial problem with projects, and practical efforts should be made to implement the following guidelines:

1 Test all decision steps by using values around the test limits. For example, if there is a test for age = >56, test with values of 55, 56 and 57.
2 Test with extreme values, like 0 and 10,000,000; for string entries, test the effect of pressing Return/Enter without making an entry.
3 Check that when an incorrect entry is detected by the program, the user is informed of the error and of what form of entry is required.

Multiple-choice test questions

1 Which of the following is *least important* in the initial planning of a program:
(a) decision trees
(b) pseudocode
(c) decision tables
(d) the programming language

2 The process of planning in outline followed by greater detail is known as:
(a) modularity
(b) stepwise refinement
(c) structure
(d) walk-through

3 Five programmers are working on a program. Each writes modules which must use as far as possible:
(a) loops
(b) calls to subroutines
(c) local variables
(d) global variables

4 The testing of a program should include:
(a) testing every possible entry
(b) testing a random set of entries
(c) testing with real data
(d) testing limit values and 'silly' values

5 A planner's documentation *must* include:
(a) the coding of the modules
(b) the algorithms that have been used
(c) the coding of the main program
(d) the instructions to the user

6 The instructions to the user must include:
(a) how to run and use the program
(b) the complete listing
(c) the algorithms
(d) the decision trees

Appendix 1 Useful texts

This list is certainly not exhaustive, but it covers some very useful reference books. The more advanced books have been omitted, such as Knuth's *Art of Computer Programming*, because it is by no means easy for the inexperienced programmer to extract information from such books.

Program design

Kernighan B., Plauger P. (1974). *Elements of Programming Style*. McGraw-Hill.

Meek R., Heath S. (1980). *Guide to Good Programming Practice*. Ellis Horwood Ltd.

Welland R. (1986). *Structured Programming*. Pitman.

Languages (elements)

Structured BASIC

Sinclair I. (1987). *Program your Amstrad PC!* Glentop.

Pascal

Kemp D. (1982). *Pascal for Students*. Edward Arnold.

Modula-2

Sinclair I. (1987). *Modula-2 on Amstrad PC*. David Fulton.

C

Sinclair I. (1988). *Simple C: A beginner's guide*. David Fulton.

Languages (advanced)

Borland. *Turbo-BASIC Manual.*
Borland. *Turbo-PASCAL Manual.*
Knepley E., Platt R. (1985). *Modula-2 Programming*. Reston Publishing.
Kernighan B., Ritchie D. (1978). *The C Programming Language*. Prentice Hall.

Appendix 2 ASCII codes in denary and hex

No.	*Hex*	*Character*
32	20	(space)
33	21	!
34	22	"
35	23	£
36	24	$
37	25	%
38	26	&
39	27	'
40	28	(
41	29	)
42	2A	*
43	2B	+
44	2C	,
45	2D	-
46	2E	.
47	2F	/
48	30	0
49	31	1
50	32	2
51	33	3
52	34	4
53	35	5
54	36	6
55	37	7
56	38	8
57	39	9
58	3A	:
59	3B	;
60	3C	<

No.	*Hex*	*Character*
61	3D	=
62	3E	〉
63	3F	?
64	40	@
65	41	A
66	42	B
67	43	C
68	44	D
69	45	E
70	46	F
71	47	G
72	48	H
73	49	I
74	4A	J
75	4B	K
76	4C	L
77	4D	M
78	4E	N
79	4F	O
80	50	P
81	51	Q
82	52	R
83	53	S
84	54	T
85	55	U
86	56	V
87	57	W
88	58	X
89	59	Y
90	5A	Z
91	5B	[
92	5C	\
93	5D	]
94	5E	^
95	5F	–
96	60	`
97	61	a
98	62	b
99	63	c
100	64	d
101	65	e
102	66	f
103	67	g

No.	*Hex*	*Character*
104	68	h
105	69	i
106	6A	j
107	6B	k
108	6C	l
109	6D	m
110	6E	n
111	6F	o
112	70	p
113	71	q
114	72	r
115	73	s
116	74	t
117	75	u
118	76	v
119	77	w
120	78	x
121	79	y
122	7A	z
123	7B	{
124	7C	|
125	7D	}
126	7E	~
127	7F	DEL

Answers to exercises and multiple-choice test questions

Chapter 1

Exercises

1 (a) 11×Q, 5×Q, 14×Q
  (b) 1010, 10110
2 (a) 0AH, 16H, 1AH
  (b) 1110, 10010, 11011
3 1001, 1110, 1100

Multiple-choice test questions

1 (b)
2 (c)
3 (d)
4 (d)
5 (b)
6 (a)

Chapter 2

Multiple-choice test questions

1 (b)
2 (d)
3 (c)
4 (b)
5 (a)
6 (c)

Chapter 3

Multiple-choice test questions

1 (c)
2 (d)
3 (a)
4 (b)
5 (c)
6 (d)

Chapter 4

Multiple-choice test questions

1 (d)
2 (b)
3 (c)
4 (b)
5 (a)
6 (c)

Chapter 5

Multiple-choice test questions

1 (b)
2 (c)
3 (a)
4 (b)
5 (c)
6 (d)

Chapter 6

Multiple-choice test questions

1 (c)
2 (b)
3 (d)
4 (b)
5 (c)
6 (a)

Chapter 7

Multiple-choice test questions

1 (b)
2 (d)
3 (c)
4 (a)
5 (c)
6 (b)

Chapter 8

Multiple-choice test questions

1 (c)
2 (b)
3 (d)
4 (a)
5 (b)
6 (c)

Chapter 9

Multiple-choice test questions

1 (d)
2 (b)
3 (c)
4 (d)
5 (b)
6 (a)

Index

Printed in France by Amazon
Brétigny-sur-Orge, FR

51786465R00105